Ben Kamin's revealing, highly readable account, l  new dimension to our understanding of the inn̶e̶r̶ ̶l̶i̶f̶e̶ ̶o̶f̶ ̶M̶a̶r̶t̶i̶n̶ Luther King—on the canvas of the modern African American freedom struggle, and the impact of the Cold War anticommunism on both the man and the movement.

- *Clayborne Carson, Professor of history and Director of the Martin Luther King Jr., Research and Education Institute at Stanford University*

Ben Kamin's *Dangerous Friendship* is a refreshing narrative that provides accessible cameos of Stanley Levison's life. Kamin creatively outlines the significance of Levison's friendship with Dr. Martin Luther King, and his influences on the civil rights movement and American politics. This text is ideal for undergraduate courses on American history and will surely be a valuable source for those interested in the more covert aspects of American history.

- *Kelley Fanto Deetz, Assistant Professor of history and Director of the Public History Program at Roanoke College*

Is it fair to say one has enjoyed a book about the putative end of segregation in America, with its miscarriages of justice, up to and including the unpunished murder of black people? It is, because Ben Kamin has honed his already formidable command of both rhetoric and exposition to create a compelling and readable tale of an unsung hero of that struggle. Stanley Levison's support of Martin Luther King Jr. described the character of American society at the time, and exposed the lengths to which even government agencies would go to prevent overturning the status quo. While Levison was unwittingly doing all that, he was also greasing the mighty wheels of change in the best ways he knew how. I learned something; no, I learned a lot . . . about unsung heroes and heroes I *thought* I knew. The entire equality struggle is much more clear to me now than it was a week ago, before Ben Kamin's lovely prose and gentle expose opened my eyes.

- *Laura Harrison McBride, author, publisher, and columnist*

No single writer living in America today can communicate the black-white story more evocatively than Ben Kamin.

- *T George Harris, former bureau chief of TIME-LIFE, senior editor of LOOK, and founding editor of Psychology Today and Spirituality and Health*

DANGEROUS
FRIENDSHIP

Ben Kamin

DANGEROUS
FRIENDSHIP

Stanley Levison,
Martin Luther King Jr.,
and the Kennedy Brothers

MICHIGAN STATE UNIVERSITY PRESS | EAST LANSING

⊚ The paper used in this publication meets the minimum requirements of ANSI/NISO z39.48-1992 (R 1997) (Permanence of Paper).

 Michigan State University Press
East Lansing, Michigan 48823-5245

Printed and bound in the United States of America.

20   19   18   17   16   15   14   1   2   3   4   5   6   7   8   9   10

LIBRARY OF CONGRESS CATALOGING-IN-PUBLICATION DATA
Kamin, Ben.
Dangerous friendship : Stanley Levison, Martin Luther King Jr., and the Kennedy brothers / Ben Kamin.
pages cm
Includes bibliographical references and index.
ISBN 978-1-61186-131-0 (pbk. : alk. paper)—ISBN 978-1-60917-416-3 (pdf)—ISBN 978-1-62895-004-5 (epub)—ISBN 978-1-62896-004-4 (mobi)
1. King, Martin Luther, Jr., 1929–1968—Friends and associates. 2. Levison, Stanley D., 1912–1979. 3. African Americans—Civil rights—History—20th century. 4. Civil rights movements—United States—History—20th century. 5. United States—Politics and government—1961–1963. 6. Communists—United States—Biography. 7. Kennedy, John F. (John Fitzgerald), 1917–1963. 8. Kennedy, Robert F., 1925–1968. I. Title. II. Title: Stanley Levison, Martin Luther King Jr., and the Kennedy brothers.
E185.97.K5K37 2014
323.092'2—dc23
2013041626

Book design and composition by Charlie Sharp, Sharp Des!gns, Lansing, Michigan
Cover by TG Design
Cover art: John F. Kennedy, Abbie Rowe, White House Photographs, John F. Kennedy Presidential Library and Museum, Boston; Stanley Levison, courtesy of Andrew Levison; Robert F. Kennedy, LBJ Library, photograph by Yoichi Okamoto; Martin Luther King Jr., Library of Congress, Prints and Photographs Division. The document used as background is courtesy of the Federal Bureau of Investigation website under Stanley Levison.

g green Michigan State University Press is a member of the Green Press Initiative and is committed to developing and encouraging
press ecologically responsible publishing practices. For more information about the Green Press Initiative and the use of
INITIATIVE recycled paper in book publishing, please visit *www.greenpressinitiative.org*.

Visit Michigan State University Press on the World Wide Web at *www.msupress.org*

For Clarence Benjamin Jones

I mean, I never really had any conversations with him over the period other than what we should be doing in connection with the Communists. We never wanted to get very close to him just because of these contacts and connections he had, which we felt were damaging to the civil rights movements and because we were so intimately involved in the struggle for civil rights, it also damaged us.

- *Robert F. Kennedy speaking about Martin Luther King Jr. and Stanley Levison, in 1964, a year after the assassination of his brother, President John F. Kennedy*

Get rid of Levison.

- *President John F. Kennedy, speaking to Martin Luther King Jr. in the Rose Garden, June 22, 1963*

I think the kindest thing I can say would be that there was resistance. . . . And it plays itself out in ways such as you're talking about with the Kennedy administration and others. Blacks are just somewhere in the sub-less department, lesser beings, lesser history, less of this, less of that.

- *Harry Belafonte, May 20, 2005, on the record with the JFK Library archival collection*

Contents

DANGEROUS
FRIENDSHIP

CHAPTER ONE

Cousin Stanley

The elderly gentleman, neatly dressed, with trim beard, round eyeglasses, and the tip of a clean white handkerchief peeking out of his lapel pocket, put down the restaurant luncheon menu. Kindness and the glint of an old Marxist shone from his thickly browed eyes. He projected the slight angst of someone who once had power and knew a lot of people but was at peace that both they—and his dominion—were essentially gone.

"I'm ninety-one years old," said Leon Schwartz, with a gravelly voice and an enunciation clear and coated with northeastern crustiness. "In the days when my cousin Stanley was around, and all the American Communists were trying to figure out whether to stick with the Party or finally walk away—this was the mid-1950s—in those days, a lunch out like this would have been very loud, very boisterous, with a spice of danger, and people shouting at each other in English or Yiddish. Maybe some Russian. Everybody was angry or passionate about something. Khrushchev's big speech at the Twentieth Communist Congress, or how the Senate had passed such a meager civil rights bill in 1957, or how Israel was turning its back on its socialist beginnings. Yes, we have a black president now but it's hard to say that the country is having a good debate about anything substantial, about the things we cared about, the unions, justice, and equality for everyone. Now the Soviets are long gone—they were a pack of liars, anyway. And the civil rights thing that Stanley cared about so much? The things he did with Martin Luther King? How they were always being wiretapped by the FBI? They were huge big deals and people caught their breath wondering if everything would turn out okay, if we'd get real labor unions, or who'd be thrown into jail by Joe McCarthy for 'un-American activities' or how many more Negroes would be lynched down south till the country woke up and gave a damn!"

Such is the memory of the jocular Leon, a cousin to Beatrice Merkin—who would marry another left-wing Jew named Stanley David Levison of Far Rockaway in Queens. Stanley, Beatrice, Cousin Leon, all progeny of an immigrant American family, born in the early part of the twentieth century, had parents and grandparents with names like Shmuel, Malka, Chaya, Isaac, Liebl, and Reuven. These ancestors hailed from places such as Ukraine, Hungary, Bessarabia, and Rumania. The European elders kept kosher, lit Sabbath candles, blessed freshly baked challah bread and were clustered in ghetto enclaves along the Dniester River, in the Pale, and beneath the Carpathian Mountains. They were born in Kiev and Lodz and Odessa. They were disliked and persecuted and sometimes murdered by their non-Jewish neighbors and in state-sponsored pogroms. Their descendants, people like Pauline and Abraham Merkin—the parents of Beatrice—and Esther and Harry Levison—the parents of Stanley—emerged along the northeastern corridor of the United States, from Providence to the Bronx to Newark to Philadelphia.

New York City was their nexus, its union halls, libraries, art galleries, concerts in the parks, theaters, nightclubs, and speakeasies. They rarely gathered in the synagogues, preferring "ethical culture" societies or humanist seminars. They were generally the first to integrate bars and hotels and gymnasiums that had barred Negroes. They were, for the most part, fervently atheist, in keeping with Karl Marx's disdain for religion as *das Opium des Volkes*—"the opiate of the people."

Their names were Americanized; for example, Leon's father first altered his name Tsolik to Saul and finally to Charles. His mother went from Tsivya to Celia; his uncle Yehudah took on the moniker of "Eddie" while selling produce and liquor after arriving here from Belaya Tserkov.

The Sabbath tables of Gdansk and Prague would give way, within two generations, to the socialist meeting lecterns of New York and Boston and Manchester, New Hampshire. In the case of Stanley Levison, a dyed-in-the-wool leftist, it eventually drifted, with Martin Luther King Jr., to the churches and sit-ins and rallies of Birmingham, Alabama, and Macon, Georgia. The road from Kiev to Atlanta, from Minsk to Memphis, however, went through Moscow. In his memoirs, Leon Schwartz identifies his leftist cousin Levison as "Rev. Martin Luther King's friend and confidante."[1]

This book, while it deals with King and the historic, postwar civil rights movement that transformed American society, focuses upon the story of a unique and mysterious man, an ultracapitalist who devoted his life and resources to the principles of communism. Stanley Levison, a poker-faced, deliberative, suit-wearing, bespectacled, chain-smoking, sometimes sarcastic man with a penchant for Armagnac brandy, was arguably Martin Luther King Jr.'s closest white friend.

This book will examine why Stanley Levison, a wealthy Jewish capitalist, was drawn to communism; why he left the Communist Party–USA and turned his attention to Martin Luther King Jr.; and why his association with King remains both heroic and hidden.

In his lifetime, Levison quietly forged a link between the civil rights crusade and the labor movement that remains the hallmark partnership of American social justice. He was a Marxist who owned some of the original and largest car dealerships in the United States, maintained huge investments in corporate real estate, and was referred to by FBI director J. Edgar Hoover as "the Mr. X" who infiltrated and saturated Dr. King's work with Communists. Hoover and others who were interested in monitoring or even shutting down King's efforts—including, for a time, Robert F. Kennedy—were never able to prove any ongoing connection between Levison and the Communist Party–USA even though they wiretapped, tracked, and subpoenaed Levison while he counseled, raised funds for, ghostwrote articles and speeches for, did the accounting of, and often bailed out King between 1955 and 1968, when the preacher was murdered.

The surveillance of Levison while he was associated with King inadvertently revealed some of King's human flaws, including his sexual adventures, and also exposed some of King's other supporters' (including Harry Belafonte's) social radicalism. It certainly made it easier for the government to tag King with the stain of "Communist affiliation." In this environment, the relationship between this Jew from New York and this pastor from Atlanta became a dangerous friendship. The ripples of this perilous alliance spread from the White House to the Upper West Side to the Edmund Pettus Bridge in Selma, Alabama. It often bristled with the domino effect of serious risk and intimidation among men who were allies but also between the government's obsession with spying and a citizen's right to expression.

Levison was a full-blooded Marxist from his youth until he severed all ties to the Communist Party in 1956. He was a man of moral seriousness and authentic activism. His name is whispered at the conclaves of aging black civil rights leaders: "Yes, Stanley—remember how much Martin loved him and depended upon him?" And then they go on, recalling the "Bloody Sunday" march across the bridge at Selma, the manner in which King improvised the unforgettable "I Have a Dream" speech, and how they were proven wrong when they begged King not to publicly dissent on the Vietnam War, as he did in 1967. They talk about those gilded days, and how this one cajoled Martin and how that one disappointed him. But they make no further mention of Levison, and one cannot help but wonder why. One cannot help but ponder the fact that Levison was the only white man in that small coterie of advisers and counselors and attorneys who truly influenced King and kept his movement afloat.

This book, while offering the narrative of Levison's special and generally unheralded connection with King and the freedom movement, will reveal why Levison was so philosophically driven by Marxism and then why he gradually grew disillusioned with, even disdainful of, the Communists.

This process was neither sudden nor spontaneous. To understand it and the disenchantment with a group of people he had held in esteem for so long, an attitude inherited through his family lineages, in favor of King and the civil rights movement, one has to examine the overall arc of the American (and notably Jewish) Communist organizations.

Levison's story is a paradigm of an entire generation's experience—a group that was weaned on hatred of the Russian czar, founded upon a deep yearning for civil liberties that could be envisioned in the United States, and was then bitterly betrayed by the cruel reality of the Soviet dictatorship. Its coordinates ranged from the 1931 racial outrage of the "Scottsboro Boys" trial in Alabama to the Hitler-Stalin Pact in 1941 to the brutish slaughter of Hungarian freedom fighters by Russian soldiers in 1956. Today, all but marginalized, the Communist Party–USA still proclaims in its literature: "The Communist Party has an unparalleled history in the progressive movement of the United States, from the struggle against Jim Crow segregation, the organizing of the industrial unions, from the canneries of California, to the sweatshops of New York."[2]

There were a number of reasons why people such as Stanley Levison were drawn to Marxism. Leon Schwartz said: "My family was all attracted to it, for very obvious reasons. Having grown up under the czar and seen the worst kind of capitalism, they were enticed by Marxism because it gave them the vision of a better world. The basic thing was the notion of social justice. A good example of that was the Scottsboro case in 1931."

It was the kind of outrage that already prompted Stanley Levison, nineteen years old at the time, to action and lobbying, and when necessary, fund-raising on behalf of defendants, who were clearly being victimized. Nine teenage boys, all black, were heinously framed and accused of rape—trumped-up charges that betrayed the very bearings of southern bigotry and apartheid. An incident had occurred near a railroad track in Tennessee; the boys were arrested in

Paint Rock, Alabama, and the rushed, blatantly illicit court proceedings, fed by rabid racism, began in Scottsboro.

It was glaringly evident that the young black men were entrapped for a crime committed by some white boys. Nobody in the South would take up their cause—and the black inmates were treated viciously in jail and had to endure three trials. The Communist Party–USA intervened and was the only group to offer and send legal representation. At one point, one of the white girls involved recanted her charge against the black men. Eventually, some of the innocents were exonerated, though others spent long terms in prison. "The case became a classic and primary one of judicial miscarriage," says Leon. "The fact that the Communist Party stepped in against something that resembled what used to happen under the czar, before the Bolshevik Revolution of 1917, made a strong impression on Stanley and people like him. We were all driven by one thing and that was to fight injustice. Those young Scottsboro boys were nearly lynched several times. The police in Alabama didn't even try to break up the mobs that gathered outside the jail. At one point, one of the defendants was just shot to death by a prison guard. We were all very proud of what the Communist Party did or tried to do."

The American socialists also found comfort in the Soviet Union's quick recognition and embrace of Israel upon its inception in 1948. "Remember, Israel was founded as a socialist state. Russia took to it at first, especially after what had happened to the Jews in Europe. The Soviets supplied it with arms from other Communist countries, especially Czechoslovakia. I'm not saying that the Marxists always liked Israel, especially when it clearly turned capitalist. That trend bothered Stanley, and he came to doubt Israel. But none of us were comfortable later when the Soviets turned so hard against Israel, which was still basically socialist, and took the Arab side in the Middle East. They even sent armaments to Egypt and Syria. It reopened some old wounds we had after Stalin made the pact with Hitler in 1941. That created a lot of bewilderment."

This "nonaggression pact" between the USSR and Nazi Germany was perceived as a flagrant betrayal by the original Bolshevik followers of Karl Marx and Leon Trotsky. Trotsky himself complained that it was an "extra gauge with which to measure the degree of degeneration of the bureaucracy, and its contempt for the international working class, including the Comintern [Communist International]."[3]

Schwartz and others also trace the early affinity of the American leftists such as Levison to the natural bond between the Communists and the labor movement. The Communists galvanized the early unions and provided the workers with principles, structure, and even meeting spaces. "Stanley liked that," said Schwartz. "He was a businessman, but he thought his wealth built on the back of working people should be used to grow the labor movement. That was what Marxists who had money did. And Stanley had brains, too. His capitalism, and his Marxism—they were just two separate worlds, like two compartments. So when he realized, as a lot of us did, by the mid-1950s, that the Soviet Union was actually nothing but a dictatorship, that its leadership did not even stand for workers and actually was prepared to deny them their rights and even kill them, like they did in Hungary, well that was about all he could take. You know, none of us here ever carried a gun or had a gun. That would have been absurd. The Soviets and their violence, it made people like Stanley Levison physically ill. When he left, he left. It was so fortunate that he happened to find King at about the same time because he was looking for a cause that really spoke to him."

In his last speech delivered as president of the Southern Christian Leadership Conference (a group basically created and underwritten by Stanley Levison), King declared:

> One day we must ask the question, "Why are there forty million poor people in America?" And when you begin to ask that question, you are raising questions about the economic system, about a broader distribution of wealth. When you ask that question, you begin to question the capitalistic economy. And I'm simply saying that more and more, we've got to begin to ask questions about the whole society. We are called upon to help the discouraged beggars in life's market place. But one day we must come to see that an edifice which produces beggars needs restructuring. It means that questions must be raised.

You see, my friends, when you deal with this, you begin to ask the question, "Who owns the oil?" You begin to ask the question, "Who owns the iron ore?" You begin to ask the question, "Why is it that people have to pay water bills in a world that is two thirds water?" These are questions that must be asked.[4]

Some would cite this as classic communistic ideology—the vision of a society devoid of class distinctions. Others would agree with Dr. King's own summation of this philosophy, which he summarized later in the same speech: "Communism forgets that life is individual. Capitalism forgets that life is social, and the Kingdom of Brotherhood is found neither in the thesis of Communism nor the antithesis of capitalism but in a higher synthesis."

Stanley Levison would have skipped past the labels and just advised King what to do, where to go, and whom to meet with next that day.

CHAPTER TWO

A Walk in the Rose Garden

Robert F. Kennedy was in a foul mood. It was a calm summer day—the cherry blossoms had receded into the blooming magnolias and orchids and the occasional, heartening smells of rosemary and mint. The irises, peonies, sugar maples, and Virginia pines absorbed the alternating interludes of sunshine and sudden thunderstorms. At the White House, the climate also staggered between talk of confidence and bursts of stress. The 1964 reelection campaign for President John F. Kennedy seemed hopeful but was again confounded by the storm clouds of Martin Luther King Jr. and the "Negro issue" in the South.

Robert Kennedy, the attorney general of the United States, had been vexed by King and his southern integration campaigns for years. It was not that RFK was viscerally opposed to what King and his allies were doing. The problem was that the Federal Bureau of Investigation, and specifically its tyrannical director, J. Edgar Hoover, were out to vilify King and prove that the preacher was some kind of Communist subversive. This caused problems for the Kennedy brothers because if they thought of helping King, the volatile FBI director could retaliate with the release of information about the president's unrelenting womanizing—or other sensitive matters that might humiliate the Kennedys. Hoover had wiretaps, informants, and guns. He also effectively had more muscle and endurance than most presidents.

But the question of King and his civil rights movement presented quandaries for the Kennedys beyond J. Edgar Hoover. The young president, who had defeated Richard M. Nixon in 1960 by a meager 100,000 popular votes, did not exactly enjoy a mandate, and JFK now sought a convincing and resounding reelection in 1964. After watching the television newsreels of black schoolchildren and adults being fire-hosed by Birmingham security, he began to be moved by the African American struggle for integration—though he remained cautious. In a landmark televised address to the nation on June 11, JFK for the first time spoke unequivocally about the human rights gap between white and black Americans: "The rights of every man are diminished when the rights of one man are threatened." However, this is was the very first time that Kennedy had actually spoken publicly about the plight of black Americans.

However, Kennedy needed to carry the South in order to defeat the likely Republican nominee, arch-conservative senator Barry Goldwater of Arizona. Southern blacks were not empowered to vote yet and whites, incited by King's freedom campaigns in Alabama, Mississippi, and Georgia, were in no mood to support a president with sympathies for King's work.

The machinations of politics were fully cranking around the White House, while, in the developing heat of the summer of 1963, blacks were boycotting businesses, integrating lunch counters and busses, protesting for school desegregation, and marching for equal labor rights. They were also being jailed, beaten, raped, kidnapped, shot, and lynched.

All of it was a mess and a headache for Bobby Kennedy—especially today, June 22, because Martin Luther King Jr. was coming to the White House. And Kennedy had a firm message for Dr. King: he had to get rid of perhaps his closest adviser, a Jew named Stanley Levison. Levison was a man with a blank face who wore quiet suits and who would hardly be noticed in a room except by those who believed that he carried secret things in his pockets.

Meanwhile, Levison knew more about Martin Luther King Jr. than any other white person in America. This made other white people anxious, curious, and hostile.

Yet another classified file dated February 2, 1962, had come out of the New York office of the FBI about Stanley David Levison, an attorney and business-man, and onetime Manhattan treasurer of the American Jewish Congress. The sealed document, one of many papers and surveillances gathered by the Bureau concerning Levison since the 1950s, a "leftist" who unquestionably consorted with Communists and other such radicals, included the following declaration:

> The NYO [New York Office] makes the following observations:
> (1) LEVISON is an Associate Director of the Southern Leadership Conference. KING as head of this organization has been closely associated in the past with LEVISON.
> (2) LEVISON's association with the CPUSA [Communist Party of the USA] is known to but a few individuals within Party circles.[1]

In fact, the name of the ministerial association presided over by Rev. Martin Luther King Jr. was the Southern Christian Leadership Conference (SCLC), founded in 1959 by King and several other prominent African American clergymen, with the financial assistance of entertainer Harry Belafonte. The discussions that led to its formation took place in the New York City kitchen of Stanley Levison, the auto dealer and real estate magnate who spent much of his adult life funding, managing, and advising the civil rights movement while acting as MLK's accountant, counsel, and close friend. King often referred to Levison as one of his "winter soldiers."

The SCLC emerged in the afterglow of the successful and groundbreaking Montgomery bus boycott, which had efficaciously desegregated the city bus system in that city, and which marked the formal advent of the American civil rights movement. The quest of the SCLC, which consisted of some sixty preachers, was to give an institutional format to the freedom efforts. Its mission was to promote civil, nonviolent protest actions against segregation in the realms of American transportation, education, labor, and housing.

A rabbi who first encountered Levison during the late 1950s, when Levison was abandoning an extended association with the American Communist establishment and completely dedicating himself to King's movement, reflected with me on the attorney's turn of heart: "He never said much, and you didn't even know if he was comfortable with his Jewishness or if that's what motivated him to work so closely with King. He carried this poignancy for struggling types and, even though he had money, he was searching for something to value. It bothered him that America seemed so largely defined by class. The Communist thing really stalled for him and he realized that it was mostly a falsehood in terms of egalitarianism. It was as if King and Levison were looking for one another. That's what you thought anyway. Stanley didn't wax too much about what he was thinking. He had this vast emotional world hidden inside himself. He could have done anything he wanted, backed any cause he chose to back. He swam in conviction when it came to King. He saw a problem and wanted to fix it."[2]

What was the problem? Fully a hundred years after the Civil War and the Emancipation Proclamation, the American South still seething with discrimination, racism, and anti-black violence, King and the SCLC sought equality, social equity, and economic fair play for black people—issues that had never permeated any presidential campaign and that remained profoundly taboo in the oligarchic southern civilization.

Stanley, a soft-spoken, philosophical man with a moderate paunch visible through his cotton dress shirts, stood out as a singular white face among the highly Baptist, black assemblage of the SCLC. "My impression of him," Rev. C. T. Vivian, a longtime associate of King's and an organizer of the Selma-Montgomery March of 1965, told me "was that he was brilliant but never really shook off his Communist background."[3]

The FBI had been monitoring Levison at various levels since his staunch advocating for known CP-USA members Ethel and Julius Rosenberg. In 1953, the couple was executed for treason and espionage—a decision that remains a haunting emblem of both the political hysteria and anti-Semitism of that era. For Levison, their plight symbolized what he viewed as America's dark, tyrannical side. Their Jewish heritage also punctuated his wrath. He lit a cigarette in his Manhattan apartment and told his twin brother Roy, "It doesn't matter what the defense said. They looked like us so they were guilty from the start."4

Levison opposed the McCarran Internal Security Act, the legislative tool of Senator Joseph McCarthy and his associates, who conducted massive investigations and defamations of alleged American Communists and "subversives" during the 1950s and promulgated the notorious Red Scare of that period. The act was passed by Congress over the objection—and the veto—of President Harry S. Truman, who called it "mockery of the Bill of Rights" and a "long step toward totalitarianism." It brought innuendo, paranoia, and a chilling atmosphere of suspicion and distrust into the worlds of Hollywood, publishing, liberally bent politicians, and scientists; it ruined lives, ended friendships, and divided Americans with incendiary jingoism and a visceral anti-Soviet obsession that did not allow for any nuances.

Stanley's lips curled in exasperation as he considered all these things. He penned letters, placed phone calls, and made recommendations with the efficient gravity of a doctor writing a prescription. His unhappiness took on the form of expectation: *What can I do?*

· · · · ·

To his exertions, and to his subsequent work with Martin Luther King and the SCLC, Stanley Levison brought his convictions, his connections, and his considerable personal wealth. His link with—and financial support—of King dated back to the Montgomery, Alabama, bus boycott, which propelled King's career trajectory from pastor at the Dexter Avenue Church to what some called "the moral leader of our nation" by this summer of 1963. Levison quietly underwrote the Montgomery Improvement Association, of which the 26-year old King was elected president in 1955. A year later, working with black activists Bayard Rustin and Ella Baker, Levison created In Friendship. This was a blanket organization that developed funding and organization principles for the first generation of southern civil rights activists.

Levison became fiercely dedicated to Martin Luther King but remained largely anonymous and unheralded about it—which suited him. He had grown disillusioned with the Soviet elders, realizing their mendacities and hypocrisies and their lack of genuine socialist principles, after the Russians brutally put down the Hungarian people's revolt in 1956. The attachment to the fledgling civil rights leader, a mere twenty-six years old at the time, was a satisfying new diversion for the prosperous businessman. Stanley, a capitalist of supreme efficacy, nonetheless was drawn to vulnerable, aching souls looking into the abyss of racialism.

He drafted articles and speeches for the preacher, prepared his tax returns, and kept the coffers of the SCLC from drying up. In 1958, Levison completed and edited King's first book, *Stride Toward Freedom*. He negotiated the publishing deal for King with Harper & Brothers.

Levison did not take money from King for his services, though King offered. Levison knew that his friend did not have the capital to pay for such professional expertise. (It should be noted that Dr. King, much to the frustration of his wife Coretta, routinely turned over his own speaking fees and royalties to the SCLC.)

"I want to pay you," Martin begged Stanley. Levison wrote to King at one point: "My skills were acquired not only in a cloistered academic environment, but also in the commercial jungle. . . . I looked forward to the time when I could use these skills not for myself but for socially constructive ends. The liberation struggle is the most positive and rewarding area of work anyone could experience."[5]

"The two men loved each other," Clarence B. Jones told me. "I know this. I worked with Stanley 24/7 for eight years." Jones was an African American attorney for King, the secret editor of King's renowned "Letter from Birmingham

Jail," and ultimately served as the clandestine intermediary between King and Levison when the two men were forced by the Kennedy administration to break off public contact.

"Stan in particular was essential in keeping us abreast of the intellectual and political climate in the progressive community in New York," Andrew Young said. "If a book came out that he thought we ought to read, he read it first and gave Martin a review, noting key chapters. Stan also had personal contacts with Walter Reuther and members of the United Auto Workers board, and helped Martin build important relationships with leaders of the northern industrial unions. Stan and his circle were admirers of social reformers like Eleanor Roosevelt and A. Philip Randolph who believed in an activist government supportive of poor and working people."[6]

In 1963, King and the SCLC were deeply immersed in a series of actions designed to break the iron-hard segregation of Birmingham, Alabama. Beyond the physical dangers to King (who was jailed more than once on convoluted charges) and to others in the movement, the SCLC was desperately in need of funds. The money was required for everything from transportation to food to lodging to bail dollars. Andrew Young reported that it was Stanley Levison who organized mailing lists from a number of northern liberal organizations and publications, including *The Nation* and *New Republic*, to effectively solicit monies—"a modern direct-mail operation for SCLC." Levison also showed SCLC staffers how to place newspaper ads for potential donors.

All this activity on Levison's part further drove the FBI's interest in the man and Hoover's personal vendetta against both Levison and King. The Bureau's now-routine wiretapping of Levison's phones failed to establish any connection beyond 1956 between him and the Communist Party. Unfortunately, the listening posts paved the way for the FBI's general, full-blown monitoring of King and his activities—which led to the discovery of the preacher's peccadilloes with a variety of women. Hoover became obsessed, though history would prove the director's blatant personal hypocrisy when it came to sexual escapades—or at least donning women's clothing. Bottom line: no direct link was ever established between Levison/MLK and Communists or any other subversive factions once Levison had embraced King. But the perception of Levison's cavorting with the left-wingers, plus his undeniable interaction with them at various points along the way, became like flypaper for those in the federal government who simply hated King.

Andrew Young wrote:

> Having labeled Stan Levison a communist, the Bureau proceeded to inform the attorney general [Robert F. Kennedy] and officials at the White House of the extent of his influence on Martin. Citing a "reliable informant," Hoover sent a steady stream of memos that was feeding information about Levison's work with King. In fact, the "reliable source" was the FBI's own wiretap. There is little indication that anyone in the Kennedy administration challenged the FBI's circular reasoning. The FBI alleged that Stan Levison was a communist and used their own unfounded assertion to generate concern over Stan's influence with Martin.[7]

Born in New York in 1912, prosperous in business, Levison was an alumnus of the University of Michigan, Columbia, and the New School for Social Research, as well as a double-degree holder in law from St. John's University. Hardly a religious Jew, he nonetheless found himself in the presence of other radical Jews who were adamant about civil liberties and human rights. These kinds of politically centered Jews, people like Leon Schwartz and the Trotsky associate Max Shachtman of the early Workers' Council, and Martin Abern of the Chicago-based Communist Youth movement, did not evolve from their Jewish spiritual roots. They were cultural Jews or simply Jews by birth. They generally voted for Henry Wallace and his Progressive Party in the 1948 presidential election. (Incumbent Harry S. Truman narrowly defeated Thomas E. Dewey.)

Levison and others in the Communist organizations (and these were fragmented, not always sharing identical ideologies or approaches) did rally around Paul Robeson, the famed African American singer-actor who worked feverishly for human rights through the structure of the Communist hierarchy.

According to Leon Schwartz, his cousin Stanley particularly supported Robeson in the aftermath of the 1949 Peekskill Riots: Robeson, already reviled by many Americans for his pro-trade union sentiments and his charges of the "American colonialism of Africa," was scheduled to perform a concert near the Westchester County community that August. He was an antecedent to entertainer Harry Belafonte, who alongside Martin Luther King Jr., would also fight for desegregation and civil rights legislation. Robeson's performance near Peekskill was designed to raise funds for the Civil Rights Congress—an agency excoriated by white supremacists and Ku Klux Klan members as "Communist."

Concertgoers were beaten with baseball bats and pelted with rocks, while a cross was burned on the grounds. Robeson escaped unharmed, but people like Stanley Levison were angered and roused. This was seven years before he would first meet Martin Luther King Jr., but a fruit was harvested in Levison's mind from a seed that had already been planted by the Scottsboro Boys incident nearly two decades earlier. Levison had spent years—and a lot of his own money—helping to create the mass industrial unions that were expressly threatened by the Republican-sponsored Taft-Hartley Act of 1947, which, despite an unsuccessful veto attempt by President Truman, was enacted and serve to monitor and control the activities of the labor unions. Levison called it "a slave-labor bill," and he expressed his concern that it particularly threatened already disenfranchised black workers. His transition to support for King by 1956 was unquestionably gestated in the context of his Marxist philosophies.

During these turbulent times immediately following World War II, there was not a high level of interest on the part of American Jews in the smoldering reality of the Holocaust of six million Jews. Perhaps it was simply incomprehensible and easier to avoid thinking about, as some Jewish leaders lamented. But Levison and others did reflect on the overall bestiality of the Nazi regime. "It helped drive him," said Leon Schwartz, "to identify with the civil rights movement." Levison, long before meeting King, was more absorbed with the plight of American blacks than he was with the new nation of Israel. Israel, in Levison's thinking, was just a pawn in the US-USSR rivalry that was playing out during the 1950s in the Middle East. He was a Communist, a movement that emanated from Moscow; he was a progressive, which tied him to unionism, socialism, and, in the mind-set of the US federal bureaucracy, thereby lumped him into an "un-American" conspiracy—regardless of when he might have exited the formal Communist Party.

The problem was, in the words of Harry Belafonte, who knew both King and Levison very well, "In those days, when it came to socialism, communism, and progressivism, the fault lines were not clear."[8]

In fairness, Levison was departing the ranks of the party by the time he was introduced to the young King. But it was not a sudden, impulsive exit. Nor was it a magical transformation from lifelong principles abruptly ignited by the persona of King. "He started asking himself some questions," said Schwartz, "when it became more and more evident that Stalin was no less a bloody dictator than Hitler had been." Levison was not deaf to Stalin's proclamation in 1952 that "every Jew is a potential spy for the United States."[9] Nor was he oblivious to the fact that by the 1930s and into the pre- and postwar periods, Stalin was physically eliminating every single Jewish figure within the Politburo and the Soviet leadership.[10]

But even the mechanism of the first meeting with King was framed in communism and tainted by controversy. It was Bayard Rustin, an openly homosexual and radical firebrand who himself was stalked by the FBI, that brought Levison and King together in the midst of the Montgomery bus boycott.

And yet: though the FBI's cabal insisted that Levison's leaving the party was just a cover for his developing relationship with King, the Bureau never actually found a hard, lasting association between Stanley Levison and the other side of the Iron Curtain from the period following 1956. In his hallmark work, *Bearing the Cross: Martin Luther King, Jr., and the Southern Christian Leadership Conference*, David Garrow writes: "The FBI kept up its round-the-clock surveillance of Stanley Levison throughout the spring and summer [of 1962]. The wiretaps detected no contacts with Communist agents, but they did allow the Bureau to furnish Attorney General Robert Kennedy with a continuing flow of reports on Levison's phone conversations with King."[11]

But circumstances, biases, and the resolve of J. Edgar Hoover, who despised King and called him "the most notorious liar in the United States," combined to galvanize government suspicion of Levison. By June 1963, with President Kennedy publicly, if reluctantly, calling for civil rights legislation in Congress, and brother Robert thoroughly convinced that Levison was so stained by communism that it would compromise the bill's chances and the president's reelection, the Kennedys were in complete consternation about Dr. King's association with Stanley Levison.

King was visiting the White House on June 22, 1963, to continue his soliciting of President Kennedy on behalf of the civil rights movement. Though the preacher had been somewhat heartened by JFK's speech on June 11, in which the president essentially equated the Negro dilemma to an American moral crisis, King had publicly rebuked Kennedy on a number of occasions for equivocation on the freedom issue—even for selling out politically. King's father, Rev. Martin Luther "Daddy" King Sr., had initially supported Richard M. Nixon for the presidency in 1960—until the Kennedys made some calls and helped to facilitate King Jr.'s release from a southern prison during the campaign. "I was grateful, of course," MLK told some of his friends, including Stanley Levison. "But I knew it was political more than anything else."[12]

For a long period of time, King was wary of Kennedy because the latter had voted against a 1957 civil rights bill while serving in the US Senate. This preserved his rapport with southern legislators that he'd eventually need for higher office. King was shrewd and practical as well: just how much would the aristocratic, astronomically prosperous, young Kennedy of Boston and Hyannis Port really know or *feel* about black people?

King was always disturbed that Kennedy systemically placed his presidential ambitions before social justice. But on June 22, 1963 (ironically, exactly five months prior to Kennedy's murder in Dallas), there appeared to be a window. The president had spoken and he was apparently committed to a civil rights bill; maybe he was rising above his own usual instincts, the kind of instincts, said Belafonte, that made the Kennedys "uncomfortable" with black people.

Taylor Branch writes in the second volume of his trilogy, *Pillar of Fire:*

America in the King Years 1963–65: "For all his tempered realism, King went to the summit unprepared for a serial bushwhacking that left him chuckling in disbelief."[13]

After a fairly ceremonial meeting with King and his delegation about civil rights in the Cabinet Room, during which President Kennedy expressed his *lack* of support for the planned 1963 March on Washington, King was first approached by Burke Marshall, the assistant attorney general for civil rights. Marshall was respected as a hands-on professional rather than a bureaucrat. He would be the eventual author of the 1964 Civil Rights Act signed by President Lyndon B. Johnson within a year of JFK's assassination. But today he was doing the bidding of the Kennedy brothers.

Marshall told King that the administration had some problems with the presence of Stanley Levison (and a second King staffer, Jack O'Dell) within the inner circle of King's advisers. "They're Communists," said Marshall. King could only chortle in incredulity—not only at the notion, but that serious men at the highest levels of government would so patronize the movement or be so bullied by rumors and insinuations. Martin King had been beaten by police, shackled, thrown in jails, and lived with a piercing fear of mortality. He dismissed Marshall's comments, ascribing them to the insipid mixture of Kennedy politics and insecurities.

But then Bobby Kennedy, intense and cold-eyed, came up to King. The attorney general and the preacher shared something of a rocky relationship. Harry Belafonte recalls a late 1960 meeting with King and SCLC staff. At the time, in between the successful Montgomery bus boycott and the 1963 March on Washington, the civil rights movement was stalled. There were no immediate major campaign victories to celebrate.

Robert Kennedy had just been designated attorney general by his brother, the president-elect. One news source described it at the time: "Famously disinterested in the civil rights movement, Kennedy's appointment seemed catastrophic to King's supporters."[14]

Belafonte remembers that King's gloomy team voiced their dejection at the turn of events. Robert Kennedy was described basically as an ambitious, hard-nosed alter ego for his brother who was focused only on advancing Kennedy agendas and had never to that point spoken a public word about segregation. King could not think of anything uplifting to say and grew frustrated. Finally, after he'd heard enough, he slammed his hand down and ordered them all to desist. "Is there nobody here who's got something good to say about Bobby Kennedy?" The reply was that there was nothing good. To this King retorted: "Well, then, let's call this meeting closed. We will re-adjourn when somebody has found one thing redeeming to say about Bobby Kennedy, because that, my friends, is the door through which our movement will pass."[15]

It was only after the assassination of his brother John that Robert Kennedy began a transformation into social justice issues and matters of equality, fairness, and, specifically, stopping the war in Vietnam. But in 1960–61, there was no alliance between the Kennedys and the civil rights movement.

Once in office, RFK was constantly trying to upbraid and manage J. Edgar Hoover and the FBI, often reminding the contemptuous Hoover that *he*, Kennedy, was actually the director's supervisor. Hoover hated both Kennedys and thought of them as skirt-chasing rich boys who had little business running the United States. Hoover also carried on his widely known crusade against King, at one point sending Mrs. Coretta Scott King scurrilous audiotapes of King in bed with sundry women while simultaneously dispatching MLK a shadowy note suggesting that the civil rights leader simply solve his dilemmas by killing himself. Robert Kennedy also routinely chafed when distinguished black leaders, including Belafonte and the jurist Clarence B. Jones, berated the Kennedys for abdicating their moral commitment to human rights in America in favor of electoral votes.

So a certain combustible quality filled the air when Martin Luther King Jr. and Robert F. Kennedy (who would be assassinated within eight weeks of each other in 1968) were in personal proximity. Bobby pressed King—on the same point just raised by Burke Marshall. "You've got to get rid of Stan Levison and Jack O'Dell," he said in a strong whisper. King shook his head in dismay while Robert Kennedy's eyes narrowed. Kennedy emphasized Levison's dangerous attributes, given Stanley's central role as a King confidante and adviser. O'Dell was African American and the New York director of the sclc. He would be more expendable for King than Stanley, but nevertheless King was shocked and upset that *this* was what he was hearing about in the aftermath of a summit on civil rights legislation. He was unconvinced and disappointed.

But now came the president of the United States. "Dr. King, let's go out into the Rose Garden."

Martin King was thirty-four years old, scion of a middle-class Atlanta family of Baptist preachers and the descendant of slaves. He was insecure about his own safety and he fretted about his sensitive light-colored skin, which tended to rash, especially late in the day. The lithe, gray-eyed Jack Kennedy, forty-six, Irish Catholic, came from a different world altogether and personified easy grace and power. Yet he too felt certain vulnerabilities: that he was too-often perceived as "weak on the Soviets," that he was tepid on issues of social justice or that conversely, he was too friendly to "Negro causes" to hold the allegiance of the old-line traditional southern Democrats. The almond-eyed preacher truly presented President Kennedy with some dilemmas. The King conundrum contained elements of all these little explosives.

Kennedy looked at King—who thought he had already had an idea of what was coming. The president reportedly indicated that he had "some bad news." The breeze was still and the scents of the daffodils, hyacinths, and tulips kissed the air of the famous garden. King glanced at the spread of roses and magnolias along the boxwood nearby.

"Yes, Mr. President?"

Kennedy reported: "Hoover says that some of your close people are communists." The president grimly suggested that King had been "infiltrated." King was practically dizzy by now from this threefold waylaying, and he later told friends that he had to hold back from laughing—although it would have been nervous laughter.

"It's a question of two of your closest advisers," Kennedy said in his Boston intonations.

King was completely dumbstruck. He actually thought that perhaps Kennedy would suggest that Coretta was one of these so-called "infiltrators." Gathering his wits about himself, and understanding that this was a very serious matter in the mind of Kennedy and his clan, he asked the president, "Who?"

It was then that Kennedy announced that the two suspects were Stanley Levison and Jack O'Dell. King's heart sank—not because he believed it, but because he knew that since Kennedy believed it, it would have devastating implications. He cared about O'Dell but he *loved* Stanley Levison. King, too, was a man of political calibrations. He had a problem.

Kennedy went on. This kind of thing, he said, could become provocative for southern segregationists and give them the ammunition they would need to derail any proposed federal civil rights legislation. If Kennedy took a major blow on the civil rights bill, well, he could lose the election altogether. He couldn't have any associations with or intimations about people in King's circle who were in any way soft on the Soviets.

But not only that: "Look at what just happened with Macmillan," said the president. Harold Macmillan was the prime minister of Britain and a scandal was developing steam around him. His defense minister and close friend, John Profumo, had recently been caught sleeping with a comely showgirl who was simultaneously seeing a Russian naval attaché based in London. Profumo had lied to a committee in the House of Commons about it and lost his position, and now Macmillan was being vilified for standing by his chum. Kennedy, deeply worried and uncompromising with King, went on. The president could not have been unmindful of his own multiple indulgences with women. He was reported to have told King: "Macmillan's going to lose his government because he was too loyal to a friend." The prophecy came true just a few months later.

In fact, Clarence Jones says that "Kennedy warned Martin that the civil rights bill couldn't be shepherded through Congress until he knew for sure that there was no danger of Martin being tainted by communist associations, because those would in turn taint the president."

"Get rid of these guys, Levison and O'Dell," warned President Kennedy, "and let me know that it's been done."

Martin Luther King Jr. left the White House that day in a daze of anguish and anger. Andrew Young, who was at King's side, said: "Martin remarked that 'if Kennedy took me into the Rose Garden to talk about this, he must be afraid that Hoover is bugging him too.'"

Reporters noticed that he seemed distant and glum while taking answers outside the gate. His answers were perfunctory and he seemed deeply distracted. In his heart, he cried for his good friend Stanley Levison. It may not have registered in his brain that Levison's presence in King's life had inadvertently brought on the surveillance and speculation that triggered this Rose Garden unpleasantness in the first place. Not that the Levison-King connection was a unique example of Hoover reconnaissance: the dogged FBI director routinely had "enemies"—real or imagined—including nationally elected officials, wiretapped, followed, and implicated.

Hoover intimidated several US presidents during his long reign at the FBI. It was no surprise that he would have pursued Stanley Levison and that Martin Luther King Jr. would have been shaken in the wake.

CHAPTER THREE

From Far Rockaway
to Montgomery

T here were still considerably more oaks and elms dotting and shading the stubborn concrete when Stanley Levison was preparing to graduate Far Rockaway High School in Queens, New York, in 1930 than there are today. The huge building on Bay and Twenty-Fifth Street spread imperially between Oceancrest Boulevard and Hartman Lane, bearing its own massive gridiron and track behind the central stone citadel and physical plant. It was cramped for parking space and had sprouted in the middle of a classically patterned, considerably Jewish neighborhood of homogenous middle-class homes with bleak stoops and miniature grass plots.

Stanley David Levison was born in that neighborhood on May 2, 1912, to Esther and Harry Levison. The house was austere in tone and structure; young Stan shared a sparse bedroom overlooking the gritty street with his identical twin, Roy. Harry worked as an accountant for Unique Specialties Corporation,

a tool-and-die firm located in Brooklyn. Esther did some real-estate management work but was primarily a housewife, dedicated to her boys, focused on
their nutrition, health, and making sure their clothes and underwear were
laundered and fresh. The boys would look out at her in the tiny backyard,
applying clothespins to their washed shirts and shorts, occasionally taking
a long breath of air while bending against the cramped weariness of her
existence. Esther and Harry seldom frolicked at the beaches. Stanley thought
his mother's face was devoid of joy, but he felt her warm allegiance.

"I want to do something to lift people out of the sameness of life a lot of
us are stuck in," he said to the principal of Far Rockaway High School, Dr.
Sanford J. Ellsworth. They were walking together down one of the high-
ceilinged hallways—the roundish-looking upperclassman in 1929 and the
silver-haired administrator in his slate-colored double-breasted suit laced with
herringbone fabric and topped off by peaked lapels. Ellsworth liked Levison
and thought the rather plain, nonmuscular bookkeeper's son would amount
to something. The principal did not know Stanley's twin brother Roy as well
and felt more of an affinity to the bespectacled Stanley at any rate. Ellsworth
detected Stanley's tendency toward asthma, and although he was a rather stiff,
formal, scientific man, he was compassionate toward and about his pupils.
Stanley had made mention once or twice of his admiration for Ellsworth's
promotion of equal educational standards for young women, and it flattered
and pleased the old mathematician.

"Use your head, Stanley. You are a thinker. But don't get radical ideas
and try to turn the whole civilization upside down. There are a lot of people
out of work and we have to find a way to rebuild the country and not getting
people to just fester."[1]

But Stanley did have radical ideas, and they were very much in his head.
He and Roy, who were raised as secular Jews exactly at the time when the
nation was reeling into the Great Depression, trafficked in the left-wing, pro-
Soviet Yiddish newspapers much more than in Hebrew prayer books. Stanley's
circumstance of being Jewish translated into an early sense of solidarity with
the working class, with revulsion at the reality of the sprouting, destitute

"Hoovervilles" of the United States, and at the growing breadlines he saw along Central Avenue and Seneca Street.

He noticed his algebra teacher, Abram Bader, reading the leftist weekly *Voch*—among a slew of dissident, Yiddish publications of the era. Though such newspapers editorialized on matters of culture, education, and literature, they were stamped with an unmistakable fealty to communism, or at least international leftist principles. Stanley, still young and impressionable, became fascinated with the unapologetic avowal of working-class values that was published in *Voch*:

> We consider the October Revolution [of the Soviet Union] to be the great-est event of recent generations. By transferring power to the workers, the Revolution simultaneously liberated national minorities, ensured their independence and undertook to help develop their cultures. We stand with the Soviet Union in its overall socialist development and in the economic and cultural reconstruction of Jewish life that the Soviet Union has undertaken.[2]

What Ellsworth, himself far-removed from such Bolshevism and a staunch patriot, did know was that that Stanley lived in the world of ideas and that he was motivated by social doctrines. The principal was a Presbyterian and supervised a student population that was predominantly Jewish. He did not particularly relate to the youngsters from what he subjectively heaped together as "Orthodox" families, often finding them aloof and difficult to understand—although they were "brainy and loyal," he'd say softly to teach-ers at the school. The principal failed to discern that there were many more meaningful strains of Judaism than just "Orthodox" and secular. A variety of practices, philosophies, and rites abounded among the decidedly pluralistic Jewish community.

Nonetheless, Stanley was "different." The boy was neither religious nor ritualistic and struck the principal as refreshingly secular, an ethical-cultural Jew who tended toward a socialist perspective. Stanley and Roy were not among the Jewish kids who demanded matzos in the cafeteria during Passover and did not wear any religious garments or skullcaps. Ellsworth also liked Albert Berlin, another Jewish student who was a three-letter athlete for the Far Rockaway Seahorses. Berlin and the Levison boys were "normal Jews," bright, literate, curious about life—young men who fulfilled the principal's long-range view of the modern secondary school as a community center and not just a "schoolhouse."

Stanley once asked Ellsworth what he thought about the rising Empire State Building soaring up into the sky right across the East River from Queens. "An amazing feat!" exhorted the principal. "When it's done, it'll be the tallest structure in the nation, 380 meters and 102 stories. Solid steel frame. A perfect mathematical accomplishment that goes almost as far down into the earth as it rises above the skyline."

"Yes, it's something," said Stanley. Then he thought about the Scottsboro incident, still fresh news then in 1931 as Stanley was completing high school and the skyscraper was just opening. He drew upon his years of reading the leftist Yiddish papers and attending meetings of the Young Communist League with his brother Roy. He said: "I wonder what will happen to all the men working on it when they finish it. The corporates will move in and what will the workers who built it then do?" Ellsworth remembered Stanley's question with considerable fondness. The principal was long gone by the time the adult Levison met and befriended Martin Luther King Jr., but he would have understood the mutual fascination.

Stanley enjoyed his adolescent life on the Rockaway peninsula, the pizza, knishes, sizzling Chinese food, watermelon slices, and lemon ices with his friends at the stands near the storied beach bungalows. Sometimes he would steal away for the tuna, bolognas, or briny salamis that were rolled in fragrant rye bread near the shore. Life was colorful and the air was salty. Exotic visitors came from the Bronx to stroll along the ocean, and there were many adventures under the hot sun of summer. Trolleys crisscrossed the venues and jukeboxes blared and bathers hollered and lovers bantered in a world in between the two world wars, unaware that in this country, we were a generation away from the greatest civil rights revolution since the end of the Civil War.

But surviving members of the family remember: Stanley was piqued about what he perceived as a lack of interest on the part of the general Jewish community in matters of real, global concern—how the subways worked, how the proliferation of automobiles was changing the landscape, how Native Americans (then universally called "Indians") were essentially condemned to reservations, how Negroes were relegated to such a reprehensible caste system most horrifically manifest in the South. Roy ultimately chose business over a vocal and active Marxism but Stanley found a way, in the words of their cousin Leon, "to keep both worlds in separate but equal compartments."

One day, Stanley showed Roy a bitter little poem, "Salute," that he found in a local paper, written by the revered Jewish lyricist, Moishe Leib Halpern. "This says it all!" he exclaimed to his brother. He read it out loud, his asthma intermittently interrupting his breath and expression:

> There's always something in our land, too,
> And where there's no lamppost that will do,
> There's a convenient tree: what's clear's
> That a Black of at least twenty years
> Hates anything tall that, in a pinch,
> Would hold you high enough to lynch.
> Although the one I saw get
> Hanged, wasn't quite fifteen yet.[3]

"What's that from, one of your Bolshevik journals?" asked Roy.

"What's the difference where it's from?" responded Stanley. "And yes, it's from *Voch*. But at least I'm reading something here that matters. Do you have any idea how many lynchings go on down in the South? It's like some kind of foreign, alien land down there *in the United States!* Negroes killed, raped, not even allowed to get schooling. My God, they're still slaves, or in some ways, worse off. At least when they were slaves they got fed."

"I understand," said Roy. Roy was so often ambivalent about many things, including his own identity, that as an adult he legally changed his last name from the too-Jewish sounding "Levison" to the less conspicuous "Bennett" and went off to Ohio State University. "I understand," he repeated. "Some of your intellectual heroes from the Jewish left are so smitten with the Soviet thing even though they managed to escape from Russia. They were in prison, a lot of them were forced into the czar's army, or their friends were killed off. Now they are Bolsheviks because they naively think there's some kind of redemption in the Bolsheviks or because half of the Bolsheviks themselves are Jewish. Trotsky this, Trotsky that. Trotsky's in exile now. He'll get lynched, too, like your Negroes down South."

Stanley was not untroubled by what Roy had to say and in the long run acceded in his heart to the violent Soviet hypocrisies that became public over the course of the decades—particularly under Joseph Stalin. But he kept Halpern's sardonic and revealing little poem in a file and it certainly helped lay down his path to Martin Luther King Jr.

Bayard Rustin introduced Stanley to King sometime in late 1955. The New York–based Rustin was a protégé of the legendary A. Philip Randolph, at the time the leader of the Brotherhood of Sleeping Car Porters and unquestionably the nation's most prominent black leader. Rustin, a fiery and skilled advocate of nonviolent civil disobedience, had become captivated by King's bus boycott in Montgomery, Alabama and decided to visit the area and examine the campaign. Rustin had led a comparable bus integration effort down South in 1947 with inconclusive results.

Not all of Rustin's colleagues in the fledgling freedom movement were enthusiastic about his traveling down to Montgomery. As David Garrow has written in *Bearing the Cross*, "[Rustin's] public record, they pointed out, included a brief membership in the Young Communist League, a prison term for draft resistance, and a conviction three years earlier for homosexual activity with two other men in a parked car. Any or all of these could be used to smear the Montgomery leadership should Rustin become associated with them publicly."[4] More than a few of the Montgomery area preachers (not unlike many of their colleagues nationally) never grew comfortable with Rustin because of his open homosexuality. Rustin was an "in your face" type of man, brilliant, ribald, always in need of money but resourceful in getting it from leftist patrons, and ultimately as invaluable to the movement as he was excruciatingly controversial. (In 1959, Levison sent Rustin a handwritten note from New York with a list of potential donors for an ongoing defense fund to help King. The eleven names included Harry Belafonte, philosopher Reinhold Niebuhr, and baseball great Jackie Robinson. "Dear Bayard," scribbled Levison at the bottom of the page. "If you need money to get this number of letters typed and for air mail, let me know. S.")[5]

Nonetheless, Rustin appeared in Montgomery and effectively assessed that the young King was as strong in his preaching and inspirational leadership as he was weak in managerial and executive abilities. Rustin called Stanley Levison down to Montgomery, shrewdly calculating that Levison would be effective in exactly the areas King needed the most help: administration, legal writing, and, above all, fund-raising. Stanley, increasingly ambivalent about the communists, was extremely eager to befriend and help King.

He felt betrayed by the Soviet insurgence in Hungary; he began to perceive that Russian communism was totalitarianism. He fought off the melancholy of disillusionment. He tried to focus even more on his various enterprises, which ranged from real estate to auto dealerships to imports. But Stanley was an activist and now he was blessed with a new cause, almost a *raison d'être.*

Andrew Young said: "Martin felt at ease around Stan because he was not aggressive with his advice, offered his analysis in rational and measured terms, and didn't jealously guard his influence among Martin's inner circle, as so many others did." In short, the quiet but focused Levison was unlike the many combative, ambitious, even covetous black clergymen who surrounded King and sometimes even sought to undermine King's growing celebrity.

Otis C. Moss Jr., now the retired pastor of Olivet Baptist Church in Cleveland and another associate of King's, told me: "This kind of enviousness, this very apparent need for some of the brothers to bring Dr. King down could not be forgiven or dismissed just because of professional rivalry. It was sometimes just heartbreaking to observe."[6]

Yet when Stanley first met King, he found a man, a beacon, who was the personification of all that Stanley deemed important. Moreover, Stanley's level head and judicious instincts were a good foil for Martin's tendencies toward depression and even morbidity. The passionate preacher was balanced by the nontheistic accountant and attorney. In a social category apart and distinct from King's pantheon of African American associates, many of whom were vying for King's attention and blessing, King and Levison quickly developed a kinship of work, purpose, and interdependence. "Yes," Clarence Jones told me, "they had something that the others close to Martin did not always understand and some resented."

"I'll never make it to 40," King would lament to Levison in darker moments of confidence. Stanley would forge ahead, hurting inside for his colleague, but charging Martin to the next task. In a 1958 letter to Martin, Stanley admonished his friend about some verbosity in a draft chapter of King's book: "The result is a somewhat bewildering profusion of ideas which submerge some of the main points and rob them of the emphasis they deserve."[7] Martin was sentimental and melancholic; Stanley was rational and impious. Yet he would cheer Martin on, at one point penning a note to King that described his friend's manuscript as "a string of pearls."

Levison had filled out in manhood: later FBI surveillance photos of him with King and with Jones reveal a more robust, intent man in a suit doing what he wanted to do. His eyes peered inward from behind his spectacles. A gray light hung above him, belying the intense glow of his loins. But his economic prowess notwithstanding, he maintained the modesty in appearance and bearing that he exhibited at Far Rockaway High School.

Years after he graduated high school, the FBI noted in its secret tracking files that Stanley Levison, unswerving acolyte of Martin Luther King, was armed with two law degrees and a network of lucrative businesses, including several Ford dealerships and a string of Laundromats. In partnerships with Roy and others, primarily an entrepreneur named Roger W. Loewi (with whom he shared a business address on New York's Broad Street), Stanley helped develop a number of ventures including Allied Laboratory Instruments, Thermo Laboratories, and Bulldog Concrete Forms. Stanley worked unobtrusively and seamlessly, his mind and hands given to effective organization, reasoned thinking, and savvy investment. In truth, a lot of money made its way quietly to King from Joseph and Sarah Filner, future parents of California congressman Bob Filner, but they never pursued the intensely personal relationship Levison coveted with King.

The twins, Stanley and Roy, were intertwined in business. "That was it," Clarence Jones told me. "Roy didn't get involved with the civil rights thing." Stanley son's Andrew Levison confirmed this with the author, conveying to me that "by the late fifties he was, like Stanley, not involved with the CP. . . . I remember him as deeply involved with the ADA [Americans for Democratic Action] and as the UN correspondent for one of the smaller British papers."[8]

During the war years, Stanley and Roy dealt in the manufacture of artillery fuse parts through the Unique Specialties Corporation, where their father worked in the bookkeeping department. Both sons were naturally entrepreneurial, though it was Stanley who was the more active in civil liberties and social justice. After the war, Roy spearheaded their first Ford dealership in New Jersey. Stanley, eclectic with his talents and acumen, actually traveled to Warsaw: the goal was to procure an import franchise for Polish ham. The effort failed, but this did not stop Stanley from spreading his wings and influence.

Linked early on with "leftist causes," such as his activism on behalf of Julius and Ethel Rosenberg, Stanley became treasurer of the Manhattan branch of the American Jewish Congress and used this base to advocate for the Jewish couple's defense and to oppose activities of the House Committee on Un-American Activities. Andrew Levison asserted to me that Stanley was an atheist with no specific interest in organized Judaism. Andrew wrote to me: "If someone had asked him if he was Jewish, he would have replied 'Yes, and Apache and African and Chinese as well. I am the inhabitant of a planet, not the member of a tribe.'"

However, Jones says that "Stanley was not a self-hating Jew. He may not have been particularly religious, but he was culturally proud of his Judaism and the social principles that he got from the faith."

Stanley quickly earned himself an ongoing file and an "SI" (Security

Investigation) number with the FBI.⁹ The Bureau hounded Stanley all his adult
life, starting as early as 1947, even pegging him then as weighing 150–160 pounds,
height five foot seven to five foot eight, of fair complexion, with brown hair,
and "wears glasses." The FBI did not note that Stanley was a chain-smoker.
Clarence certainly remembers that: "Oh, there just never was a time when he
did not have a cigarette lit in his left hand and a pencil or pen in his right. He
wrote and smoked for long periods at night about labor issues, fund-raising
projects for the SCLC, or just editing some article that Martin was struggling
with. He was constantly in a ruminative state. I remember his raspy voice and,
sadly, the asthma that afflicted him for decades."

Levison was married to Beatrice Merkin and they lived on 104th Street on
the Upper West Side. An earlier, three-year marriage to Janet Alterman ended
with acrimony—it was not about sexual matters but about the woman's clumsy
betrayal of both Stanley and Roy to the FBI. She apparently informed on the
brothers when they originally became members of the American Communist
Party. It was an extremely odd, even inexplicable series of concentric circles
that eventually had a hazardous impact on Harry Belafonte. The entertainer
and ally of both King and Levison would learn later that Janet Alterman was
his psychoanalyst! This story is detailed in a later chapter but it contains
another twist: Janet eventually married a key business partner of Stanley's
named Jay Richard Kennedy, yet the entire crowd remained on sociable terms.

However, this "Mr. Kennedy" (a pseudonym) was eventually found out as
a major FBI snitch that pursued a notorious career of infiltrating other people's
lives, from Frank Sinatra to Gene Kelly to Belafonte. This Mr. Kennedy was
also Belafonte's personal manager and financial adviser—much to the calypso
singer's eventual consternation and disbelief.

A typical-looking, almost wooden businessman in a suit, Stanley Levison
nonetheless always remained something of an enigma.

In January 2011, journalist Matthew Schuerman filed a story for New
York's WNYC News—one of very few dispatches that have been published about
Stanley. Schuerman wrote: "One of the Rev. Martin Luther King Jr.'s most
important political advisers, Stanley Levison, has remained largely hidden

from public view—even 40 years after King's death."[10] Later that same year, Clarence Jones, then a vigorous eighty-one years old, sat with me at the King Research and Education Institute, located on the Stanford University campus.

A loop earring in his left ear, grief in his eyes, Jones declared: "I have gone from anger to sadness on this. Since Stanley Levison's death in 1979, I have been dismayed that the magnitude of Stanley's contribution, financially and otherwise, to Martin Luther King Jr. and the Southern Christian Leadership Conference, has been diminished, overlooked, or ignored. Not even Harry Belafonte, Harry Wachtel, Bayard Rustin nor I match the depth, quality or 24/7 length and breadth of Stanley's support of Dr. King. I saw this firsthand. Why his photo or even a bust of Stanley Levison is not found in the King Center in Atlanta or at the Lorraine Motel National Civil Rights Museum in Memphis defies all logic." Jones rubbed his neatly trimmed beard, shook his head—the years of perilous toil, studied partnership, court sessions, having phones tapped, derision by the FBI and many government figures, and finally, the "invisibleness" of his "beloved Stanley" all thundering in his voice.

Yet there was a time when a special troika, Clarence B. Jones, Martin Luther King, and Stanley Levison danced together in a bittersweet, sometimes treacherous circle that quietly changed the United States of America.

CHAPTER FOUR

The Communist

t should have been a normal trend of thought for the untold thousands of African American soldiers, sailors, and air corpsmen: having served with valor and shed their blood against the forces of the Axis, they aspired to share in the spoils of victory. Black men helped save the world from the fascists, and they distinguished themselves in the war in tandem with their white counterparts. So they assumed they'd come home to equality. They believed that the old way of racial humiliation would now disappear.

Granted, they fought in segregated units and too often were relegated to inferior or more tedious or treacherous duties, as cooks, ditchdiggers, mail runners, mechanics, butlers, mine sweepers. But they carried a vision, against the blinding incongruity of the battlefield, from the Philippines to Normandy, that the war—and their ultimate brotherhood with their better-fed and more often promoted white counterparts—would pave the way to an America that was also liberated.

Sadly, this dream proved as difficult as it was for GIs to traverse the steep cliffs of Pointe du Hoc on D-Day. The lurid grip of state-sanctioned segregation in the South, known as Jim Crow, was unaffected by the military success of the Americans. Jim Crow was unimpressed; he remained grim, unyielding, and evil. Men who had faced an incomprehensible enemy in war came home without a trace of the euphoric aura that seized the nation. The postwar prosperity, the suburban expansion, the sense of optimism and of America's new positioning as the world's leader—these had nothing to do with the black veteran who limped back and still found himself in the rigid apartheid that held firm from Texas to Mississippi to Georgia to the Florida panhandle. He could die with his white comrade in Italy, but he still could not drink from the same fountain in Louisiana.

He had helped free children of all creeds from despotism in France and North Africa, but he could not send his own children to the same schools as his white equivalent. He could personally recount the history of the greatest armed struggle for human dignity ever fought, but his children could only read about it in substandard, unheated, poorly ventilated school buildings relegated to separate neighborhoods and using hand-me-down desks, chairs, blackboards, and even textbooks that had been disposed of by white schools. He was drafted to serve his nation, but he returned to still being denied the right to vote. He won the war but still lost the peace.

He was often enough bitter, disappointed, and angry about it. Black Americans had never been passive about the systemic degradation that pervaded their lives, the lynching, the denial of education, unionization, housing, or even the opportunity to own property and gain a promotion. As early as 1900, black indignation about American racial arrangements fueled trolley-car boycotts in a host of southern cities. Race riots were not uncommon, though they were generally suppressed by the iron hand of white supremacists whose philosophies were buttressed by state laws that at best upheld the "separate but equal" doctrine and at worst simply dishonored black folks and crushed them with heartless consistency.

It simply wasn't a real crime to gang-rape a black woman, to lynch a young black man who allegedly looked "the wrong way" at a white woman, to kidnap and smother a child who happened to venture into a prohibited white zone. Blacks were fair game in the South; their lives amounted to group dehumanization and, all too often, a collective surrender to enforced subservience and self-contempt. The fact is that black servicemen were met with a vicious wave of racial murders in the South as they returned from World War II.

Decades before Martin Luther King, the fiery black intellectual W. E. B. DuBois attacked the more compliant black leadership (particularly Booker T. Washington) and its policies of "adjustment and submission." DuBois howled in 1900: "The problem of the twentieth century is the problem of the color-line."[1] He unabashedly called for a new "pan-Africanism," which was nothing less than an early cry for what later was called "Black Power." The tall, sinewy, mustached professor, who feared no one and wrote in the vivid language of unbridled wrath, created the Niagara Movement in 1905. This was an original civil rights association that demanded "a mighty current" of change. Revealingly, the group of radicals had to assemble on the Canadian side of Niagara Falls. From the safety of Ontario, they declared: "We do not hesitate to complain loudly and insistently" about the shameful plight of their dark-skinned brethren.[2] Few in white America listened or cared—especially when W. E. B. DuBois came to espouse socialism as the national cure for racial bigotry.

Four years later, the National Association for the Advancement of Colored People (NAACP), largely funded by Jewish patrons, was established in New York City after a particularly savage antiblack riot in Springfield, Illinois. It was not lost upon the founders that Springfield was the birthplace of Abraham Lincoln. This spawned a growing black radicalism that spread into unions, launched more African American legislators at local, state, and federal levels, and created an increasing sense of daring on the part of black citizens protesting for their basic rights in cities and towns across an industrializing country that needed their muscle and labor. Things were changing in terms of labor and the economy: cotton fields were yielding to soybean harvests that gave way to factories, railways, and even automobile plants.

Yet the experiences of black Americans ranged wretchedly, from steady, outright violence to the polite understandings that smothered the ability of even the most sympathetic white neighbors to reach out to them or even mix with them. In places like Birmingham, Alabama, and Albany, Georgia—two sites for Martin Luther King's eventual freedom campaigns—there was literally no difference between the local police and the regional Ku Klux Klan. Ruthless, savage men wore civic uniforms by day and ghoulish sheets by night. Their women had very little compassion when it came to the Negroes; nobody thought that the triumph in World War II changed anything.

For Stanley Levison, this American grief was rivaled only by his anguish about the betrayal by the Soviets of cultural freedom, glaringly revealed by the effects of the war. It had started before the war and prior to Stalin's infamous and ill-conceived "nonaggression pact" with Hitler. Robert Harvey summarized it in his book, *A Short History of Communism*:

> From around 1930 the ideological restrictions on cultural activity in Stalin's Russia grew increasingly sharp; officialdom decreed that artists should become virtual propagandists for the Communist Party and the state, and 80,000 censors ensured adherence to the Party Line—every one of them fearful for their lives in case they missed some heresy not yet invented. . . . in the sixteen years leading up to Hitler's invasion of Russia, [Sergei] Esenin, [Vladimir] Mayakovsky, and Marina Tsvetayeva committed suicide, while Osip Mandelshtam and the short-story writer Isaak Babel both died in prison camps.[3]

These were among many Russian poets and novelists and musicians whose lives were crippled or ended by the Stalinist regime. Musicians and composers, including the legendary Sergey Prokofiev and Dmitry Shostakovich, came to endure virtual cultural exile. Stanley remembered that the Soviet state, which he still glamorized at the time, had been able, in the mid-1920s, to transfer to actual paper currency rather than trading in precious stones. Were the Soviets now trading Marxist values for paper statements?

This unhappy condition, this skewing of righteous civilizations, was on the mind of Stanley Levison in the years following the war. Stanley was like a man in secret mourning for an unrevealed grief; his plaintive countenance, shrouded by cigarette smoke and framed in thick glasses, seemed drawn into the crypt of black suffering in America and artistic strangulation in Russia. He began to withdraw from the Russian situation and drew nearer to the clear and present denigration of black people in his own land.

He liked to quote an old African proverb to his brother Roy and to anyone else who'd listen: "You can't turn the wind, so turn the sail." Stanley was successful in business but did not consider himself as rich. He considered himself obligated. He felt an unsuppressed affinity for the peripherals of American life; the poor, the unemployed, the blacks, the Native Americans, the people left behind in the flush of national exhilaration following the surrenders of the Japanese and the Germans.

He struggled, in his deep and somber soul, between the traditional values of elite society and an intensive rebellion against them. Like many white sympathizers, Stanley believed that only a socialized economy could resolve the second-class citizenship of America's blacks. Lighting an unfiltered Lucky Strike one night, he told Clarence Jones, as Jones sipped on his favored vodka cocktail: "It's about capitalism, Clarence. I am part of it, I know. But I also know that capitalism breeds racial prejudice. It's so clear to me. The white capitalists pit the Negro workers against the white ones just to exploit them both. As long as capitalism holds, the Negro will never have a chance."

But before completely turning his attention to the Negroes, Levison became agitated about the case of Ethel and Julius Rosenberg—a married couple accused of sedition. Julius Rosenberg, born in 1918, hailed from a family of Jewish immigrants in New York City. The family settled in the Lower

East Side around the time Julius was eleven. Like so many new Americans, the parents worked in the shops and tenements of the Lower East Side. Julius graduated from Seward Park High School. Not unlike Stanley Levison, Julius was bewitched by socialist attitudes, and he quickly climbed to leadership in the Young Communist League–USA. This happened while he studied at City College, from which he graduated in 1939 with a degree in electrical engineering.

Julius was like so many other impressionable and passionate young people in those days, many of them Jewish: drawn culturally and philosophically to civil libertarian causes, not the least of which was a deep-seated conviction about racial equality. Life was cruel for the working classes and even more so for the socially segregated—most notably black people, who were more than ever shackled by Jim Crow.

It was before the harsh revelations of Soviet tyranny and oppression, most notably the invasion by Russia of Hungary in 1956 and the regime's staggering, tank-driven suppression of a popular uprising by the people of that satellite nation who just wanted to be free. The attack further tarnished the idealism of even party acolytes such as Stanley Levison. But in the late 1940s and early 1950s, the New York intellectuals who fancied leftist principles still believed that the Soviet system was truly communal, open, and a balm for the oppressed and underprivileged. One scholar of communism has written: "Recruits of a Jewish background found that their practice in dissecting contentious passages of the Talmud fitted them well for discussion of the finer points of Marxian texts."[4]

Of course, to a vocal and powerful segment of American legislators, most conspicuously Senator Joseph McCarthy, the Soviets were simply the evil "Reds" and the Jewish-dominated American Communist sympathizers were nothing more than treasonous traitors.

Julius Rosenberg found love and a political ally in Ethel Greenglass, who was three years younger. Ethel dreamed of becoming an actress and singer, though she ultimately settled for secretarial work at a shipping company. But she was not content to type. She became embroiled in labor disputes and then joined the Young Communist League. There she met Julius, and they were married in 1939, just as the Germans were preparing to launch World War II. It made sense to the Rosenbergs and other young Communists that the United States and the USSR would be allies in the crusade against fascism, though no one in the Roosevelt administration really trusted Joseph Stalin or the Russians as much as they just needed them.[5]

By 1940, Julius Rosenberg was busy at work with the Army Signal Corps Engineering Laboratories at Fort Monmouth, New Jersey. He functioned as an engineer-inspector and gained access to a bevy of sensitive technological, electronic, radar, and missile data. Suspicious army superiors fired Rosenberg when they discovered his previous membership in the Communist Party. He would use such information in the 1950s when he connected himself to a Soviet mole and, according to investigators, he and Ethel sold military documents and secrets to the Russians—who were starving for covert material to augment their atomic ambitions.

The Rosenbergs were indicted in 1950, tried, convicted, and executed for treason in the electric chair at Sing Sing in 1953. Even an appeal from Pope Pius XII directly to President Eisenhower did not stay the verdict.

The notorious couple was not alone in their espionage; hosts of other Americans were caught spying for the USSR in that era. Julius and Ethel were the only two civilians put to death for it. There was an undeniable sense, particularly among American Jews, that ethnic prejudice played a role in the severe punishment. Moreover, the use of the chair, seen as abhorrent by some, fueled the bitterness and even second-guessing about the decree.

Julius died instantly from the voltage. Ethel, who was smaller in frame, suffered through five charges of electricity before finally succumbing. It was reported that her heart was still beating through the fourth current, and that when she finally expired, smoke curled up from her head.

Among the most ardent of advocates for the defense and exoneration of the Rosenbergs was Stanley Levison. At the time of their executions, Stanley had established himself, quietly, out of the public eye, as one of the key financiers of the Communist Party–USA. The FBI, driven specifically by the fervor of J.

Edgar Hoover, and fanned by the "red-baiting" activities of Senator Joseph McCarthy and the House Committee on Un-American Activities, was well aware of Levison's activities. Stanley, the poker-faced alumnus of Far Rockaway High School, was nonetheless extremely active in the machinations of the Left, and the government was keenly interested.

The eminent King biographer Taylor Branch summarizes the irony of Stanley Levison, as he was being monitored by the FBI during the early 1950s—before he met and embraced Dr. King: "A leftist radical since his college days during the Depression, Levison nonetheless had a firm capitalist side to him. He was a forty-four-year-old socialist who had grown rich off real estate investments, a lawyer who shunned law books and had never practiced law. He had owned car dealerships but never learned to drive." Levison was sure of himself, nonetheless. At one point in 1958, two years after he had severed his ties with the Communist Party, he chastised Dr. King about a potentially lucrative lecture tour for the reverend.

"You can't do that," said Stanley.

"Why not?" asked Dr. King, who made a habit of donating much of his salary and all his stipends to the movement and, frankly, needed money.

"Because the kinds of people that you will be preaching to about nonviolence are too poor to pay for your lectures." King immediately acquiesced. He not only agreed with Stanley, but found himself in a moral box: Levison always refused any payments from King for Levison's services as a consultant, accountant, fund-raiser, and ghostwriter. But what King did pay for, in a broader sense, was Levison's indisputable association with Communists in the 1940s and early 1950s.

The problems for Stanley began in 1951 and were circuitously triggered by the heart condition of one old man and the cancer of a young man. Morris Childs, the elder, had been the chairman of the Illinois chapter of the CP-USA. Morris was born in Kiev to Russian Jewish parents as Moishe Chilovsky. His father, Josef, was a revolutionary who fought against the czarist regime and suffered an exile in Siberia. The family, including Morris's younger brother,

Jakob (later Americanized to Jack), was able to make its way from Ellis Island to Chicago—their strong Bolshevik sensibilities intact.

Morris developed serious heart problems in his late forties and was summarily dismissed as editor of the Communist Party's newspaper, *The Daily Worker*, in 1947. Morris, his Ukrainian blood boiling, took this poorly and began to reevaluate his loyalty to the party. The situation was exacerbated a year later, in 1948: his brother, Jack, also a party functionary, was dealing with the cancer of his young son. The lad suffered the loss of an eye from the disease. When Jack turned to the party hierarchy for some financial help with this medical crisis, he was rebuffed. The two brothers, deeply angry now, brimming with resentment, quit the party. This made them both great bait for the FBI, which was always lurking, looking to recruit informants.

Before long, the brothers Childs were firmly enlisted as informants for the FBI. The Bureau had a special interest in how the CP-USA was able to bankroll itself. That was an easy matter for Jack Childs to discuss: he had served as assistant to the party's fiscal director for several years. Jack regaled his handler-agents about secret meetings with donors and about furtive cash depositories. At some point, he disclosed that the twin brothers, Stanley and Roy Levison, had been making substantial donations, in the thousands annually, to the party. Morris corroborated the connection with Levison. Morris had a particular gripe concerning "this visitor from New York" because Levison had been dispatched to talk with Morris and find out why the latter had not been keeping closely in touch with the party. Was there a problem because of Morris's health, Levison inquired?

Moreover, an FBI memo file states that once Jack Childs stopped working for the Party's monetary department, "he transferred to Stanley Levison all cash, bonds, and lists of depositories and records . . . under the informant's control." The FBI monitored a cloak-and-dagger type meeting between Morris and Stanley in front of the New York Public Library on a gray, blustery day in November 1952. In time, the Childs brothers divulged and uncovered a vast inventory of rendezvous, documents, bank records, hotel receipts, and conversation trails that unequivocally linked Stanley Levison to the top financial levels of the Communist Party–USA. Stanley even acquired various business firms and interests to which he consigned a percentage of profits to the Party and its work.

In one of his detailed narratives of Levison, Taylor Branch reports about what happened when the chief financial officer of the CP-USA died in 1954. Stanley and his wife Beatrice called upon the widow at her Manhattan apartment. During the course of the visit, Stanley looked through the deceased's personal files and removed a batch of party-related bank statements and ledgers. A few days later, Levison met with Morris Childs at the Statler Hotel and acknowledged that he, Stanley, was now going to be managing the financial interests of the Party. The FBI, deploying wiretaps and other surveillance, and relying directly upon the Childs brothers, was now vigorously scrutinizing Stanley Levison—who had emerged from the shadows and was absolutely and incontrovertibly a key underwriter and promoter of the American Communist movement.

The operation, initiated by Jack and Morris Childs, and code-named Solo, persisted for twenty-five years until Stanley's death in 1979. It became difficult to absolutely link Stanley to the Communist Party after 1955, and certainly after 1956, when he turned his focus to assisting the emergent Reverend Martin Luther King Jr.—who was quickly ascending in prominence following his stewardship of the bus boycott in Montgomery, Alabama. That did not stop the FBI, however, from illicitly attempting to link King to the Communists by default—one of the most sinister government plots in postwar history. As David Garrow has written, "Stanley Levison and Martin King were only two of thousands of Americans whose lives would be forever changed by Jack and Morris Childs."[6]

Operation Solo was remarkably successful, and it garnered the Bureau an immense trove of information about the Party's flow of money, its management, and its clear association with high-ranking members of the Soviet regime. So valuable was it to the government's mission of undermining the leftists that the FBI put up for decades with Morris's egomania and Jack's slyness.

Solo employed wiretaps, photographic evidence, the interception of mail and courier traffic, and the reconnoitering use of double agents and informers. The wealth of once-secret government documents, some redacted, some startlingly unmarked, prove that Levison had devoted a significant number of his years—and vast amounts of his money—to the Communists. The transcripts expose his involvement (until 1956) in secret subway encounters, so-called bag-jobs, and shadowy business ventures (from luggage stores to bolt-manufacturing concerns to "reserve funds"). Levison wrote articles and gave speeches decrying the McCarran Act, a tough immigration law, as well as the Eisenhower administration itself. His pleas for, and his energetic fund-raising on behalf of, Julius and Ethel Rosenberg, were a natural outgrowth of his belief that the American government tended toward fascism.

He exploited his budgetary leadership of the American Jewish Congress in favor of the socialist community, though the Congress was, at that time, decidedly left-wing anyway. Stanley had dubious feelings about the newly founded state of Israel. Even though the country was originally socialist-structured, replete with a comprehensive national health care system, he dismissed it as yet another "western" nation. Stanley saw Israel as being aligned with the ignominious economic doctrines of the United States, Great Britain, and other capitalist nations. Stanley Levison was no Zionist.

Stanley and Beatrice's only child, Andrew, a successful attorney and writer in Atlanta, wrote to me in 2011: "Stanley respected the cultural heritage of Judaism but he was a firm, lifelong atheist and a passionate believer in universal human values. He did not speak a word of Hebrew, never entered a synagogue for spiritual purposes and never taught me to consider any human culture superior to any other." Clarence Jones has a slightly altered view, telling me that "Stanley was not a self-hating Jew, not at all. He may not have been so observant or interested in the theology of the religion. But he drew from the Jewish heritage of social action. After all, he served as treasurer of the American Jewish Congress and was active with the American Jewish Committee."

Regardless of how pious Stanley was or was not, the vast majority of his colleagues in the early days of his political activism—before he committed himself to Dr. King—were Jews. The hierarchy of the Communist Party–USA was significantly born of Jewish families. Jack and Morris Childs were Jewish refugees from Russia; they, more than anybody else, exposed Stanley's dominant role in the party and thus brought significant harm to both Levison and ultimately to King. It was Solo that shed light on things: where some of the dollars from the Levison brothers' Ford dealership in New Jersey were winding up; what Stanley was really doing in Poland when he supposedly was looking to import Polish sausage; why Stanley was mysteriously investing in laundries in Ecuador.

But then, midway through 1955, it began to change. Perhaps Stanley, like some other members of the Communist circle, had never quite made peace with the stunning Soviet-German pact that put the Russians on the Nazi side originally in World War II. (This alignment changed when Hitler then invaded Russia in 1941. The Führer would regret opening the eastern front, and the Russians lost 20 million people stopping him.) Maybe the folksy socialist poems and essays that Stanley once read in *Voch* were not holding up against the mounting dictatorial nature of the Stalinist regime—this was not really socialism, but just another form of totalitarianism.

The record shows that by 1955, certainly by 1956, Stanley was no longer involved in the clandestine financial dealings of the American Communists. Martin Luther King Jr. may have been waiting in the wings for him, but it was not a simple matter of switching one cause for another. Jack Childs was no longer pursuing Levison, and they had no further contact. The FBI—for the time being—had no more trail to follow in the matter of Stanley Levison. Soon enough, the Bureau dropped Levison from its list of prominent persons within the American Party. The FBI became convinced that Levison was no longer active and that he was developing an interest in the evolving civil rights movement.

Indeed, the government decided that Stanley, like the Childs brothers before him, might be a great catch as an informer. During Levison's early years with Dr. King, the FBI approached Levison twice to discuss the possibility of his becoming an informant. Stanley did talk with agents but categorically declined the invitations. Very little is known about these conversations but for the fact that they took place in New York City and that Levison would not be recruited.

David Garrow summarizes the narrative:

> The FBI's information tied Levison to the Communist party only for the years before 1956, and not for those after. While Jack Childs could supply firsthand testimony that Levison had been directly involved in secret Communist activity in 1954, activity that almost certainly made Levison privy to the party's financial link to the Soviet Union, the FBI possessed no evidence that connected Levison to any CP activity in the years after he and Martin Luther King, Jr. first became acquainted.[7]

Andrew Levison, Stanley's son, told me that his father often laughed about the FBI's interview with him about becoming a mole. The elder Levison recalled that one of the agents offered some sanctimony: "Do it to serve your country."

Levison would tell friends: "I could not have asked the agent for a better setup line. I drew myself up and said: 'I think I'm serving my country a whole lot better by helping Martin Luther King to dismantle southern segregation than by going back into the CP to spy on a pathetically isolated and irrelevant bunch of guys half of whom are already working for you.'"[8]

The US government then essentially lost interest in Stanley, until the FBI deviously gave the Kennedy brothers the impression, starting in 1962, that Levison *and* King were controlled by, and sworn to, the Communist Party. This was based on the disingenuous use of the Solo files and wreaked havoc—and wiretaps—on King, Levison, and others, including Clarence Jones, Andrew Young, and Harry Belafonte, as we shall see.

Meanwhile, on December 1, 1955, a seamstress named Rosa Parks refused to stand up and move from her seat on a Montgomery, Alabama, city bus. She was arrested for taking the seat of a white rider. "I was just tired of standing," she told the press. A new, twenty-six-year-old Baptist preacher in town named Martin Luther King Jr. had recently assumed the pulpit of the Dexter Avenue

Church. He had taken the post to get away from the shadow and sternness of his father, Martin Luther "Daddy" King Sr. of the Ebenezer Baptist Church in Atlanta.

The other black ministers sensed in young King a special gift for oratory. Besides, he was too new in town to have earned the traditional hostility of the white establishment. So they elected him the president of the Montgomery Improvement Association, and King stepped into history.

Stanley Levison of New York was not far behind.

CHAPTER FIVE

In friendship

" just can't sing a song; it has to be part of my marrow and bones and everything," Libby Holman, the dark-skinned, exotic, Jewish performer and philanthropist told an interviewer in 1966.[1] Holman, who died five years later, was a particularly fervent, though not widely known, patron of Martin Luther King Jr. and a kindred spirit of Stanley Levison.

The better-known actor and dancer Clifton Webb gave her the nickname "The Statue of Libby." Elizabeth Lloyd Holzman was born May 23, 1904, in Cincinnati to a lawyer and stockbroker, Alfred Holzman and his wife Rachel. She was affectionately known as "Libby," and while she is remembered for her career in theater and for allegedly killing her husband with a gunshot blast in 1932, she is also revered in civil rights circles as a generous ally of Martin Luther King Jr.

In Little Rock, Arkansas, one night in 1939, Libby and her cabaret partner,

Josh White, ran into some trouble. Josh was a black man, lyrical and athletic, and the two of them had just alighted at a local club to prep for their performance. Josh, with a guitar in his hand and a fire in his soul, was used to adversity. He had been challenging discrimination all his life; he mixed his rhythm and blues with social protest songs, and he thrust his throbbing music into the face of segregationists and racists. Just as Stanley Levison would become Martin Luther King's closest white friend and adviser, Joshua White became Franklin Delano Roosevelt's closest black friend and comrade. The wartime president would call upon the lyricist for advice and counsel about the mood and yearnings of the black community.

That did not help Josh with the rampant critics of the time. Because he sang about human rights, because he danced for freedom, because he spoke at political rallies and cried out for black liberation, and maybe even because he was a friend of FDR, the McCarthyites assumed he was a Communist. They tarnished him with innuendos, they painted him "red," and his career was ultimately damaged. Like Stanley Levison, and so many intellectuals and artists who yearned to democratize the country, Josh White was ostracized and cursed. Stanley saw and heard Josh entertain at Greenwich Village's famed Café Society—a trailblazing club where blacks and whites mingled comfortably in the 1930s and 1940s and where artists such as the Jewish comedian Jack Gilford and the incomparable Billie Holiday performed together.

In that spirit, and with gritty determination, Libby Holman, with her overbite and moxie, her mulatto complexion and moral indignation, linked up with Josh and toured the nation.

Libby and Josh were the first such interracial duo to perform together on the road, but they could not readily find venues that would permit such a production. They made movies together, recorded albums, and petitioned the War Department to perform in USO concerts for American servicemen during the war. Eleanor Roosevelt wrote them a special letter of recommendation. Nonetheless, the department rejected the duo, citing them as being too provocative. Again, black men could fight the Nazis, but they not could sing in front of GIs. Especially with a Caucasian woman. Particularly when that

Jewish woman's husband had reportedly committed suicide in a hotel room and many law enforcement authorities contended it was a murder.

Libby knew it wouldn't be easy for Josh as they ventured into clubs and bistros in the South. In Little Rock that night, they sought a beer. Josh was denied a drink, pushed out of his seat, and thrown out. Libby quit the bar immediately and attended to her friend—who was also restricted from the whites-only hotel she stayed in, who could not use the same bathroom or kitchen or drinking fountain visited by the same white audience members whom he would later regale in the establishment. Of course, the curtain would rise only after Josh had to access the service entrance; he was not permitted to enter through the front doorway.

It was natural that Libby would find inspiration in the evolving work of Martin Luther King Jr. The grandiloquent young preacher was thrust into the national spotlight by 1955, and she was moved by his soothing voice and his quiet bravery—his filmed remarks following the bombing of his Montgomery, Alabama, home, admonishing people to refrain from a violent, vengeful response, moved Libby.

Clarence Jones was dispatched by Stanley Levison to connect with the actress. Stanley knew that she'd be sympathetic and that she was wealthy. Even though her first husband, Zachary Smith Reynolds, had died from that mysterious gunshot wound (Libby was acquitted of any wrongdoing), the R. J. Reynolds family, cosmically rich due to their tobacco holdings, remained close with Libby. She would never want for money, and she was always driven by her ethical contentions with society.

"Libby Holman Reynolds?" Clarence Jones retorted broadly with recollection when I asked him about the famed chanteuse. "Oh yes, I knew her well. She was formidable," he stated, emphatically. "Stanley sent me to see her and discuss the movement."

This came as no surprise; Stanley was the supreme fund-raiser for King, and he did not hesitate, even if Libby was controversial, outspoken, and known to dabble in bisexual liaisons. None of this mattered to Stanley. By 1955 and the launch of the Montgomery bus boycott, when he latched on to

King, Stanley was working closely with Bayard Rustin—a man fundamentally communist and openly homosexual. Even though King himself occasionally lampooned Rustin's personal behavior, on one occasion fretting that Rustin might "grab one little brother 'cause he will grab one when he has a drink,"[2] Levison simply withheld judgment. He directed Clarence Jones to convene with Libby Holman.

"Yes," Clarence recalled. "I met with her a couple of times at her New York townhouse. She gave me $25,000. And then she donated another $25,000 after a second meeting. The money went to the SCLC Foundation."

Libby's friendship with King would continue over the years, though she never publicized it or wove it into her résumé. She would think about the indignities suffered by her onetime stage comrade, Joshua White, as he churned out Piedmont blues and protest psaltery while being humiliated by white separatists. That part of her that was Jewish, though she ultimately practiced Zen liturgies and was eulogized in a Quaker ceremony after her suicide in 1971, nonetheless fed her empathy and zeal for the outcasts of civilization. Moreover, still young, she had lost a son, Topper, and never quite came to terms with her grief—this fed her compassion for others.

In memory of her boy, Holman created the Christopher Reynolds Foundation, which still exists today. Through this fund, Libby underwrote Martin Luther King when he visited India and had the opportunity to meet Prime Minister Jawaharlal Nehru—an experience that galvanized the preacher and his belief system till the day he died.

By sometime in 1956, Stanley Levison had completed his dissociation from the Communist Party–USA. "One of the things that really plagued him," said Leon Schwartz, "was that as much as the Communists did for black people, the party organization was always ambivalent. At one point, the party called for a separate nation for them, in what they called 'The Black Belt' of some of the southern states. Since the black problem was confined to that specific group, the problem could not be viewed as part of the global revolution. It was actually a plank passed at the Comintern in 1928 or so. That was something that Stanley and a lot of us thought was pretty crazy. So while they did good things often enough, all too often the Party itself took these bureaucratic positions that were neutral or even hostile to civil rights. They seemed to get themselves into a box. The blacks were an American issue and they were always stuck on the so-called international workers crusade. Mind you, besides a few headliners like Paul Robeson or Bayard Rustin of course or A. Philip Randolph, the Marxists never really attracted a lot of African Americans."

Eventually, Levison had stopped raising or diverting funds for the Party and had desisted from manipulating his own businesses, and that of his brother Roy, in favor of the Party's treasury. The FBI may have decided to profess that Levison was still infatuated with the Soviets, a deceitful practice that continued for many years after his separation from them. But Levison's disillusionment with the American Communists had been brewing for many years; it culminated, according to Levison's son Andrew, because of a "rigid, cult-like intellectual atmosphere," and Stanley could not tolerate such staleness. Echoing Leon Schwartz's comments, Andrew Levison wrote to me that his father felt that the CP-USA "had become completely isolated and irrelevant to the larger trade union, Negro freedom and other progressive social movements of the era."[3]

For years, Stanley had struggled with the conflict of knowing that the Communists were feckless and knowing too many good people who were being hounded, disgraced, and even jailed simply because they were leftists. He couldn't just walk away from old friends and colleagues just because the organization was corrupt and deceitful—laundering both its false egalitarianism and Soviet intransigence. It was hard for his colleagues not to see—and appreciate—the dependable character aspects of his viscerally autonomous and independent nature.

According to his son, Levison would come to say: "The honest people who broke with the party before I did considered me a real first-class 'sucker' for not realizing the absolutely appalling nature of Stalinism at that time, and, in retrospect, they were entirely right. At the same time, though, I felt that a lot of the people who were recanting and naming names back then weren't acting out of high principle but were just groveling in order to save their own lousy skins, and, in retrospect, I was also right."

But Stanley was turning his attention, his skills, and his assets to the emerging pastor of Montgomery's Dexter Avenue Baptist Church, Martin Luther King Jr. There was a context for this; it wasn't a sudden, incongruous turnabout sprung by the Soviet invasion of Hungary in 1956 or any one specific incident. After all, King was divinity and Levison was skepticism.

Levison had been working with a publication called *The Churchman* in the mid-1950s. This was a journal of religious pacifism and, even though it was theologically based and Levison was wholly secular, the bulletin's penchant for social radicalism suited him fine. The writers were psalmists, peacemakers, liberals, believers in justice—they despised racism and economic injustice. Unlike some hard-core secular leftists who dismissed religionists out of hand, Stanley was not so narrow in attitude. As he came to know King and heard King's decidedly progressive religious language, and he understood that the pastor was actually something of a social militant himself, it was easy for Levison to align himself with the man. And Stanley, nudging away from Soviet hypocrisy, was looking for something or someone else with whom to hook up.

King was twenty-seven years old, almond-eyed, smooth-complexioned—a rather short man with a certain roundness about him that in a few years would soften into plumpness. But his countenance, sharpened by the trademark pencil moustache and firm lips, was masculine, handsome, and emitted a delicate combination of intelligence and vulnerability. Few people knew that he had extremely sensitive skin, highly prone to rashes—so much so that King could never use a razor to remove his daily stubble. Only his wife Coretta and his closest traveling colleagues, most notably Ralph David Abernathy, knew of and put up with the rotten-eggs smell of King's required shaving emollient that unpleasantly dissolved his whiskers.

King came to his first pulpit in Montgomery over his father's objections. The senior King saw Martin as his associate and successor at the prestigious Ebenezer Baptist Church on fabled "Sweet" Auburn Avenue in Atlanta. "Daddy" King, a towering sledgehammer of a man, a man of severe doctrines who stubbornly swore allegiance to America in spite of the nation's shameful history of racial travesty, was committed to the successful emergence of a black middle class.

He preferred reasonable social compromise to black militancy, he wanted to work with the greater Atlanta ministry, and he had old-line views on the role and place of women that were shared by many of his white colleagues. He had little tolerance for feminism or homosexuality and was deeply suspicious of the Communists. Daddy King was (until a late turnabout for JFK in 1960) a Republican who liked Dwight D. Eisenhower and approved of Richard M. Nixon's presidential aspirations until the Kennedy brothers helped to get his son Martin Jr. out of a prison stay during the 1960 campaign.

But "Mike Jr.," who in 1955 completed a Ph.D. in Systematic Theology at Boston University, and studied philosophers from Socrates to Augustine to Gandhi, did not want to start out in his daddy's considerable shadow. So he jumped at the chance to assume leadership of the distinguished Montgomery pulpit. He had little idea that concurrent events, from the heinous kidnapping and murder of fourteen-year-old Emmett Till in Money, Mississippi, to the bus boycott in Montgomery, would suddenly catapult him to a celebrity that he both accepted and dreaded.

By the time Bayard Rustin, who had ingratiated himself into the Montgomery community and protest, introduced Levison to King, those two outside events had given a significant boost to white indignation (primarily in the northern and western states) about the pitiful and dangerous plight of southern Negroes.

Till was a fourteen-year-old African American from Chicago who was sent down to Money, Mississippi, in order to spend time with relatives. Unfamiliar with southern ways, he was a bit too brash and upbeat for a black teenager. He did not know about some of the oligarchic taboos that were as endemic to the Delta as fireflies and bourbon. He was further handicapped by a lisp; people were not always sure what Emmett was saying or trying to say. At times, when he spoke, what emerged sounded something like a whistle.

Exiting a little five-and-ten store in the center of Mississippi, Emmett allegedly hooted at an attractive young white woman—although he may have just been trying to speak to her, maybe even offer up an "Excuse me, ma'am" as he passed by. It didn't matter; people thought Till had whistled at the woman. By nightfall, a group of local vigilantes overran the house of Emmett's relatives, and dragged the shrieking, terrified lad out. They methodically proceeded to terrorize him, pummel him, and shoot a bullet through one of his eyes. They then dumped his body in the Tallahatchie River and were satisfied that justice was done. The crickets resumed chirping in the woods as the moonlight paled over the muddy, bloodstained river.

The swollen, ripped, and shattered body of the teenager was recovered under the steaming sun of daylight. Members of the Till family were numb, traumatized, yet they kept their mouths shut. A sham of a trial would ensue, with the killers set free. Fortunately for history, an enterprising and gutsy black photographer named Ernest C. Withers dispatched himself to the vicinity in his old wood-paneled station wagon to record the scene. Withers, a veteran and decorated photographer-soldier of World War II, was well known for his uncanny ability to be present at timely and revealing events—the publicizing of which created outrage and concern in the general public. With his camera, he had brought a young Negro League baseball prodigy named Willie Mays to national attention; he would routinely snap Martin Luther King in critical moments; he would now publish a photo of the corpse of Emmett Till, with a hollow socket where his eye had been and the crusted horror of a trampled, doomed, drowned body lying across a coroner's slab. In Chicago, Emmett Till's mother had belligerently insisted that the gruesome print be distributed to the newspapers, crying out, "I want them to see what they done to my boy."

Stanley Levison took note of this gruesome episode, and it grabbed his soul and shook it. Why? He brooded to himself. How can human beings do this to other human beings? By the time of the Till incident, he had quit the Communists, taking all the jagged parts of his long fealty to them and fitting them together into something else.

Levison was working with A. Philip Randolph, the legendary chairman of the International Brotherhood of Sleeping Car Porters and—prior to MLK—the unrivaled principal of the fledgling civil rights movement. Stanley's mission was to help Randolph and his associates capitalize on the historic 1954 Supreme Court decision, *Brown v. Topeka Board of Education*, which (on paper) sanctioned integrated facilities for blacks and whites in schools, hotels, community venues, and the like.

Ironically, the Communist movement did not particularly endorse or support *Brown*, although on the surface, such a ruling would be consistent with the prevailing Communist doctrine of social equality. Again, the Communists rather scorned such arbitrary judicial diktats, aspiring instead to "total world revolution" in order to realize their economic utopia. The Negro, opined serious Bolsheviks, had to push for a kind of separate national development to achieve his place in the new order—as suggested at the 1928 Comintern.

"That's a lot to ask," Stanley once muttered to the unswervingly Communist Bayard Rustin, "given that the Negro people can't even vote in the South or send their kids to college even when the kids are smart and qualified."[4]

By the time of the Emmett Till murder, Senator Joseph McCarthy's power in Washington, and the brazen red-baiting witch hunts that destroyed the lives of so many artisans, performers, and scholars, were waning. The Senate had seen enough and gone so far as to censure the Wisconsin ideologue and to halt his unwarranted persecutions of innocent intellectuals. Stanley had tired of it all, and his entry into the black human rights struggle was an appealing alternative for the onetime taciturn kid from Far Rockaway. The cast of characters changed for him, but he still loved loners, outsiders, undesirables, people who traveled through the world without light. He was literal-minded, but he was drawn to dreamers, men and women of audacity—for these he sought to be an enabler, just as his old school principal, Sanford Ellsworth, had envisioned.

In Montgomery, the bus boycott sparked by Rosa Parks's refusal to get up from her seat after another long day's work ("I was just tired," she told reporters) on December 1, 1955, was dragging along for months. With tenacity and an aroused clergy-leadership, carpools were formed, people just walked, and Montgomery's businesses began to feel the impact. Local and state authorities refused to buckle even as the nonviolent protest began to captivate the nation. The only problem, vexing and persistent, was the fact that the Montgomery Improvement Association, which had elected the young newcomer Martin

Luther King Jr. as its president, was running desperately low on funds. White philanthropists were, at best, not interested; at worst, downright hostile. Black people were generally too poor to contribute but, in Montgomery, they gave with their feet, grit, and faith.

Bayard Rustin, the fiery and flamboyant New Yorker, was on the scene and recognized the historicity of this flashpoint. Emmett Till's murder added a sense of urgency to the mix. Like the community ministers in Montgomery, Rustin recognized in young Martin King a remarkable, almost messianic aura. His oratory was rhapsodic—as the featured rally speaker at Holt Street Baptist Church spurring the community to pick up where Rosa Parks had left off, King even surprised himself with the power of his speech to move the crowd: "There comes a time when people get tired of being trampled over by the iron feet of oppression. . . . If we are wrong, the Supreme Court of this nation is wrong. If we are wrong, the Constitution of the United States is wrong. If we are wrong, God Almighty is wrong!"

Rustin, working the old Communist network, brought Stanley Levison into the loop immediately after the Emmett Till tragedy. The two of them, spawning a long partnership, met in New York City. Rustin shrewdly perceived that Levison, loaded with monies and with strong natural gifts for administration, was ripe for a cause like that of the blacks of Mississippi and Alabama. The Montgomery boycott needed a sympathetic and practiced, behind-the-scenes executive director in order to survive and prevail.

There was other Jewish money being funneled into the Montgomery boycott. Former mayor (and former congressman) Bob Filner of San Diego remembers the work of his father, Joseph Filner, the onetime secretary of the Pittsburgh division of the Communist Party–USA. "Dad had these Sunday breakfast meetings all the time," Bob Filner told me. "They would talk politics, eat bagels, smoke, and carry on about all the indignities suffered by the poor people, black people, and others. I remember Stanley Levison being at these Sunday gatherings a lot. Dad read about Dr. King and was really impressed. So he picked up the phone and called King in Montgomery. He asked King how much money they needed down there. King was shy about giving a number, but he mentioned his traveling expenses now that he had to fly all over and speak about the cause. Yes, Stanley was in on it. Even before he ever met Dr. King."

Joseph Filner had served in World War II and personally saw what the Nazis had done to the Jews; he was among the GIs who liberated the Dachau concentration camp, taking the smell of mass death into their nostrils, and witnessing the heaps of contorted corpses and the living dead who limped around the murdering fields in what was left of their skin and bones. He related these experiences to his business associate and friend, Stanley Levison, when they both lived in New York and talked of freeing the masses from tyranny. Filner had done very well both in the bakery business and in stainless steel scrap metal, though he was a dedicated organizer of various industrial unions. He and his pals sent Martin Luther King over $100,000, which, said Bob Filner, "truly helped King to put his Southern Christian Leadership Conference on a sound financial footing."

But Joseph Filner and his circle never really left New York and, though they sent checks, did not actually jump into the fray of what was starting in Montgomery and then would be spreading to Selma, Alabama, Albany, Georgia, Birmingham, and Memphis. Not so Stanley Levison. Influenced immediately by Bayard Rustin, Levison went to Montgomery and, hands-on, forged a unique relationship with King and all the key men and women in the new movement.

Working with his old friend A. Philip Randolph, with an outstanding, emerging civil rights activist named Ella Baker, and with the regional offices of the NAACP, Stanley Levison created an entity called In Friendship in 1956. It was a fund, basically, designed to help and rescue the innumerable black victims of Klan brutality in the South and of general white complicity. This is what Stanley did with particular adroitness: he funneled and raised dollars, wrote press releases and newspaper ads, and created investment dividends for the cause—just as he had done before on behalf of the Communist Party–USA.

A defining event, completely engineered by Levison, was a star-studded benefit and gala to benefit the boycott, held in 1956 at New York's Madison Square Garden. Stanley, soft-spoken but resolute, seasoned at compelling people to put themselves out for a good cause, got both Harry Belafonte and Duke Ellington to perform, *pro bono*. He convinced Coretta Scott King to appear as well. (Mrs. King did not require her arm to be twisted: she was already feeling left behind somewhat in the wake of her husband's bounding fame.)

Profits from the concert (the first of two such events) went to the MIA and to the NAACP. An additional $10,000 was deposited into the Victory Savings Bank in Columbia, South Carolina, to assist the bank in offering loans to indigent tenant farmers. Stanley was in gear. He moved deftly among celebrities, particularly Belafonte, while keeping himself below the radar. "We have to connect the Negro struggle with the labor movement," he told Belafonte, standardizing a principle that would be embraced by King throughout his thirteen-year tenure as the *de facto* head of the freedom campaign. It was no coincidence that when King was shot in Memphis in 1968, he was there helping the sanitation workers accredit their labor union. In light of the Montgomery boycott, labor organizations ranging from the Sleeping Car Porters to an assortment of car assembly workers and fishermen's unions contributed to the cause. Individuals such as Tallulah Bankhead and Marlon Brando pitched in. Stanley, said Harry Belafonte, was "a brilliant tactician and tireless fund-raiser." From the moment that Stanley met King, he was cast under the preacher's spell, and his own life had an unwavering focus.

The occasion of their meeting, arranged by Rustin, impacted both men deeply. Stanley felt King's "vulnerability" and "power." Taylor Branch wrote: "King's revealing directness deeply impressed Stanley Levison, who resolved at that moment to get to know him better. As for King, he found nothing objectionable about Levison, least of all his radical connections."[5] King was no Communist, but he supported the Communists' historic empathy for oppressed peoples and for their fierce argument with racial inequality. He was immediately grateful for Stanley's organizational know-how and his unabashed habit of giving the preacher strong advice—even when Levison would harness King's tendency to overstate things or speak with too much imagery and a degree of hyperbole. Time and again, Clarence Jones has told me that the two men "just liked each other and trusted one another implicitly." King never shunned white people in any general way, but Stanley was unconditionally Martin's closest white friend.

A river of events pulled Levison away from the Communist infrastructure and into the complex tapestry of what was then called "the Negro work." Libby Holman Reynolds, with her sultry, offbeat liberalism and tobacco money, influenced King to move in the direction that Bayard Rustin had calibrated via the Stanley Levison introduction.

Then came the Twentieth Congress of the Communist Party of the Soviet Union in February 1956. In a seismic speech, the Russian premier, Nikita Khrushchev, strongly condemned the crimes of Joseph Stalin. He denounced and repudiated the "cult of personality" that he claimed surrounded Stalin and stained the international socialist revolution that was better represented by the legacy of Vladimir Lenin—who was truly for "the masses." Khrushchev powerfully exposed Stalin's appalling legacy as a genocidal despot who did anything but liberate the Russian people. Stalin was revealed as a traitor to the original Bolshevik doctrines. Stanley Levison was affected by this landmark oration, and it further demoralized him about the Soviets.

Meanwhile, Soviet tanks were preparing to squash and kill Hungarian workers. The ranks of the Communist Party–USA were radically depleted; longtime members were harshly awakened from their utopian dream and their identification with Moscow. Thousands of them were prosecuted in the United States via the Smith and McCarran acts.

From Hollywood to New York, onetime stalwarts were fleeing, disappearing, or simply reeling in anger and disillusionment. A martyred teenager named Emmett Till and a formidable seamstress named Rosa Parks turned their collective nightmare into a new *cri de coeur*. Stanley Levison was in the thick of this painful realignment, and he was ready. As Leon Schwartz said, "It was already too hard to defend the Marxists or rationalize their behavior. There were just too many questions coming too often."

The Montgomery bus boycott continued for 381 days. At its zenith, 90 percent of the city's blacks stayed off the buses. It was grueling hard work, walking long miles in rain or steaming heat, taking in fewer wages, organizing car pools, suffering through the emotional and physical bullying of many whites. In November 1956, the Supreme Court upheld a prior district court ruling citing segregation on city buses as unconstitutional. On December 20, King formally declared the end of the boycott. The next morning, he and three other local leaders boarded an integrated bus. King told reporters: "We came to see that, in the long run, it is more honorable to walk in dignity than ride in humiliation. So we decided to substitute tired feet for tired souls, and walk the streets of Montgomery."

A few weeks after this news conference, King opened a letter in Montgomery he received from Levison in New York. Dated February 11, 1957, Stanley concluded his note with this paragraph:

> We saw your television broadcast and our enthusiasm was matched by everyone with whom we spoke. It had a compelling, persuasive quality and many of our friends were deeply impressed with the profundity of your observations and their highly effective presentation. All we need now is a sponsor to give us a half-hour weekly—we have the star.
>
>   Warmest personal regards. Stanley[6]

The civil rights movement had its leader. And Martin King had Stanley Levison.

CHAPTER SIX

Harry Belafonte, Janet Levison, and a Totally Different "Kennedy"

Besides Stanley Levison, another notable person who met Martin Luther King Jr. for the first time in 1956 was Harry Belafonte. King phoned the rising calypso star in New York, and according to Belafonte's memoirs, said, simply: "You don't know me, Mr. Belafonte, but my name is Martin Luther King Jr."

Belafonte, astonished, replied: "Oh, I know you. Everybody knows you."

King's unpretentiousness was neither unusual nor misplaced. Although he had electrified the Montgomery community with his Holt Street Baptist Church charge to arms regarding the boycott (a presentation for which he had twenty minutes to prepare), been arrested twice, had his home bombed, and was the undisputed leader of the remarkable and unprecedented campaign, he really did not gauge his already global prominence. The distinguished

Reverend James Lawson, ensconced in India following his own prison term for refusing to serve in the Korean War, read about King in a newspaper and was exhilarated by the notion of black people taking on the white establishment in a nonviolent, Gandhian action that, in Lawson's mind, directly mirrored the Mahatma's stunning crusade to remove the British from colonial India. Lawson, a black Methodist with strict and austere disciplines, would eventually ally with King in a number of efforts, including, and finally, King's participation in the Memphis sanitation workers' strike that cost King his life in 1968.[1]

Stanley Levison had told King: "You should get in touch with Belafonte. He could be very valuable in our work." King was headed for New York to raise funds for the Montgomery boycott, which was moving along but was desperately short of cash. Stanley knew that Belafonte was atypical among Hollywood celebrities. Belafonte was a man whose talent and charisma were matched by his zeal—his anger—regarding the historic oppression of blacks by the white establishment. Like Libby Holman's friend, Joshua White, the entertainer was not wrapped up in his own hard-won celebrity. He would take unparalleled physical risks himself in his proactive, very present participation in a number of protests, most notably the Montgomery-to-Selma march in 1965 to secure voting rights for African Americans. As Clarence Jones told me, "Martin was not always smitten with the Hollywood lifestyle of consumption and superficiality, but he found a genuine confidante and constant resource in Harry."

Belafonte was well aware of the preacher who was already intoning his refrain from pulpits and community lecterns, "There comes a time when people get tired . . ." Unlike other media luminaries, Belafonte was not drenched with vanities, nor did he confine his recording artistry to pop and his trademark West Indian rhapsody. His music was sung in the lyrics of his political activism and international humanitarianism—from the Freedom Rides of Mississippi to the 1963 March on Washington to the famine fields of Rwanda. He experienced racial discrimination firsthand, often barred from performing in southern clubs and theaters. He was blacklisted by the McCarthyists, hounded by FBI surveillance, and tracked by Klan members and their small-town police acolytes.

He never disassociated his fame from his outrage and, in time, became a key underwriter of King's and the civil rights movement in general.

Before encountering King, Belafonte already admired and sat at the feet of black militants such as W. E. B. DuBois and Paul Robeson. He maintained a long friendship with, and admiration for, Eleanor Roosevelt, about whom he said: "She [invited] me directly to link up with her for her cause. She was very interested in the development of people in the black community, particularly children."

When King called Belafonte, the preacher asked if they could meet at Harlem's Abyssinian Baptist Church. King was en route to recruit other ministers to the cause. It was agreed that they would talk following King's sermon. Belafonte wrote about the first encounter:

> When I met him in a reception room, I was struck by his sense of calm. He stood surrounded by at least two hundred well-wishers, yet he seemed unaffected by the crowd, at peace with himself, as if he were standing alone. . . . I felt an unmistakable edge of excitement meeting him. "I'm so delighted you were able to find the time to meet," he said, looking up at me. "I can't tell you what it will mean to me and the movement if I can just make you aware of what we're trying to do."[2]

There were photographers and gawkers in the area. King politely motioned them away and led Belafonte to the basement, which was used as the Sunday school class. Belafonte recalls that the room was nondescript, with a simple chalkboard, a folding table, and some wooden chairs. King closed the door; "it was just the two us," remembers Belafonte. "We got right into a very easy place. I made him feel comfortable; he certainly fascinated me. Above all, I was taken by his humility. It wasn't false humility; I knew the difference. Nor was it humility in the service of charm. This man was both determined to do what he saw as his mission—and truly overwhelmed by it. 'I need your help,' he told me more than once. 'I have no idea where this movement is going.'"

Wherever the movement was going, Harry Belafonte was coming along.

The two men conversed for some three hours. It was transformative for Belafonte. "All I knew was that here was the real deal," Belafonte added, "a leader both inspired and daunted by the burden he'd taken on." For the remaining twelve years of King's life, the musician would be at his side, listening to Martin divulge his deepest fears, his frustrations with his marriage, even his profound guilt about his infidelities, as well as his remorse about creating so much danger and anguish for the many people, black and white, whom he also conscripted into the service of the movement. Harry would find himself in the role of King's executor of estate—along with Stanley Levison—after the 1968 assassination. Belafonte, although he would grow disenchanted to a great degree with Coretta Scott King and later with King's adult children and their notorious squabbles, nonetheless funded innumerable undertakings and often pulled the family and their endeavors out of financial calamity.

Harry always remembered one thing: "I felt [Martin] pulling me up to that higher plane of social protest. . . . I'd find I wanted to live by those values myself, both to help the movement and to wash away my personal anger."

Belafonte's friendship with King undoubtedly complicated his life, though, as Clarence Jones told me: "Harry does what he wants to do and his choices are not marred by the challenges involved." Belafonte recruited Sidney Poitier to the cause, though Poitier was never quite as disposed to be physically on the scene in hostile southern towns. Belafonte immediately connected with Stanley Levison, just as Bayard Rustin had calibrated. The actor was less complacent about Levison's Communist past as was King himself. The Cold War still pressed in those years of *Sputnik* and the Hungarian revolt and the 1956 Suez War involving Israel, Egypt, Britain, and the Soviet Union. The US government was pursuing any and all alleged Communist sympathizers. Belafonte assuredly loved Levison but still has confessed that he sometimes thought that the attorney was a functioning Communist, "taking his orders from Moscow. . . . But then I would talk to Stan again, and think, nah, impossible. The guy was a mensch. And he was."[3] Belafonte's dilemma was paradigmatic: Levison may have divorced himself from the CP-USA by 1956, but this book does not assert that he ever divorced himself from communism.

Belafonte's connection to King also made things more problematic for King—directly because of Belafonte's heavily monitored contact with Stanley Levison. By the time John F. Kennedy assumed the presidency in 1961, FBI director J. Edgar Hoover was completely hyperventilating about "the troublemaker communist King." Hoover issued a celebrated, venomous memorandum to all his regional directors, known as the "Why Not?" memo.[4] Why has the FBI not thoroughly investigated King and proven he's a Communist? Subordinates in every sub-bureau combed their files. No direct link between MLK and the Communists was ever—or has ever—been uncovered.

In 1987 Clarence J. Karier reported the following:

> At every step along the way the FBI was there with its COINTELPRO (FBI's acronym for its covert program against American citizens and domestic groups). It was a thorough, ongoing program that extended to the point of repeatedly persuading universities not to give King an honorary degree when they were considering it as well as directly attempting to prevent him from meeting with the Pope or receiving the Nobel Peace Prize. When he did receive the Nobel Peace Prize, the agency took great pains to interfere with and disrupt any welcoming-home ceremonies. The attack was vicious and amounted to psychological warfare. The agency monitored King's psychological stability and took every step it could that might give extra stress and pain. For years the agency tried aggressively to break King psychologically to the point where it openly tried to persuade him to commit suicide.[5]

The FBI took advantage of the associations and tête-à-têtes (many wiretapped) and public appearances involving King and Belafonte and Levison. Lacking any adhesive evidence of King's Bolshevism, the FBI stubbornly maintained that King was a Communist and that Belafonte was a partisan and that Levison was a spy. Ironically, the record shows that the black Americans were never as a group particularly influenced, recruited, or inspired by the Communists. Granted, King had given in to relentless questioning during a Cleveland television interview in 1961, saying that it was "remarkable" more blacks hadn't become Communists, given the history of racial oppression. But King was never affiliated with the Party, even if the FBI audaciously put his name on a "Reserve Index" of people who would be rounded up and interned during any national emergency.

Yet even Burke Marshall, assistant attorney general under Robert F. Kennedy, a man of integrity and meticulous standards, not one given to innuendo, concluded that King's bond with Belafonte and Levison was "ominous."[6] Reluctantly, he asked for all the files on the two men—this was as late as 1963. The Kennedy brothers were getting ready to banish Stanley from King's inner circle. The FBI stage-managed the entire drama by keeping both Kennedys in the dark about Levison's long-prior departure from the CP-USA and Belafonte's complete innocence in the matter. The FBI hierarchy also quietly controlled which, and how many, files Burke Marshall could examine, citing the cynical canard of "national security."

But it was a matter of personal security (in matters of money and discretion) that almost threw a wrench into the friendship between Harry Belafonte and Stanley Levison. Belafonte has written and spoken publicly about this matter, including during a 2011 television documentary entitled *Sing Your Song*. This wrinkle, this uncertainty, was a complex drama, tinged with secrecy and inscrutabilities, involving Stanley's first wife, Janet, and his onetime business associate and nemesis—a man who renamed himself Jay Richard Kennedy. Here was a chameleon, a fraud, and a con man that was suspiciously intertwined with Stanley even as he caused Stanley a lot of distress.

The trouble between them dated back to the 1940s, just after this Jay Richard Kennedy had legally altered his name from the one he was born with: Samuel Richard Solomonick. Samuel was an intensive, forceful man, a native of the Bronx with multilanguage skills, and wily instincts, a man who worked at hard physical jobs and even harder at winning people over to his political convictions. He was a vociferous anti-Nazi (understandably) and crusaded against an array of ideologies, ranging from fascism to the publishing regime of the Hearst family. Solomonick was the circulation manager for the Communist *Daily Worker*—until the Hitler-Stalin Pact of 1939 enraged him and he quit.

The disgust with the Nazis and the sympathy for workers were about the only two conditions this individual shared with Levison.

The Levison brothers, Roy and Stanley, came to know Solomonick in 1940, when he was a co-owner of a Brooklyn real-estate firm for which both Levisons worked. Europe was becoming increasingly dangerous for Jews; New York Jews cloistered together in jobs, educational societies, labor unions, and avant-garde bistros. Solomonick was already "Kennedy" when Stanley and Roy encountered him, but there was no question about what he was culturally. "Kennedy" was by now living behind his lifelong facade that would eventually affect, even harm, both Stanley Levison and Harry Belafonte.

David Garrow recounts the transformation of Samuel Solomonick to Jay Kennedy: After Solomonick walked out from the *Daily Worker*, he discovered that his former Communist colleagues were going to make it hard for him to work—just out of spite. The strident Solomonick, with thick wavy hair, a charming smile full of teeth and magnetism, and bright, busy eyes, was walking along a New York boulevard with a friend, bemoaning his professional prospects. He looked up and saw the name Kennedy on a billboard. Checking for his friend's approval, he made the decision on the spot: Samuel Richard Solomonick became Jay Richard Kennedy.

In Great Britain, Joe Kennedy Jr., the eldest son of Ambassador Joseph P. Kennedy, and the intended future president, was preparing to train as a special US naval aviator. Joe Jr. would die in 1944 during a high-risk mission known by the code "Aphrodite." He and his copilot were vaporized when their converted B-24 suddenly exploded over Suffolk, England. As a result, Ambassador Kennedy made up his mind that his second son, John, would inherit the mantle and become the Kennedy president someday.

Back in New York, Solomonick's name change also improved the new Jay Kennedy's prospects. "Look at this guy go," Stanley said to Roy in 1940, not without acidity, as Jay consolidated his resources, bought a big share of the real-estate firm, and then went on to establish his own "Kennedy Management Corporation." He would move on to radio, movie projects, war propaganda documentaries, even a failed film biography of President Franklin

D. Roosevelt—access to whom was arranged by his general business partner, Stanley Levison.[7]

Jay Richard Kennedy smoothly created a lot of government contacts during and after the war years. He glad-handed people in the Defense Department as well as the Bureau of Narcotics. Before long, history would reveal, the chameleon that eventually wooed and became the personal business manager for Harry Belafonte, also slipped into the shadowy role of CIA operative and informative.

Stanley and Jay fell out of amity soon enough—there was only so much Levison could stomach of Kennedy's beguiling and questionable lifestyle. But then it got even more complicated.

Stanley and Janet divorced in December 1941—just after the Japanese launched their surprise attack on Pearl Harbor and America was drawn into World War II. Stanley would remarry, to Beatrice Merkin, with whom he had his only child, Andrew. Meanwhile, Janet remarried as well—to Jay Richard Kennedy.

Any personal rancor or resentments among the four principals in this unlikely quadrangle were subjugated to the overall business interests of this oddly blended family: Janet and Jay Kennedy relocated to California, though the former Solomonick kept firm reins on his Manhattan firm. Meanwhile, Stanley and Roy continued to manage everything in New York; according to Garrow, "The entire group remained on friendly terms."[8]

The former Janet Levison, now Janet Kennedy, was a trained psychotherapist. She also was a leftist, with Communist ties that she shared with Stanley during their brief marriage. Belafonte maintains that when the marriage broke off, Janet went off with Jay Richard Kennedy—with whom Stanley had strong business ties, including "a chain of car washes or laundries in Latin America." Belafonte did not know that Janet Levison, who became Janet Kennedy, was ever married to Stanley until many years after the fact.

As improbable as it would seem, Janet the psychotherapist eventually took on a clinical patient: Harry Belafonte. One has to fast-forward to August 1963 to learn how and why Belafonte fell into this startling relationship.

It was the very hot, muggy day of the March on Washington, August 28. Martin Luther King Jr. spoke at the end of the long program, in front of the unexpectedly overflowing crowd of 250,000. Besides Harry Belafonte, who was on the podium, the galaxy of Hollywood stars clustered about the Lincoln Memorial included Marlon Brando, Burt Lancaster, Charlton Heston, Lena Horne, Diahann Carroll, Paul Newman, Mahalia Jackson, Shelley Winters, and Sammy Davis Jr. It was Mahalia Jackson who called out to King as he plodded through the first segment of his delivery: "Tell them about the dream, Martin!" This lifted King to suddenly extemporize a theme he had already tested at a speech in Detroit a few months earlier: "I have a dream," he began to practically sing.

President Kennedy and his brother Robert had opposed the march. They had deep concerns about King's alleged Communist ties and, as stated, they did not want to compromise southern electoral votes in 1964 by being too friendly to the Negro cause. Yet after the wildly successful—and entirely peaceful—march, King and his entourage were invited to the White House for congratulations.

Harry Belafonte remembers that after everything was concluded, he and others in his Washington hotel suite were relaxing and watching television. There was a live interview being broadcast involving King and some of the other civil rights leaders. Belafonte reeled with disbelief when he realized that the moderator of the program was none other than his former financial manager, Jay Richard Kennedy.

Belafonte became deeply concerned and agitated, knowing from his own experience with this Kennedy and from general intuition that the man was not to be trusted. This Kennedy was at best, an opportunist; at worst, an FBI mole or informant. "I had a higher obligation now, to make Martin aware of what a dangerous character Kennedy was," wrote Belafonte. The matter was discussed and evaluated with King and then with Clarence Jones and, of course, with Stanley Levison. Nobody seemed to know or say too much about Jay Kennedy—at least not initially.

Belafonte met with Levison several weeks later in New York City. Stanley, normally "unflappable," in Belafonte's word, was rather tense. He had something to share with Belafonte.

"What is it?"

Levison proceeded to tell Belafonte that Stanley's former wife, Janet, was actually Belafonte's onetime psychoanalyst. Belafonte, a proud man, caught his breath. He had been in therapy with this person for a long time and confided many things to her, from his love life to his rage to his most delicate matters of career and finances. He had shared confidences about Martin Luther King and other public figures. Harry could not believe his ears; he was totally caught off-guard and felt bewildered and possibly compromised.

How was it possible that Stanley had never, in all those years, mentioned this improbable situation? But that was not all that Stanley would now reveal. Matter-of-factly, Stanley told Harry that after their divorce, Janet married this same Jay Richard Kennedy that Belafonte saw on television, interviewing Dr. King, back on August 28, 1963. Belafonte wrote that Stanley simply held up his hands, and said, cryptically: "I don't know what it means but it happened."

"Now my mind was totally blown," Belafonte has stated. It seemed to be the most implausibly convoluted, dangerous labyrinth of circumstances that anyone could have imagined. Jay Richard Kennedy? As far as Harry Belafonte was concerned, this person was "very malevolent" to both him and Stanley. Was this all part of some gruesome setup, with Janet passing secrets she learned in their therapy sessions to this nemesis and rogue who was her husband? Was this perhaps some dark tunnel of forbidden information, garnered in a privileged setting that started in the analyst's office and wound up in FBI files? Were people like J. Edgar Hoover or Robert F. Kennedy reading summation memos drawn from the most concealed statements of Harry Belafonte?

Stanley did not say much of anything else about the matter. As in so many things, he was circumspect and reserved, sometimes taking on the aura of a mandarin. Perhaps the turn of events, the divorce, the fact of Janet winding up with the likes of Jay Richard Kennedy—Stanley's onetime business ally and longtime antagonist—hurt Stanley as much as these revelations alarmed Harry. In the end, Belafonte has made it clear that he retains nothing but admiration for Stanley Levison. When pressed, he leaves it at that. The fact is that Stanley chose to share the story with Harry. And Stanley's unwavering, *pro bono*, and risky support of Martin Luther King Jr.'s life, moods, work, and finances speaks for itself as a matter of history.

Five years after this conversation, in the darkest hour, the trust between Harry Belafonte and Stanley Levison was ultimately corroborated. Dr. King was cut down by a single .30-caliber rifle bullet while standing on the balcony of the Lorraine Motel in Memphis at 6:01 P.M. on April 4, 1968. The question of who would succeed King as the president of the Southern Christian Leadership Conference and thus the de facto leader of the civil rights movement immediately arose from the gathering darkness of that evening.[9]

Everyone assumed, and the outcome was, that Reverend Ralph David Abernathy, who had known, counseled, and safeguarded King since the early days in Montgomery, would be the new president of the SCLC. They traveled together, ate together, and went to jail together. Though different in temperament (Abernathy was generally sunnier and certainly simpler), they shared an extraordinary bond of experience, pain, and secrets. King didn't really take to all the roaming; Abernathy, who had served in the army, adjusted easier and helped King adapt to the motels, the homes of strangers, the buses, the greasy spoons, the prison cells. Abernathy intuited King's moods, laughed heartily when King began to brilliantly mimic other preachers, and comforted King when he would telegraph his angst, his guilt, his migraines, and his frequent bouts of profound spiritual loneliness. In airport lounges, when it was just the two of them waiting for nocturnal connections, Abernathy would literally sit on the pouch of funds they had collected that day, protecting both the money and King, even as the latter would scribble and anguish over the next day's schedule and speeches.

On a long drive across Georgia in 1967, King spoke to Abernathy (who handled the wheel), and said, "David, if something were to happen to me, I want you to succeed me as president of the SCLC."[10] (In private conversations,

Martin called Abernathy "David" and Ralph called King "Mike.") King mentioned that even if this was already written into the bylaws of the organization, he wanted to personally declare his wishes. Abernathy, who died in 1990, had written that this was the last thing he wanted to discuss, and that is surely a plausible assertion.

But not all the inner circle agreed with this assessment of the SCLC's future at the time of the King assassination, and not everyone was so enamored of Abernathy. Georgia Davis Powers, the former Kentucky state senator and the known inamorata of King's at the time of his death, told me: "All Abernathy ever wanted to do was be in every photo of King. Just look at any picture. There he is, just hanging on to Martin. He was an opportunist."[11]

But it was more significant that both Harry Belafonte and Stanley Levison opposed the accession of Abernathy. Belafonte has stated categorically: "Was there no one else who could truly lead the SCLC? Stan Levison and I agreed that of all the candidates, only Andrew Young had the necessary temperament and charisma." Belafonte added, clearly without enthusiasm, "By default, the job was Ralph Abernathy's to take, and he took it."

In fairness to Abernathy, it is important to point out that in one of the many bitterly poignant moments of 1968, Robert F. Kennedy instinctively went to Abernathy for a private meeting just prior to King's funeral in Atlanta. They talked quietly for a while; everyone, including Belafonte, was cognizant of Bobby's genuine transition before and during the presidential campaign from aloofness to the civil rights movement to a heartfelt empathy for and with blacks, Native Americans, Latinos, and the poor. As some of the late King's aides also joined the emotional session, the exhausted Abernathy—about to eulogize his dearest friend—rose up and wordlessly embraced Senator Kennedy. The room was steaming with heat and acknowledgment: Abernathy's embrace of Kennedy signaled that the torch of symbolic leadership for the freedom movement was now passed to the senator.

Robert F. Kennedy, only forty-two, was killed by an assassin's bullets eight weeks later in the kitchen of the Ambassador Hotel in Los Angeles, just after winning the California presidential primary.

Still: Levison's distaste for Abernathy was significant, and, given the power he had wielded for several years within King's inner circle, it transferred over into his discussions with Coretta Scott King following the assassination.

In the transcript of a wiretapped conversation between Levison and Mrs. King held in the summer of 1968, Levison first discusses an impending speech Mrs. King will deliver—which he was helping her to write:

> LEVISON: Since you are going to have to read a good part of this speech, do what Martin often neglected to do and that is read the speech two or three times so that when you are beginning a sentence you know where it ends. . . . Sometimes I would listen to Martin and know that he hadn't read written materials and feel bad because I knew how much better he could have delivered it if he had read it beforehand.[12]

Then Levison proceeded to the main thrust of his telephone call, which was to criticize the attitude and behavior of Ralph Abernathy:

> LEVISON: I must tell you a story. Bayard [Rustin] just called me. Bayard doesn't often call me. He wanted Ralph's home telephone number. . . . Ralph called him several times. Most urgent. There is a very important women's conference taking place this Tuesday night and Juanita [Abernathy] hasn't gotten an invitation to it, and he thinks the first lady of civil rights should be invited to it . . . and he wants Bayard to wangle an invitation to it.

Rustin had succeeded in "wangling an invitation" to the event—at which Coretta Scott King was to be the featured speaker. Stanley continued to complain to Coretta:

> LEVISON: . . . And he was calling Juanita to tell her she could come. So I told Bayard that this was sort of pathetic for him to have to do this sort of thing, and told Bayard that you are the featured speaker. I assume that Ralph knew you were the featured speaker.

CORETTA: I wonder if he did. Isn't that funny?

LEVISON: I get the feeling that it became important because you were the featured speaker, and therefore Juanita had to be there. That old competition.

Coretta proceeded to be diplomatic, saying she'd been "out of touch," and maybe had offended Ralph and Juanita inadvertently. Stanley could not particularly contain his resentment.

LEVISON: I have always felt that making these calls that everyone knows are meaningless is hypocritical. . . . As long as Ralph has the approach, which he articulates, that Juanita is the first lady of civil rights, you have a problem with him because she is not. You are and there is no compromise on this. Bayard was telling me that everyone he comes in contact with, from the lowest Negro to the top Negro, the question they raise with him is why Coretta King doesn't take over. So for him to pit Juanita against you when people are pitting you against him is an absurdity.

CORETTA: (Laughing) It doesn't make sense. It is completely absurd and very awkward. I think it's going to be very hard . . . and I don't look forward to it at all.

The conversation eventually turned to how Abernathy had dressed for King's funeral.

CORETTA: [Someone] raised the question of him going to the funeral in those clothes. What was your feeling about that?

LEVISON: My reaction wasn't as strong as yours because they had come directly from Washington and this was the garb they were wearing but I don't know that I'm right.

CORETTA: She said that people felt it was disrespectful and sort of rubbing it in, and that Dr. King wouldn't have done that.

LEVISON: You're probably right. People do dress up for a funeral. It is part of the respect you show and they did have other clothes.

CORETTA: His shirt tail was out and he looked like a mess.

The two of them, the patron/consigliore and the widow, continued to discuss matters for a few moments, their words and sentiments framed by fresh sorrow and crammed bitterness. In the deepest corners of their hearts, they had both known for years that Martin would be killed and that they would be in this position of trying to alight in a dreadfully altered world. There was almost an obsessive relief in gossiping about Ralph Abernathy—the underwhelming successor who did not want the position before he got it and now was a bit infatuated with it. Further along in this wiretapped banter, Stanley, truly aggrieved for his murdered friend, let off a salvo about the whole lot of Martin's colleagues who he felt were not standing up to the weak Abernathy: "They will say one thing privately but then engage in the hypocrisy of telling Ralph that he is the leader."

In another taped conversation, about the same time in 1968, Levison was talking with Bayard Rustin. Rustin, who had been with King since 1955 and the Montgomery bus boycott, and had brought Levison in, was bewildered and angry about Ralph Abernathy's antics in the aftermath of the succession. Stanley, who with Harry Belafonte, so wanted anybody but Abernathy to be the leader, spoke up:

LEVISON: You know that over-eagerness used to put him in a silly position . . .
RUSTIN: Why does he do these things?
LEVISON: Well, why did he always do these kinds of things? The same problem of ego.

Stanley Levison had been so close to Martin King for so long, had corrected the texts of his speeches, done his taxes, edited his books, found him donors and attorneys and bail money, advised him on matters ranging from his sex life to how to criticize American foreign policy, and had effectively edged out Ralph Abernathy as the ultimate confidante. Ralph was Martin's friend; Stanley was Martin's conscience. It is notable that in Abernathy's 1989 autobiography,

And the Walls Came Tumbling Down, he mentions Stanley Levison but once in the 600-page document. Is there any stronger evidence of what a threat Stanley was to Ralph?

And when Harry Belafonte, fiery of song, gallant of soul, wondered for a moment or two, in the aftermath of the disturbing revelations about Jay Richard Kennedy, if Stanley was really legitimate, was there any question that Belafonte would still believe in him?

CHAPTER SEVEN

A Stabbing in Harlem

SEPTEMBER 1958 | HARLEM, NEW YORK

N o one will ever know what actually compelled Izola Ware Curry to take a seven-inch letter opener to Blumstein's department store on the evening of September 20. Martin Luther King Jr. was signing copies of his first book, *Stride Toward Freedom*. The book had been largely edited by Stanley Levison—who also negotiated the publishing deal with Harper and Brothers. About fifty people, almost all either black or Jewish, had gathered in the rear of the shoe department where King had been occupying a table and was cheerfully greeting folks and inscribing books. He had been criticized by some for choosing the Jewish retail store over a black-owned bookshop in Harlem, but this was a reality of King's patronage. Some Harlem residents grumbled: the signing at Blumstein's was considered a "snubbing" of the community's leading black bookseller—the National Memorial African Bookstore owned by Lewis Michaeaux. Around kitchen tables, in pool halls, and at bars, some blacks muttered things about "the Jews controlling King."

Izola Curry, wearing a blue raincoat, concealed her weapon underneath. She approached the preacher and asked if he was Martin Luther King Jr. King affably nodded and told her, yes. Taylor Branch describes what happened next:

> The woman's hand came from under her raincoat and flashed in an arc. King reflexively yanked his arm up just enough for the razor-sharp blade to cut his left hand as it plunged deep into his chest. A quick-witted woman next to King knocked the attacker's fist from the handle before she could pull it out for a second stab. The attacker stepped back, making no effort to flee, and shouted, "I've been after him for six years! I'm glad I done it!"[1]

King was able to identify the assailant while being prepared for treatment at Harlem Hospital. Izola Ware Curry, an African American maid, was diagnosed as a paranoid schizophrenic. She was dangerously focused on King and, in a series of courtroom rants before being committed to a state asylum, accused him of both disparaging Roman Catholicism and being a Communist. Curry had reportedly attempted to alert the FBI about King's purported leftist views. She was criminally insane and came very close to killing King that evening.

Witnesses to the shocking event noted how calm King had remained in the immediate aftermath. Stanley would report to Bayard Rustin: "He sat in the chair all the while people tried to stop the bleeding. He sat there, not moving, even while the paramedics came and got him to the hospital." Stanley, not a religious man, nonetheless uttered to himself a prayer of thankfulness when he learned that King would recover.

It was extremely fortunate that King remained composed and motionless during the ordeal. The blade of the Japanese-made letter opener came to rest just alongside his aorta. The doctors marveled at the situation: the slightest movement on King's part—even a sneeze—would have ruptured the artery and King would have died quickly in his own blood.

Gabe Pressman, a reporter and commentator for WNBC in New York, recalled how he got to King's bedside within hours of the stabbing: In 2012, Pressman reminisced: "After managing to get into King's hospital room, I was amazed at how calm he was. He said that he had no bitterness against Izola Curry, the woman who stabbed him in the sternum. 'I think she needs help,' King told me. 'I'm not angry at her.'" Years later, Pressman discovered King visiting homeless people in a New York ghetto community; the preacher was without any guards or security. Recalling how effortlessly he had found King the night of the stabbing, Pressman hailed a passing NYPD cruiser and demanded better protection for the civil rights leader.[2]

King relied on the safeguard of people who gravitated to him—people like Stanley, Harry, Bayard, Ralph Abernathy, and a handful of others. These people did not carry firearms.

Meanwhile, as Levison and Belafonte assisted Coretta King to quickly fly into New York, and helped arranged interim housing for her, Dr. King's condition worsened. He developed pneumonia, and the medical team was alarmed. The danger passed, however, and by the third day, King was able to sit up and contemplate a mountain of greeting cards and flowers that filled his room. He was hospitalized for two weeks, and the full convalescence required some three months.

King always remembered—and often quoted—from one card in particular. It arrived from a schoolgirl in Westchester County who made note that she was white, "though it should not make a difference." The youngster wrote that she read the doctors' statement in the newspaper that if Dr. King had just sneezed, he would have died. "I'm glad you didn't sneeze," the child had written. Martin reveled in that little missive, shared its sentiments with Stanley and the others, and frequently used the refrain, "If I had sneezed, I would not have been there to see . . . ," in speeches that reflected upon the milestones of his civil rights journey. He even recalled the little white girl and her "I'm glad you didn't sneeze," in his long, plaintive, and final speech, "I've been to the mountaintop," on the last night of his life, Memphis, April 3, 1968.

The stabbing, meanwhile, interrupted the nascent advance of both King's first book and the momentum generated by the SCLC in the victorious aftermath of the Montgomery bus boycott. (In fact, the boycott was the key narrative of the book, which also included a great deal of King's philosophies regarding racial and economic justice.) Stanley and Martin had some pitched battles about some of King's writing as the manuscript developed.

"You are too hard and too sweeping, the way you write about the southern white workers," critiqued Stanley on the manuscript. "I know you better, Martin. You don't want to come across as hateful, especially since you don't have hate and you do want the races to work together." King had written in the raw draft of *Strive Toward Freedom* that working whites in the South were guilty of "acts of meanness and violence" against black people. He indicted them as a group, asserting that they carried "abnormal fears and morbid antipathies" when it came to African Americans. Levison understood that King was affected negatively by the resistance and contempt of white working people during the bus boycott in Montgomery. But he, Levison, was truly concerned about the manner in which King had originally written—with indignation—about "uneducated masses" that inflicted cruelty and contempt on black folks. He exhorted King to remember that white mobs, from Montgomery to Little Rock, also included degreed people, businessmen, housewives, and aristocrats.[3]

Levison understood King's hurt: the minister just wanted white laborers to "get it"—that the bond among workers transcended, even yoked, black and white people. In truth, though individuals like J. Edgar Hoover and Robert F. Kennedy often suggested or believed that King was a Communist, the real deal was that King saw social struggle defined as much as an economic crusade as it was a civil rights mantra. He decried racism in the unions with special vigor; he genuinely believed that the labor movement "must concentrate its powerful forces on bringing economic emancipation to white and Negro by organizing them together in social equality."[4]

Martin Luther King Jr., stabbed in the chest in Harlem on September 20, 1958, saw the covenant of labor—color-blind, inclusive—not unlike the way that new immigrants viewed the Statue of Liberty. Stanley understood this, and he pleaded for moderation in certain of King's texts.

"All right, then," Martin told Stanley. "I'll rewrite some of this stuff." In fact, a committee of people, including Levison, Bayard Rustin, and another white thinker named Harris Wofford who advised the Kennedys and would become a US senator, did most of the writing and rewriting. Clarence Jones eventually joined this group, although he primarily functioned as King's personal attorney. The book was ultimately an amalgam of voices, sometimes a little patchy, that more or less delivered the labor-centric freedom message of King. It was a clarion call to nonviolent civil disobedience that took on established leaders (including President Eisenhower) who were often heard to say that laws could not change the way people felt about other people.

Stanley was pleased with King's famous retort in the book that "morals cannot be legislated, but behavior can be regulated." King told Levison, and ultimately wrote in the book, that "the law cannot make an employer love me, but it can keep him from refusing to hire me because of the color of my skin." Stanley also had to settle with the fact that King tempered his criticism of white working people but he did not remove the phrasing about white "morbid antipathies." In the end, it was King's book, even if it was written in the language of several sympathetic men.

Stanley was also not thrilled about the fact that Ralph Abernathy replaced King as leader of the 1958 SCLC convention, which took place in Norfolk in October while King was convalescing. "Nothing's going to happen at that conference," Stanley muttered to Bayard. Stanley would close his eyes at night, trying to imagine what it felt like for Martin—having a steel blade plunged into his chest, so close to his heart. The image made him tremble even during the day, as he tried but failed to concentrate on what he was writing, whom he had to call, or a detail he had to remember. He saw that his right hand was shaking as he went to light up another Lucky Strike. *Martin, Martin.* So vulnerable and kind and stubborn, all at once. How could he have the mettle to sit so serenely in that chair as they lifted him out of Blumstein's? How did he know not to sneeze? The drops of blood on the floor. The screams, the sirens, and then Martin so quiet and poised. Like an angel. His face blank yet with a trace of a knowing smile. It will happen again and Martin knows it. The hot slivering pain in Martin's flesh. How will I live without Martin?

Stanley looked aimlessly into the main closet of his Manhattan apartment one afternoon. It was bitter outside and the iciness and gray crept into the place. Stanley shivered with cold and fear. *Hmm . . . where is that topcoat I once lent Martin? He must still have it. Get better, Martin.*

And, indeed, nothing much transpired at the 1958 SCLC convention. King was not there, and there was hollowness to the proceedings. No new programs were announced and no initiatives were floated. Stanley was frustrated, and he missed Martin's presence keenly and personally. He resented Abernathy's cloying attempts at stewardship; he was too good at spotting weakness and unrealized abilities in other men, regardless of their color. "We have got to move from Montgomery to getting voter registration work done across the South," Stanley exhorted people in a quiet but firm voice. Abernathy resorted to platitudes, as far as Stanley was concerned. And without Martin present and in the absence of his voice and authority, little was harvested from the resulting meager sales of *Strive toward Freedom*, in spite of the generally warm reviews the book was receiving. Izola Curry had cut into even more than Martin's chest.

In fact, as 1958 closed, the SCLC was teetering financially, there were significant staff tensions, and the recovering King had to fire the executive director, John Tilley—by mail. The fiery and well-respected Reverend Fred Shuttlesworth, who more or less took on the rabid segregationists of his Birmingham, Alabama, community single-handedly, pressed King on the failure of the SCLC to seriously confront and disrupt the sinister troika of Klansmen, police, and state government. Dissatisfaction and impatience were pouring in, despite the success of the Montgomery boycott victory; King was overwhelmed with schedule demands, weary, fighting depression and guilt, and still physically and emotionally healing from being stabbed.

David Garrow wrote: "If it were not for Bayard Rustin and Stanley Levison in New York, dozens of small but important tasks never would get done. Rustin was receiving a salary of $50 a week as King's executive assistant, but the well-to-do Levison refused any compensation and continued to do a myriad of jobs: preparing King's tax returns, drafting articles and speeches, and keeping an eye on Harper's promotion of *Strive Toward Freedom*."[5]

From his New York apartment on Thirty-Ninth Street, Stanley wrote Martin a long letter on December 11, 1958. There was a lot on Stanley's mind, most especially the marketing and distribution of the book. Stanley pictured the convalescing preacher, mostly healed, thankfully. He saw his friend's soft face and reflected on the grandiloquent Martin's strange and inherent bashfulness. It was "shyness," Stanley once said, that "was accented . . . with white people." Stanley chuckled to himself about the habit the still newly famous King had of rushing his words when speaking in public.

In the December 11 letter, Levison wrote to King about a push for Christmas-related publicity that would help book sales, placement in book catalogs, and the running of newspaper and magazine ads. All this legwork Stanley did with diligence and without taking any money from King. He went into significant detail about publishing percentages due King: "I just completed the negotiations with them around the [book] deal and substantially improved the terms as far as your royalties are concerned." Levison laid out the discussions in microscopic detail, noting the "vigorous debate" he had with the distributor about the remunerations, specifying in dollars and cents and per book how much King would have lost had he, Levison, not made a better bargain across the board. It was as though Stanley was reporting to a supervisor. He had even negotiated a split deal for book profits that would help the treasury of the Montgomery Improvement Association, basically sparing King a double division of fees, "so that your royalties on these sales would continue at the forty-four cent level." Stanley's four-page, single-spaced letter was a blend of deference, minutiae, and loyalty. He expounded to Martin:

> In the circumstances this is a maximum arrangement. Both Marie and Joan [King's literary agents], as well as I, are convinced that our problems with them stem from the religious department. In that department, they seldom if ever, have to deal with agents or lawyers, since their writers are not people

schooled in the subtle deceits and tricks of business, they are able to get away with anything. I pulled the rug out from under them when I discovered in reading the contract that the clause by which they had reduced your royalty to fourteen cents, did not actually apply to an arrangement of this type. They thought they had a free hand under that clause to make any deal without consent from you, but they were stretching the interpretation beyond any reasonable basis. When Marie made it clear to them that I would not permit it, they dropped this arbitrary position. They now assure us, very virtuously, that they never dreamt of enriching themselves at your expense. What they have not yet explained is how they drew a contract and were on the point of signing it which did exactly that.[6]

Like any relationship, the one between King and Levison had to be tested. It was only after this particular exchange, well into the third year of their alliance, that this test happened. Levison had swiftly moved in, quietly taking control of King's business affairs, assuming the role of white liaison, protecting King from presumed lechers and opportunists, coaching the evolving leader of the American human rights crusade, serving as his *pro bono* barrister, editor, and public relations proxy, and unassumingly managing King's dire fund-raising requirements. Levison gave of his time, talent, and treasury. He routinely brushed off King's awkward and intermittent protestations about wanting to pay Stanley back. Stanley knew that King could not pay him back—perhaps that gave Stanley even more control. But it's not hard to wonder if Levison ever wanted something back for his selfless efforts.

In a request that one historian has termed "revealing," an old topcoat became the subject of a little test between Stanley and Martin. At the end of the same letter dated December 11, 1958, after reviewing some other matters not directly related to book royalties, Stanley brought up a personal matter: "While on the subject of small items, a couple of years ago, I loaned you my top-coat."

After occupying some ten paragraphs carefully analyzing royalty charts, expense lists, and mailing costs, Stanley was now focused on a coat that he had thought about while looking in his closet. He typed:

If you had a use for it I am delighted, but if it is sitting in a closet somewhere, I would appreciate it if it could be sent back to me. I am ready to discard the one I've been using and before getting another one, I thought I would check with you. Please don't take it off anyones [sic] back, including your own, but if it is only keeping a hanger warm in your closet, I'll find use for it.

I spoke on one occasion with Clarence Jones about what, if any, obligations Stanley thought Martin might have incurred to his advocate and champion. Jones replied clearly: "Stanley never asked for, expected, or received anything from Martin. He did everything *pro bono* and considered it to be an honor." Jones then requoted, verbatim, from the text of a letter (in fact, it was from Levison's very next letter to King, after King had sent an apology for holding on to the topcoat and again pleading with Stanley to allow some form of compensation for everything): "It is out of the question. . . . I looked forward to the time when I could use [my] skills not for myself but for socially constructive ends. The liberation struggle is the most positive and rewarding area of work anyone could experience."

So why did Stanley specifically bring up the topcoat when he had the means to purchase manifold topcoats and spare Martin Luther King Jr. any guilt? One can only speculate that even Stanley, though smitten with the person and stature of King, fully aware of his own invaluable—and incalculable—use to the movement, still wanted some act, some gesture, through which the preacher could tangibly reveal his gratitude and approval. There is no question that Stanley Levison would have never taken any fees from King. But he did provide him with "warmth," as it were, and he was not without need for appreciation, even if this need were subconsciously felt. If he did not want to invoice King, he nonetheless wanted King to ask about it, and not take anything—even an old coat—for granted.

Finally, in that same lengthy letter of December 11, 1958, Stanley made a reference to the stabbing that King had miraculously survived: "I hope your recovery has been proceeding and that you are not interfering with it. Don't forget, we want you to be around for that future, we are all working for."

Did Stanley know that his friend Martin had grown a scar across his chest from the emergency surgery he endured to remove the blade from near his heart, and that the scar had taken the shape of a cross?

CHAPTER EIGHT

Stanley Knew Better

The South may have lost the Civil War militarily, but it hardly surrendered psychologically. The firebombing of Reverend Martin Luther King's house in Montgomery, Alabama, during the bus boycott of 1955–56 was but one of thousands and thousands of incendiary acts, terrors, murders, lynchings, rapes, assaults, intimidations, and criminalities committed by white citizens against black people, individuals and groups, from the formal end of the Confederacy in 1865 through the twentieth century.

The atmosphere in southern towns and cities, from Biloxi, Mississippi, to Valdosta, Georgia, to Jasper, Alabama, was fluid and perilous—for African Americans and their white sympathizers. People had lived in these places a certain way for generations; homes were maintained, businesses established, trade done, churches built—all on the foundation of the southern segregationist tyranny. It was as endemic as the boll weevil and the cotton fields. There was a certain white intimacy that bowed to the great woodlands of Alabama, the red soils of Georgia, the verdant mountains of Tennessee, from porch to porch, dancing, like the fireflies of the old Confederacy, amid the mint juleps and under the twilight of long drawls, clinging traditions, and polite understandings.

In fact—as Stanley Levison knew well—the South had not only failed to be enlightened by the outcome of the Confederate insurgence, it had digressed and coiled over in its contempt for both the Negro people and for progress in general. After World War II, after the brave exploits of the Tuskegee airmen and of black servicemen by and large; after the folding of, and the disillusionment with, leftist groups that were betrayed by Soviet treachery and brutality; the disavowal of both the 1954 *Brown v. Board of Education* ruling and the tepid 1957 Civil Rights Act; southern blacks were left facing rabidly separatist governors like Lester Maddox of Georgia and George C. Wallace of Alabama. Even Senator John F. Kennedy, the emerging Democratic nominee for president in 1960, had voted against the limp, boiled-down civil rights legislation of 1957—which had been stripped of any real social impact because of the powerful grip that southern Democrats held in the Congress.

The civil rights movement, lifted by songs and marching feet and bloodied faces and too many corpses, was a brash, people's uprising that—with funding by northern radicals like Levison, Joseph Filner, Libby Holman, and so many others, was the difference between a southern illumination and its steady submergence into communal turbulence.

At one point, Stanley said to Martin: "You have to absorb some kind of real philosophy, or a doctrine that sets you apart from other leaders and makes you more than just an after-dinner speaker."[1] Stanley was worried that the drifting of the SCLC, exacerbated by a robust share of infighting, along with the vacillations on civil rights exhibited by both the likely 1960 presidential candidates, John F. Kennedy and Vice President Richard M. Nixon, would combine to make Montgomery a footnote in history. King had long taken a deep scholarly interest in the life and work of Mohandas Gandhi: why not make a pilgrimage to India and encounter both the land and the living disciples of the Mahatma—the trailblazer who had been assassinated in 1948?

An author and curator of black literature named L. D. Reddick had just written the first biography of King, called *Crusader Without Violence*. The timing was propitious; why not have Reddick and Coretta accompany Martin to India? King wanted to absorb Gandhism as a living philosophy, and this journey, carefully publicized, replete with high-profile meetings, would serve both to imbue King with what he wanted to learn and to further catapult him into the role that A. D. Randolph would declare for him: "the moral leader of our nation."

Levison worked with Libby Holman's pacifist foundation, along with other charities, and the trip was underwritten. King's congregation at the Dexter Avenue Baptist Church remained patient and supportive; they were proud of their minister, even though he was increasingly absent on Sundays. King struggled with that, just as he wrung his hands over so many conflicting needs and goals and people wanting him, exhorting him, scolding him. He looked for advice and talked to Levison.

"You should meet Nehru," Stanley told Martin. "Go to a place where masses of people are really suffering but where the leadership of the nation is at least talking about it. Neither Nixon nor Kennedy is saying much at all about the Negro situation. They are both too busy trying to appease the Southern bloc and so they have no conscience, either of them. Go over there and see what it's like and then bring it all back to your pulpit and your people in the church will not resent your absence. They will be proud of you." Levison thought King would grow through such a journey. And the publicity would also spike book sales.

King was nearly traumatized by what he saw—especially in the first days, in Bombay. He had never even imagined such a travesty of life, such hunger, blight, mass vagrancy, homelessness, and rampant disease. King himself had not grown up poor, and though he had certainly seen the ravages of African American poverty and displacement, the neglect born of negligible health care, and the physical and spiritual emaciation of poverty, he had never seen anything like this. The stench of it stung his nostrils; he could barely set eyes upon the dense rows of people, shrunken and disconsolate, that filled the narrow, filthy streets of Bombay and New Delhi.

He was reportedly embarrassed by his many trunks and baggage and had some difficulty with the dietary impositions of the trip and the sometimes strenuous physical demands of travel in India, which included exhausting jaunts with Hindu gurus, even while flailing off the unyielding waves of beggars, pickpockets, and pesky vendors. He fought off headaches, and his stomach was turned not only by some of the food but also by the shocking manifestation of India's caste system. Martin was dismayed at the contemptuous treatment given to the so-called Untouchables—it was something he would never forget and that would shape his social ministry till the day he died. He thought about it incessantly even while sojourning with Coretta in the grand New York residence of Harry Belafonte upon their return from this pilgrimage.

When Stanley stopped by, Martin said to him: "Here I am in Harry's palatial apartment while over there, families are piled on top of one another, starving to death, with no hope whatsoever."

"I understand, Martin," Levison replied quietly. "The important thing is to get Harry to agree to another benefit concert because we need the funds to carry on." Belafonte did enthusiastically consent to perform again on behalf of the SCLC. And the FBI was listening, although not to the lyrics.

But Levison was busy with more than his counseling of King. While in New York, the preacher took part in A. Philip Randolph's second Youth March, which would make its way from Manhattan to Washington, DC—stumping for voting rights. Randolph made no bones about his Communist associations and, notably, made an open declaration of thanks to Stanley Levison for his assistance in organizing the youth campaign.

A secret FBI transcript entitled "YOUTH MARCH ON WASHINGTON" was dated April 22, 1959:

Of interest is the fact that Washington Field Office reported . . . that A. Philip Randolph, March chairman, publicly announced that one Stanley Levinson (phonetic) was partially responsible for setting up the mechanics of this demonstration as well as a similar-type activity in 10/58.

We may assume that Levison's connection with the captioned activity was at the behest of King who was one of the motivating forces behind this demonstration. Levison's activities in last Saturday's demonstration may have also been at the direction of the CP as we do know that the CP was extremely interested in the demonstration, giving it widespread coverage in "The Worker," as well as issuing instructions to the CP throughout the eastern United States, particularly that this activity should be supported and individual CP members and their families should participate in it.[2]

Indeed, it was 1959: the Kennedy family was putting together John's imminent campaign for the presidency, and J. Edgar Hoover got wind of the Randolph-King-Levison troika of "fanatics" who were agitating out of New York. The fact that King had traveled to India and was making fanciful speeches about Gandhi's loincloth populism only deepened Hoover's suspicion and hostility. "He's a subversive," muttered Hoover. "And that Levison, he's nothing but an old Commie."

In fact, officials at the highest levels of the government of the United States were, as 1960 approached, beginning to pin the socialist/radical label on Martin King—essentially because of the dubious connection they imposed via Stanley Levison. What were King and Levison talking about as the new decade approached, an elderly president retired, and NASA launched the Mercury manned space program with its seven crew-cut, Caucasian astronauts? They were not talking about communism. They were talking about the ascetic philosophies of Gandhi while King was wrestling with whether or not he should even own any property or have any money (much to Coretta's understandable chagrin). Levison would often tell people: "Martin is so convinced, now that he's been to India, that materialism breeds corruption.

He's filled with guilt and misgivings and thinks he shouldn't own anything. He practically condemns all his awards and honors, saying they don't belong to him but to everybody in the movement."

No, Levison and King were not talking about communism, nor were they taking any calls from the Politburo. In fact, even though the relatively new state of Israel was highly socialist, built on the communal kibbutz movement, Levison was critical of the nation. An FBI recording of Stanley and another Jewish businessman in the 1950s was summarized as follows:

> Stanley said that Israel had moved over to the West and now was a real danger spot; that Zionism had become a major menace, and that Israel is now an enemy state—a Fascist state just like Poland, Latvia, Lithuania, and Estonia had been. Stanley said that a year ago Israel pretended to have a foot in each camp.[3]

King spoke at Morehouse College in Atlanta after his return from India. His position on international alignment was *against* alignments. His passion was for global social democracy, and he implored both superpowers to share their wealth and resources with the world's "wrinkled stomachs." He actually condemned "the destructive rage of the Communist revolution" even as he raged against the "guided missiles and misguided men" of the United States. He implored America to transfer its rotting surplus of wheat and foodstuffs to Calcutta and other centers of hunger and malaise. And in a decidedly prophetic exclamation of his eventual denunciation of the Vietnam War a few years later (which led to a bitter split with President Lyndon B. Johnson), King protested in 1959 that America would sooner "send 10,000 tanks to the French in Indochina" than deliver sustenance to the hungry in poor nations.

As 1959 wound down, Martin King was mulling over resigning his Montgomery pulpit and returning to Atlanta. Stanley Levison was assiduously writing letters, some via a typewriter, and others in his own handwriting. A flowing communicator, Stanley was haphazard with the mechanics, pecking away at the keys with just two fingers. Lips pursed, he would stare down at the board between the ashes and smoke of his continuous cigarettes. The thick eyeglasses would slump down and he readjusted them. His forehead would crease with concentration and manual frustration. In the end, his wife Beatrice would sit and do the typing for him. Their son Andrew remembers: "He wrote almost everything in longhand and Bea typed it. He also had the habit of writing on whatever paper was nearest at hand when a thought came to him or he was drafting something like a letter that was less than a couple of pages long—he'd use the backs of manila envelopes, the flip side of old stationery."

Meanwhile, one of the tensions that gnawed at Martin Luther King was his growing national profile and his equivalent inability to minister to the parishioners at Dexter Avenue Baptist Church. Martin pondered this; Stanley, mindful of his friend's dilemma and guilt, managed King's emergent prominence. Stanley was thinking one day of another African American star, Jackie Robinson—known worldwide because he was the first black player in major league baseball. The phenomenal Robinson became the second baseman for the Brooklyn Dodgers in 1947; if King was renowned, Robinson was a living legend.

"You know," Levison remarked to King over the telephone in September, "you really ought to consider a syndicated column." Levison had been working with a publisher on the idea and was inspired by the success of such a column being ghostwritten for Jackie Robinson. King could make anywhere from $125 to $175 a week and the exposure could only energize the fund-raising endeavors of the debt-ridden SCLC. Not only was the SCLC losing support and momentum, it was mired in competition for dollars and prominence with the NAACP. The NAACP president, Roy Wilkins, was suspicious of King and resented the latter's public successes; turf issues were rampant among the personalities, egos, and domains of the black freedom movement. In 1958, Wilkins had written a long letter to King, outwardly polite, which nonetheless betrayed the strains between Wilkins's NAACP and King's SCLC. Wilkins reminded King:

> You were present in Atlanta November 15–16 when we held a meeting of repre-
> sentatives of the NAACP from ten Southern states together with representative

of several other groups who are working on the task of increasing registration and voting among the Negro citizens in the South. The delegates to Atlanta remember your inspiring remarks and your joining with others in the theme of close cooperation in carrying forward the campaign.[4]

It was faint praise coming from Wilkins. The letter was the catalyst for accelerated charges of a "serious rift within Negro ranks." An article in the *Atlanta Constitution* carried strong assertions from Georgia's attorney general Eugene Cook that "NAACP leaders are opposed to King's independent operation and want all integration and voter activity funneled through their organization." The day after the article appeared, King sniffed at it and dismissed and criticized it as being beneath a response. In private, Stanley muttered about the "cynical style" of Roy Wilkins. In a note written to King, Levison described his view of the thinking of Wilkins and the NAACP hierarchy: "Therefore, the SCLC and King can drop dead. Whatever they do is duplicatory." The NAACP, Stanley would complain, was guilty of "faking cooperation."[5]

This kind of intrablack rivalry dogged King continuously, and it added to the prevailing sadness of his life—a condition that has not always been faithfully documented by his biographers and devotees.

Levison was keenly aware of King's depressions and tried to keep him focused. He understood King's uncommon talents, his increasingly mesmerizing oratory, and King's own healthy love of a good audience. Sensing King's ambivalence about a newspaper column that fall, he wrote his friend about it, asserting: "I nevertheless feel quite strongly that this may be a very valuable opportunity and substantial effort should be made to utilize it." He continued:

> I say this particularly because Jackie Robinson's column is doing a great deal of good generally and for him as a public figure. Of course, it is not being written by Jackie, which brings me to my point. Possibly, a division of labor between you, myself, and Bayard could simplify the task and yet produce a column of importance hitting the main issues and resting on a good foundation of accuracy and timeliness. . . . Please give this some careful thought

because it may be an excellent opportunity arising just at the right time in terms of your total picture.[6]

What was King's "total picture?" In Levison's mind, King had outgrown his pulpit in Montgomery and needed to accede to his national prominence. In short, Stanley had anointed Martin as the undisputed leader of the civil rights movement—an assessment certainly shared by the press and resented by some of the other well-known black principals. Moreover, none of the others, from Wilkins of the NAACP to Randolph of the labor movement to even the legal giant Benjamin Hooks of Memphis, were being called to television studios, meeting with presidential candidates, or being physically menaced by white thugs as was Martin Luther King Jr.

Not only was Stanley trying to help Martin out of Montgomery, he was smoothly reconfiguring the administrative stewardship of the SCLC. Ralph Abernathy would be happy to succeed King as president of the Montgomery Improvement Association; that would placate Ralph and eliminate him from consideration for the much-needed position of executive director of the SCLC—of which King, of course, would remain president. Levison respected Abernathy's devotion to King but regarded him as irritatingly depthless.

On the issue of executive director, Stanley had determined that the best person for the job was Bayard Rustin, and Stanley quietly gathered the support of other financial heavyweights such as Joe Filner for this objective. There was a logistical problem: in late 1959, Rustin was sojourning in Africa; this was somewhat confounding for the mastermind, Levison.

Bypassing the typewriter, Stanley wrote Bayard a letter in his own hand about the developments with Martin and the need for a new administrative direction within the SCLC: "I feel like I used to during the war when I had a partner in my war plant, who was the technical man, and I had to prepare a bid in a big contract when he was out of town. There's nothing like a solid collaboration when a major fine conclusion has to be reached. Needless to say, hurry home, soon."[7]

About the other underwriters whom Stanley had lined up in support of

Rustin's candidacy, Levison added: "They were painfully miserable to learn that you are in Africa."

Just a few weeks later, Levison wrote again to Rustin, laying out his thoughts on paper and then having his wife Bea transfer the copy onto their Olivetti typewriter. Stanley informed his old colleague that "the conclusion was unanimous that you be sought."

> Martin's position, of course, you know. Ralph is so strongly for you that if you were not to come he would not consider the job as Executive Director. [Stanley wrote this knowing that Abernathy would not be considered and that Abernathy preferred the security of pulpit life] . . . Martin said one or two [members of the committee] had reservations. Of course, none related to respect for you, but only the possible public relations problem [referring to Rustin's homosexuality]. Their reservations were, however, not so deep or firm that they would vote against you or abstain. They voted for you.[8]

Levison elaborated about King's mind-set:

> Now, naturally, he is more vividly conscious of the public relations problems involved in the move and is deeply dependent on your guidance and imagination. While he feels that the SCLC needs an early program of action, he's primarily concerned that this move should not turn out to wash him out as a leader. I did not feel that this was vanity or opportunism. He knows how much the group rests upon his prestige at present. As an aside, I might say, in discussing meetings he has addressed in recent months, I was strongly impressed with the fact that his popularity remains high. . . . Neither time nor Roy Wilkins appear able to destroy him. He is extremely eager to have you start as early as the first part of December in order to deal with the transition.

"The transition" had more to do than with just the election of a new executive director. After struggling with many concerns and qualms, King decided to give up his Montgomery pulpit and accept his father's long-standing offer, or rather, demand that he return to Atlanta and become associate pastor of the Ebenezer Baptist Church. The junior King was conflicted about this; Daddy King was notoriously authoritarian and opinionated and had never really taken to Coretta King. It's doubtful that he would have wholeheartedly approved of any woman his son took as a wife; Martin Sr. idolized his namesake son and was disposed to regard no one as good enough for Martin Jr.

But Stanley knew that Ebenezer was the right pulpit for Martin—serving as his father's associate-successor in his hometown pulpit would free Martin to assume his national platform without the duress of a solo congregation in Montgomery. Moreover, Atlanta was the emerging capital of the South, a world-class city, cosmopolitan, less prone to the enduring racial incivilities of the smaller communities and outlying areas of the old Confederacy. There were more clergy of all faiths with whom to dialogue and a much more viable press and media. It was time.

And so Stanley included a revealing bit of information to Bayard Rustin within this same letter, sent to Africa on November 1, 1959: "The reason for Martin's urging me at present is that he has now resolved his doubts and is definitely making the move to Atlanta. He plans to give his church notice December 1st and to move in February." Rustin would read the letter and comprehend the text and the meaning behind the text; it was he, Rustin, who in 1957 had prepared an extensive memorandum for King as the preacher prepared to meet with then-vice president Richard Nixon about the plight of "more than 11 million southern Negro citizens." That same year, Rustin and Levison had tactically discussed the possible movie rights for King's *Strive toward Freedom*; Rustin knew well that King was the *de facto* chief of the American civil rights crusade. Rustin had traveled extensively in India, even before Gandhi was assassinated, and he perceived the impact upon King of the latter's journey there. He understood the rhythm and motion of all that Levison was writing about and orchestrating, just as he had known in 1955 that Levison's skills were needed as black folks began boycotting the buses in Montgomery.

Rustin did not ultimately succeed to national leadership of the SCLC. His homosexuality and his radical political history undermined him throughout his career. Harlem congressman Adam Clayton Powell actually drove Rustin out of the SCLC altogether by 1960 by threatening to reveal Rustin's sexual orientation (and 1953 criminal prosecution) in the House of Representatives. But the fact remains that as the new decade opened, a white Jewish lawyer from New York and a gay black activist from Pennsylvania were collaborating—as they had been for several years—in the libretto of Martin Luther King Jr.'s life.

· · · · ·

Even before he entered law school, Stanley Levison had examined a milestone, if disreputable Supreme Court case, decided in 1896, and known as *Plessy v. Ferguson*. The court upheld the constitutionality of a doctrine known as "separate but equal," which effectively opened the way for legal racial segregation in all phases of public life. Blacks were barred from "whites only" accommodations, transportation, schools, stores, and toilets. Jim Crow was given a free hand to divide out children with black skin from community swimming pools, playgrounds, parks, drinking fountains, soda counters. They could not attend the same public schools as white kids, and the buildings to which they were confined were unmaintained, underfunded, poorly heated, and rarely to code. They had access only to textbooks that had been previously used by white students and were now discarded. Their world was separate indeed, but it was not equal.

Levison was born only sixteen years after *Plessy v. Ferguson*, and he came into his own world of leftist ideology and social outrage well aware of this disparity in American life. The original appeal of Marxism to leftist Americans is further well summarized by Robert Service:

> The USA bore similarities to the old Russian Empire. Factory working conditions and wage rates were abysmal and the influx of European immigrants made it difficult for trade unions to secure betterment. The labour movement was persecuted. Police and courts supported employers. Violent gangs were paid to break strikes. . . . Oppression had made heroes of the Bolsheviks in

the eyes of radical opinion before 1917, and the tsarist authorities had not succeeded in extirpating Bolshevism. Communists in the USA hoped for a similar denouement.[9]

Meanwhile, state-sanctioned segregation may have been a southern phenomenon but in Stanley's mind it was a national disgrace. *Brown v. Topeka Board of Education* in 1954 and the Montgomery bus boycott of 1955–56 helped to reset the old, fierce tapestry of southern life, but the reality was, as Dwight D. Eisenhower was retiring from the presidency and John F. Kennedy was envisioning a New Frontier, that African Americans were still in a state of general humiliation, degradation, and civic division.

White Americans were flocking to the suburbs and agonizing about *Sputnik*. They were buying refrigerators, washing machines, Chevrolets, watching *I Love Lucy* and Milton Berle while munching TV dinners; they were ruminating about nuclear war with the Soviets. They knew a lot more about Nikita Khrushchev than they did about Martin King. The human rights of black citizens, their access to voting booths and their admission to colleges, their ability to seek mortgages and buy Cokes at a movie theater—none of these items were on the collective consciousness of the typical American as both the New York Giants and the Brooklyn Dodgers were relocating to sunnier baseball diamonds in California.

Civil rights was simply not an issue taken up by the presidential nominees, Nixon and Kennedy, in 1960. Nixon harangued Kennedy about his youth and inexperience; Kennedy successfully exploited the relatively new medium of television to develop an image of vitality and dynamism. His famed Inaugural Address of 1961 ("Ask not what your country can do for you, ask what you can do for your country"), in fact a Cold War call to arms, made not a single reference to what Americans could do for their fellow citizens that were living in a state of apartheid. Kennedy was going to the moon; he wasn't going to Montgomery.

The president's brother, Robert, the new attorney general, was in 1961 trying to outmaneuver FBI director J. Edgar Hoover in his own efforts to neutralize Cuba, track down gangsters, and keep Communists away from the administration—or even the friends of Communists. Neither of the Kennedy brothers actually had any Negro friends or personal acquaintances. Jacqueline Kennedy, the elegant, French-speaking First Lady, carried a personal aversion to Martin Luther King Jr. and dismissed him as a sexually obsessed, party-loving colored man and opportunist that she preferred would not visit the White House or hang around too much with her husband.[10] The "Negro work" was not part of the culture the Kennedys originally brought to Washington.

But then something happened at Harveys Department Store in Nashville, Tennessee, in 1960. For the better part of two years, a group of black activists, led by Reverend James Lawson and a particularly brave woman from Chicago named Diane Nash, had been conducting workshops for college students. Deriving strategy from the principles of Gandhian nonviolent civil disobedience, the youngsters were training for the peaceful integration of downtown Nashville lunch counters. African Americans were tolerated in the department stores but were forbidden to eat in the restaurants. (There were other restrictions as well, from Nashville to Louisville and back down to Tallahassee: black people could not try on clothing before purchase; heaven forbid a white person might later buy the same item and be exposed to the contamination.)

The lunch counters were chosen as targets because they were highly visible and extremely public. Reverend Lawson (who would later move to Memphis and be crucial to the 1968 sanitation workers' strike there that brought King to his final campaign) and other leaders had met with the owners of Harveys and asked that blacks be allowed to sit at the counters. After the request was refused, an action took place at that department store as well as another, Cain-Sloan. Young men and women sat at the counters for several hours, menus in hand, receiving only invectives and no service.[11]

Over the telephone from Chicago, Diane Nash told me how frightened she was, at twenty-one years of age in 1960, a black woman "way in over my head." She said: "We were children, really. We were bright and filled with idealism but we were up against these powerful white men, decades older, and they ran the city and police and the courts. What had we been thinking while we were sitting around in Jim Lawson's workshops on civil disobedience and nonviolence?" Nash chuckled to herself, a laugh filled with bittersweet wisdom and fleeting grief.[12]

Stanley read with fascination about these gallant efforts in 1960, the evolution of the "Nashville Movement," and the spread of these sit-in protests to such places as Greensboro, North Carolina, and Chattanooga, Tennessee. In some cases, the young demonstrators were brutally beaten by law officers, servers, and other customers. One of the emerging captains of this movement was John Lewis, the burly, taciturn, idealistic rural lad who idolized the comely and steely Diane Nash and evolved into a primary subordinate to Martin Luther King and, eventually, a renowned member of Congress from Atlanta. But during the several months of the sit-ins, many of the protestors were jailed, there were bombings and shootings, and James Lawson—a divinity student at Vanderbilt University—was expelled from the school due to his involvement.

By May 1960, the tenacity of the sit-in protestors paved the way for partial agreements in several cities: the lunch counters would be incrementally desegregated. But the full realization of equal access to service and facilities would not be realized legally by African Americans until after the Civil Rights Act of 1964, passed by the US Congress and signed into law—with Martin Luther King present—by President Lyndon B. Johnson.

In 1960, some people in the protest movement criticized King for his lack of presence in the landmark campaigns. King did speak at Nashville's Fisk University in April and cited the valor and exemplary organization of the sit-in crusade. He also preached to a rally of some one thousand people at the White Rock Baptist Church in Durham, North Carolina, exhorting the students to remain steadfast in their fight for personal freedoms. But it might be understood if King was distracted during those months: he faced the real possibility of arraignment and prison time just after relocating back in Atlanta.

In what can only be regarded as an act of racial spite, the state of Alabama decided to extradite King from Georgia and indict him for alleged income tax felonies. The charges were trumped up and disingenuous, invented by malice and fed by a turncoat minor official of the Montgomery Improvement

Association. The defector had charged that King misappropriated funds from the MIA and SCLC treasuries in 1956 and 1958 and used them for himself. If anything, it was a case of sloppy bookkeeping—nobody knew better than a furious Stanley Levison that Martin was as fiduciary and modest about money as he was impossibly inept when it came to budgets and line-keeping. When Stanley heard in New York that two deputies had walked, unannounced, into Martin's study at Ebenezer and presented both arrest warrants and extradition papers, Stanley felt pummeled. He was further devastated to learn that King was handcuffed (hardly the first time) and taken for booking at a downtown Atlanta police station.

Stanley's heart ached with anger and fury. He courted despair but then just pushed it away. Memories of Martin with the letter opener sticking out of his chest always flashed into his head when these crises occurred—he threw them out of mind and refused any valedictory retreats. What Stanley knew was that Martin's soul was a chamber of need. When the forces of what he perceived as evil turned upon Martin, Stanley drew his short breaths in and turned everything back on the enemies, determined to demonstrate that he was better informed and gutsier than any of them.

Levison sprang into action. A bond of $2,000 was quickly arranged, and it was recommended to King that he waive extradition and report to Alabama freely and with dignity. Over a tense phone line, Stanley advised his friend to react with calmness and poise. "He seems to be all right," Stanley told Bea. "But I know him. Inside, he's destroyed and afraid. He's always been terrified of prison, especially in the South. Who could blame him?"

Ironically, the sit-in campaign was just spreading to Atlanta, but even King's critics could not condemn him for being unavailable to participate. David Garrow records the period in *Bearing the Cross:*

> In public King put forward a strong face, but in private he was overwhelmed. "I had never seen Martin affected so deeply," Coretta wrote. The tax charges "caused Martin more suffering than any other event of his life up to that point." He was deeply worried that people who knew him from a distance

would presume the allegations were true, and lose faith in him. Stanley Levison and other close friends explained that King could prove that he had done nothing wrong by showing at the trial, with the best possible defense, that the allegations had no basis in fact. King should not let the matter worry him to death, for his New York friends would raise the money for a first-rate legal defense.[13]

In 1958, a black woman had stabbed Martin Luther King to within an inch of his life. Now, a black man had potentially condemned King to a long prison term—another form of slashing. And again, an asthmatic but determined white Jewish attorney from New York would step in and help save the day.

CHAPTER NINE

Senator Kennedy Is Calling

artin Luther King did fear prison—and for good reason. Even if one wasn't so well known, the dangers were clear for any incarcerated black man or woman in the South. Certainly, many of the African American inmates were criminals; some had done hideous things to members of their own families or communities. Yet prison guards (overwhelmingly white) were merciless and too often were engaged in this line of work to feed their very racial demagogueries and social dysfunctions. Wardens and other corrections officers were clinically engaged in a culturally based pathology that freely permitted the mistreatment, abuse, and murder of Negro prisoners. If you were black in a prison in the South, you didn't close your eyes at night, breathing in the stale snuffle of caged men, hearing the nocturnal horrors of deranged souls, depending upon the mercy of your worst enemies, not certain where or what you'd be in the morning light.

The viral system of Jim Crow was applied at his harshest within the walls and cells and holes of the southern jail system. Belts, axes, tortuous prongs, and ruptured human standards were applied against the bodies and beings of dark-skinned convicts caught in the labyrinth of Dixie machismo. The blacks were not clothed, educated, fed, or given medical attention in any way proportional to white inmates—regardless of the latter's crimes. Men, chained-gang in the daylight, disappeared in the darkness of night without reason, explanation, or any accounting.

For King, the dread was wired by his innate fear, and certainty, of being eventually killed. His heart pounded with panic at the first shout of "Come over here, boy!" that initiated every arrest or seizure. Over and over again, he was manhandled, shoved, hit, handcuffed, and thrown into police cruisers or into the backs of steel vans. He repeatedly heard insulting references such as "nigger," "coon," and the like. Always dressed in a neat preacher's suit, often donning a fedora, the minister and Ph.D. was treated like the most vulgar felon or scoundrel.

Whatever his weaknesses or vanities, the one person who often enough accompanied King to jail was Ralph Abernathy. Sometimes, Abernathy happened to also be arrested; at times he voluntarily escorted his mentor to confinement with solidarity and to simply offer his comforting presence. Stanley Levison and Harry Belafonte—among others—may have disapproved of Abernathy's cloying habits or even called him out for opportunism. But for King, Abernathy was a brother, a sweet foil, and a confessor. No matter how close King was with Levison, only Ralph was Martin's best friend.

Ralph and Martin had a bit of an emotional scuffle as King was leaving Montgomery for Atlanta. Unlike Stanley, Martin wanted Ralph to also move to Atlanta and become the executive director of the SCLC. Abernathy clung to his cozy pulpit and its perquisites. King was stung by Abernathy's refusal; he was nervous about succeeding his father at Ebenezer and about being judged by the considerable Negro leadership in Atlanta. Many of these people remembered "Mike" King as a child. So now he wanted the familiar face and rhythm of his steadfast deputy, Ralph. They exchanged some impatient words (referring to each other, as they did in private, as "Michael" and "David"), but then embraced the reality and the future.

That future seemed in jeopardy when King was presented with the Alabama subpoena so soon after his return home to Georgia. So much was already pressing upon King at the time: the white establishment in Atlanta had made declamatory noises about King's move: he was "a troublemaker" and "a rabble-rouser," and his presence in any community, they blathered, always precipitated riots, lawbreaking, and general unrest. People in the black community, especially other ministers, were indeed comparing King unfavorably to his father. Meanwhile, King was dismayed by the increasingly brutal response of police and state militia to the valiant lunch-counter activists. He even attempted to communicate with the retiring President Eisenhower about this, but his protestations were ignored. Now he faced extradition and jail time. He missed Ralph, but he needed Stanley.

Again Levison bounced into action. He was already keeping a watchful eye on the evolving student sit-in movement. He had written to King: "This is a new stage in the struggle. It begins at the higher point where Montgomery left off." Stanley was advising a cadre of young attorneys who were defending a host of protestors being held in southern jails. He was fund-raising and organizing and managing the SCLC staff operations still limping with penury and without professional guidance. He was pulling Harry Belafonte into the fray in order to fill the treasury and he was, by phone and by mail, galvanizing eastern labor unions to support both the sit-in campaign and now the grave legal threat being faced personally by Martin Luther King.

He assured Martin on the phone: "The response is heartwarming." Privately, Stanley was chain-smoking addictively, coughing and hacking with his asthma, even while remaining poker-faced and focused. Not even Beatrice knew how deeply he worried about Martin, money, and the future.

It was March 1960 and Stanley had rapidly created and launched the Committee to Defend Martin Luther King and the Struggle for Freedom in the South. The chairman was A. Philip Randolph, and the executive director of the committee, in charge of its immediate development goal of $200,000, was

Bayard Rustin. In a stroke of typical administrative genius, Levison formally linked the two issues of the Alabama perjury charges and the southern segregations into one powerful fund-raising appeal. It was as though Levison had to put these things together in order to redirect and channel his feelings of dread for Martin, his intuition about King's susceptibility and danger. Stanley knew that the turn of events that came out of Alabama like a legal banshee would exhaust Martin of his remaining will and resolve; he knew that Martin was traumatized and humiliated.

In his *Parting the Waters*, Taylor Branch describes King's state of mind at this juncture:

> The confluence of the sit-ins and the perjury indictment slapped King with a cruel irony. Just as he was deciding that he should aim his political influence at filling the jails with idealistic young protestors, Alabama struck at the most sensitive spot of such resolve. If convicted on tax charges, even in the white courts, he would take to prison the tarnished public image of a lying, greedy, sham preacher. This was everything King had resolved most devoutly not to be himself and to change in his church if he could. . . . Never before or after was King so distraught about his future.[1]

On February 17, just after the indictment that day, King had spoken to a reporter from the Atlanta television station WSB. Even in the grainy, black-and-white video, he appears utterly drained, wan, and barely able to run words together—though he does succeed in a jaded manner that betrays his brutal inner anger. "No, I didn't have the slightest idea that I'd be arrested today," he says, his head slumped somewhat to the left, his mouth working as if it is not connected to his face, his tie struggling to remain neatly affixed to his collar. His eyes blink frequently; he shares his dignified, if weary, response mechanically and not without a form of draining resentment: "I have always said that if it is necessary for us to go to jail in the midst of this struggle, we should do it willingly and we should do it with love in our hearts. And maybe, through our willingness to suffer and accept this type of sacrifice, we will be able to arouse and awaken the dozing conscience of many citizens of our nation."

King pauses at this point and awaits the next question from the white reporter. In an undeniable flash of cold fear and anxiety, he uncharacteristically appears to be out of words, out of resolve, out of hope. Both of his eyes shift nervously to the left, at the newsman, and one can actually see the utter vulnerability of the young man and one can practically taste the dryness in his mouth. He comes to life, somewhat, when the reporter asks: "What do you think lies at the root of this indictment against you?"

King answers forcefully: "Well, I believe it's just a new attempt on the part of the state of Alabama to harass me for the role I have played in the civil rights struggle. This seems to be a pattern . . . of harassing individuals working in the area of freedom and integration and brotherhood."

The reporter asks: "Are you ever afraid?"

"Well, I wouldn't say that I have totally risen above the shackles of fear. But I live every day under the threat of death, almost . . . and I have had to develop something within me to keep me going amongst all these, uh, difficulties. . . . I am strengthened from the realization that in the struggle we have cosmic companionship and that the cause is right. And there is a great spirit that comes to an individual when he is engaged in something he believes is right and something he will ultimately win."[2]

On March 29, the Committee to Defend Martin Luther King placed a full-page ad in the *New York Times*. The bold headline read "HEED THEIR RISING VOICES." In the upper right-hand corner of the page, the ad quoted from a *New York Times* editorial that had been published just ten days earlier: "The growing movement of peaceful mass demonstrations by Negroes is something new in the South. . . . Let Congress heed their rising voices, for they will be heard."

Levison had solicited the signatures of eighty-four prominent Americans and King supporters, from Jackie Robinson to Eleanor Roosevelt to Harry Belafonte. Belafonte had reportedly edited the text in tandem with Bayard Rustin. The flier began:

As the whole world knows by now, thousands of Southern Negro students are engaged in widespread non-violent demonstrations in positive affirmation of the right to live in human dignity as guaranteed by the U.S. Constitution and the Bill of Rights. In their efforts to uphold these guarantees, they are being met by an unprecedented wave of terror by those who would deny and negate that document which the whole world looks upon as setting the pattern for modern freedom. . . .

Decent-minded Americans cannot help but applaud the creative daring of the students and the quiet heroism of Dr. King. But this is one of those moments in the stormy history of Freedom when men and women of good will must do more than applaud the rising-to-glory of others. The America whose good name hangs in the balance before a watchful world, the America whose heritage of Liberty these Southern Upholders of the Constitution are defending, is our America as well as theirs. . . .

We must heed their rising voices—yes—but we must add our own.

We must extend ourselves above and beyond moral support and render the material help so urgently needed by those who are taking the risks, facing jail, and even death in a glorious re-affirmation of our Constitution and its Bill of Rights.

We urge you to join hands with our fellow Americans in the South by supporting, with your dollars, this Combined Appeal for all three needs—the defense of Martin Luther King—the support of the embattled students—and the struggle for the right to vote.[3]

The appeal was successful—it recouped in donations several times more than its own cost. But there were political costs: Alabama state officials were incensed and, again, the feathers of the NAACP were ruffled. Roy Wilkins and his colleagues, begrudging of King exactly at his moment of supreme peril, complained that the SCLC was taking too much credit for the voter registration efforts in the South and that it was coveting the position of the NAACP in these exertions. The state administration of Alabama publicly implied that it would sue the *New York Times* for libel and everyone who had signed the ad. There were demands for retraction. So, while the ad raised money, it also raised the temperature of the whole controversy, and King reportedly went into the coming trial with great doubt and trepidation.

King had even managed to try the patience of his two special advocates, Belafonte and Levison, during those stressful days leading up to the court date. While the three convened to talk strategy, King would confound them with sudden dissertations about fees, guidelines, and proprieties. The preacher was terribly conflicted over—at once grateful for, and resentful of—the powerful professional services he was acquiring from lawyers, celebrities, and publicists pro bono or at greatly reduced rates.

"I don't know what's right here," he moaned to Stanley. "If I made a mistake, or even if people think I made a mistake, I'm not sure what category that falls under when it comes to charitable help and especially if it involves any money from the movement. Maybe this is all a personal matter and shouldn't be resolved like a political problem."

"For heaven's sakes, Martin," Stanley responded, with an edge. "I'm having enough problems getting all the other attorneys to pitch in like I'm trying to. Don't make it more complicated. Look, this is about Alabama versus the civilized world. It's political, okay?"[4]

When Stanley told Harry about this type of bewailing from Martin, or when Belafonte heard it himself, he rolled his eyes. Sometimes Martin just doesn't get it, the entertainer thought.

King was drowning in despair and struggling with demons even as he was sorely grateful for all of his supporters and sponsors. He needed them even as he so desperately wanted not to need them; he was as embarrassed about his helplessness as he was painfully shy. Meanwhile, white racists were out to get him, while black adversaries were not about to save him. He was only thirty-one years old and carried the anguish of several lives.

· · · · ·

During those especially trying days, Stanley visited, phoned, and posted letters to countless politicos, jurists, patrons, journalists, and clergy. His mantra was simple: the charges against King were "a gross misrepresentation of fact." Alabama officials insinuated that King had earned some $45,000 in 1958 and that he had perjured himself on the issue. Stanley was livid and upset; as King's accountant, he knew this imputation was wrong and deceitful. "My God," he'd scream into the receiver, his voice straining with anger and cigarette burn, "Martin's income never even approached $45,000. Ludicrous!" Levison was well aware that a guilty verdict could result in a five-year sentence—and the end of both King's career and the civil rights crusade. This was serious business, and everybody, from Bayard Rustin to the contentious (and singular) female SCLC executive Ella Baker (who was critical that King did not let the students control their own sit-in campaigns), just had to close ranks and get the job done!

The entertainment lawyer Clarence B. Jones would soon come into King's orbit during the grim litigious days of 1960. Jones told me: "The Alabama tax thing practically broke Martin in half. His worst dreams were turning into a living nightmare. And he was just plain scared. Imagine his situation right there and then."

Jones shared that even while King waited in torment for the trial to get going, "other things hit him. Somebody burned a cross in their front yard one night in Atlanta. And then he was speaking about the sit-ins at Fisk in Nashville and there was a bomb scare. It was a false alarm, but everything like this accumulated for him and for Coretta and added to his sorrow and fear. Oh, and he and Coretta were driving Lillian Smith, the white author and a good friend, somewhere in Georgia. So some state troopers pulled him over just because they saw a white woman driving with a black man. This was in the 1960s! They harassed him and threatened him because he was using an Alabama driver's license and it was past the three months or whatever the limit was that you had to change over to a Georgia license if you were a new resident. I don't know why, but they let him go with a warning. Life was a problem for Martin 24/7."

Happily, King's luck—which was never considerable—did hold out at the trial. Historian David Garrow's succinct sentence has often been quoted: "It was the first time Alabama had ever prosecuted someone for perjury on a tax return." The trial began on May 25 and quickly demonstrated that the state had no hard evidence with which to penalize King. After only three days of testimony, a jury of twelve white males deliberated for less than four hours and exonerated the civil rights leader. "Not guilty!" King was astounded and remained stoic and dignified. Stanley lit one cigarette after another in a cloudy exhalation of relief. It would only be a reprieve, however, during an extended period of heavy anxiety, great apprehensions, and turbulent ups and downs for King, Levison, and the small, weary circle that held together the civil rights campaign even as John Kennedy was headed for the presidency.

Kennedy's relationship to King, never a priority for the glamorous and youthful candidate, proved to be an accidental—and possibly decisive—issue in the 1960 campaign.

While Martin Luther King Jr. and John F. Kennedy are generally linked in history as allies in the civil rights saga, in fact their relationship was tentative, even adversarial. King took a dim view of what he viewed as Kennedy's craven senatorial record on civil rights, often asserting that Kennedy was more interested in the presidency than in moral values. But now, on June 13, 1960, a meeting was held between the two men.

Harry Belafonte had already met—and been relatively fascinated—with the candidate, recalling Kennedy's "cool, clear gaze." Belafonte has shared that Kennedy really did not discern King's importance in the black community—which betrayed his basic ignorance of the playing field. It was clear that Kennedy figured that "a key Negro" would be Jackie Robinson or even Belafonte himself. Kennedy seemed "puzzled" when Belafonte emphasized that King was the linchpin among African Americans.

Belafonte was discouraged by Kennedy's "lukewarm" attitude about the concerns of blacks, especially those living in the South. Kennedy demurred that a Democratic president was handcuffed by the preeminence of southern Democratic segregationists. Belafonte recalls telling the senator: "Six years after *Brown v. Board of Education*, schools in the South are still segregated, Negroes are being lynched for trying to vote, and a lot of us aren't going to take it anymore. Civil rights is a freight train and it's headed your way."[5]

In spite of the inconclusive nature of their meeting, Belafonte resolved that Kennedy, though "unschooled" in civil rights, was "whip-smart and knew how to listen." Belafonte urged King to meet with the candidate if an opportunity arose.

The brief meeting of King and Kennedy on June 23, held in the opulent New York residence of Kennedy's father, Joseph P. Kennedy, proved useful to both men. If Kennedy did not seem to grasp the concept of civil rights, he did become focused on the *voting* rights that were the natural entitlement of every American. In spite of his patrician ways, something about Kennedy's instinct for leadership impressed and reassured King. He would not endorse Kennedy, but he left the session with a positive feeling even as the SCLC's official stance of neutrality in the election spared him the necessity of making an endorsement. Martin told Stanley: "I really don't feel much difference between Kennedy and Nixon though I suppose I lean towards Kennedy."

"Don't stick your neck out for anybody," said Stanley.

King and the Democratic nominee met again in September, and Kennedy was forthright: "I need the Negro vote." Some Kennedy advisers wanted King to stand with Kennedy and make a case for civil rights; King was skeptical. He was not about to be manipulated. A suggestion was made that the SCLC, though nonpartisan, invite both Kennedy and Nixon to appear at one of its gatherings; Kennedy had no interest in that. But he would take an interest in what happened after King reappeared in Decatur, Georgia, on September to deal with the vexing old issue of driving in the state with an Alabama driver's license while showing expired plates on the car.

The proceedings at the De Kalb County Criminal Court rapidly snowballed into a cold and ominous situation for King. He paid a fine and accepted a year's probation. He did not, however, realize that the judge had signed off on another part of the decree: King could not violate any laws anywhere in the United States for that year without being subject to stark legal consequences.

Subsequently, King participated with sit-in students in a demonstration against Rich's department store in Atlanta. One of the Student Nonviolent Coordinating Committee (SNCC) leaders at the time was Julian Bond, the future NAACP chairman and now a professor at both American University and the University of Virginia. Over the phone, Bond recalled for me when he and other student leaders pleaded with King to physically join them in the protest. "I told him, 'Martin, you just have to come along.' The others were even more adamant. We just felt that, well, how could he be making all these speeches about filling up the jails, about 'jail, not bail,' without actually being a part of it? He heard us and came along."[6]

The decision was fateful for King. He, along with others, was promptly arrested for trespassing. This is when he found out about the severe amendment to his sentence back in Decatur—he had left himself open to harsh new ordeals and to serious time in prison. King had effectively violated probation, and the white court system would seize upon this breach. Taylor Branch described the scene at the time:

> The students reassembled outside the Fulton County jail . . . in a vigil of support, waiting for King to be transferred to De Kalb County for Judge Mitchell's hearing. A group of white theology students, in Atlanta to encourage the sit-ins, joined them in quiet prayers until the first sight of King turned all their hopeful apprehension into cold fear. Emerging from the jail between two De Kalb County deputies, King wore not only handcuffs but also leg and arm shackles. The students fell silent enough to hear the clang of metal as King was marched briskly to a squad car and put into a backseat next to a police dog. . . . As for King, who was trying not to look at the ferocious German shepherd beside him, it was a sudden return to the terror of his first arrest . . . in Montgomery, when visions of lynching had undone him.[7]

Mercilessly, the probation was revoked, and he was sentenced to four months at hard labor in state prison, assigned to a road gang. He was dragged away, his limbs frozen in shock, his eyes devoid of life. Every black person in the South knew what road gang bondage meant for a Negro, especially one of such prominence, especially Martin Luther King Jr.: inmate justice, brutish treatment, shadowy murder. "What was there," Harry Belafonte has reminisced, "to keep some white supremacist on the gang from killing him with a blow of his pickax?"

A crescendo of terror and pure dread for King's life sent Stanley Levison to reinstate his rotation of anguished phone calls to attorneys and politicians and led Belafonte to petition for help and financial support from his many Hollywood friends and colleagues. The latter reached out to everyone he knew, from Nelson Rockefeller to Frank Sinatra to Sammy Davis Jr. to Jackie Robinson. Belafonte bitterly recalls the absolute silence of the Richard Nixon campaign. But the pleading din made its way out of Georgia, New York, and California and was heard in the Kennedy campaign.

It should not be assumed that either John or Robert Kennedy had a proactive concern about helping Martin Luther King get out of prison. Any sign or action on the part of the Kennedy campaign to assist King could be devastating to Kennedy's campaign in the South. Stanley knew this all too well. "Never mind that a man's life is absolutely in danger," he muttered to Beatrice. "The Kennedys won't do anything that might cost a single precinct. There isn't a moral ounce of marrow in them. We have got to figure out a way to help them understand that this will be good for them, that it could swing a whole lot of Negro votes their way and actually deliver the South."

A key figure in what the Kennedys eventually did was Harris Wofford, an adviser to John, a believer in King's work, and a comrade of Levison's. Wofford was torn in half: on one side was his loyalty to the Kennedys and his primal political understanding of the situation and the grave risks if any Kennedy tried to intervene; on the other, his genuine compassion for King's personal plight and an ethical impulse to act against an obvious legal outrage that was toxic with racism.

Wofford, a tall, elegant-looking man with establishment roots but a penchant for Gandhi and civil disobedience, received a frantic telephone call from Coretta Scott King. "Martin's in Reidsville prison!" she screamed. Wofford, truly panicked, contacted Kennedy's brother-in-law, Sargent Shriver. Harry Belafonte also claims to have worked Wofford over on the phone, imploring that Senator Kennedy make an official statement demanding King's release for safety and humanitarian reasons. Meanwhile, it was learned that King had arbitrarily been placed in solitary confinement.

Robert Kennedy, a grim realist without much sentimentality in his life to that point, obsessively dedicated to his brother's presidential success, was steadfastly opposed to any meddling in the King case. He saw it as an out-and-out political calamity that could cost JFK the election. Shriver, who would create the Peace Corps, was sympathetic and had to wiggle carefully in the matter. He was able to talk directly with John Kennedy and to persuade the ambivalent candidate that calling Coretta King would be a decent gesture that would also reflect well on the campaign.

Shriver had the number and John Kennedy agreed. Shriver placed the call to the King home in Atlanta; when Coretta answered, her voice trembling, he announced: "Mrs. King, Senator Kennedy is calling." The conversation was as follows, according to Taylor Branch:

> KENNEDY: "[Mrs. King,] I know this must be very hard for you. I understand you are expecting a baby and I just wanted you to know that I was thinking about you and Dr. King. If there is anything I can do to help, please feel free to call on me."
> MRS. KING: "I certainly appreciate your concern. I would appreciate anything you could do to help."[8]

Miraculously, King was released from prison on a $2,000 bond. But it was not the call from John Kennedy to Coretta King that set up this happy reversal—that just got the Kennedys very good play in the black community and even caused Daddy King to publicly switch his endorsement from Nixon to Kennedy. No: according to Harry Belafonte, Robert Kennedy experienced a change of heart after initially resisting any intermediation. The caveat was that no one in the Kennedy campaign was permitted to comment about, let alone reveal, that John had called Coretta or that Bobby had gotten upset enough about what was done to King to place some covert and effective calls to Georgia. The story did not get much play in the media at the time (to the Kennedys' relief) even though it immediately became legendary in the black community. To this day, the hagiography among many African Americans is that the Kennedys saved Martin Luther King Jr. from state prison because they were morally alarmed.

In fact, what prompted Robert Kennedy to act secretly was not his concern for King as a black man trapped in a potentially lethal prison predicament. Robert didn't even discern the issue as having a racial flavor. What dismayed Kennedy was a purely legal problem. This is how Harry Belafonte summarizes Bobby Kennedy's strange turn at that simmering moment: "Apparently, what moved him to action wasn't anyone's pleading. Instead, as a lawyer, he felt affronted by the county judge's flouting of fundamental law. No one charged with a misdemeanor was supposed to be denied bail—period. Bristling, Bobby had called the judge to remind him of that."

So, because of a legal flagrancy detected by Robert Kennedy—and not any social outrage—King was sent home and the Kennedys captured a wave of black electoral support in the South. Many historians credit the presence of Lyndon B. Johnson on the Kennedy ticket as the reason Kennedy ultimately garnered enough southern support to narrowly defeat Richard Nixon that November. Johnson, the wily Texan, did campaign vociferously up and down the South and undoubtedly helped swing the tide. But no one should discount the sudden surge of black voters in the South who were galvanized to choose John F. Kennedy in the aftermath of this bitter little drama; it may have been the difference.

Meanwhile, the question in the civil rights group was, what should King do to express his gratitude to Kennedy? Stanley, flush with relief and ecstasy that Martin was again safely delivered, returned reflexively to serious analysis.

"Martin, you must not endorse Kennedy, even after this." King thought he should and argued with Stanley that even Daddy King had dramatically reversed himself and openly sanctioned JFK.

"Your father is not the leader of America's Negroes. You are that man. You must resist your emotional temptation here and remain above the fray. If you endorse the Kennedys, they will own you." Stanley was adamant, as were Harry Belafonte, Clarence Jones, and others in the inner circle.

And it was Levison who drafted a statement that King read to the press a few days after his discharge. King thanked Kennedy for his help and commented that the senator "served as a great force in making my release possible." But he fell short of any endorsement, citing his role as a civil rights leader, which forced him to remain nonpartisan.

"He did really want to endorse Kennedy," Clarence Jones told me. "He had gone through a hellish experience and it was his nature to give something back. Harry was convinced that Martin shouldn't fall into that trap and then sort of become a house Negro for the Kennedys. But it really was Stanley who helped Martin come to terms with the whole thing and come to the right conclusion."

CHAPTER TEN

Martin, Stanley, and Clarence

At the end of the day, Martin Luther King Jr. was a preacher, an oratorical wizard, who knew how to play music with people's emotions. Ironically, he hadn't spent a lot of time as a child and teenager, very much in the looming shadow of his father at Ebenezer, fancying himself as a pastor. His vast intellectual curiosity, his embracing of philosophers and ideas, generally led him to think of himself as a future campus professor or even the president of a college.

He may have truly discovered his own pulpit powers—and may have been entrapped by them—that evening in Montgomery in 1955 when he stood up and spoke out for the city's blacks and their right to dignity in the buses and streets of that city. Recruited to the presidency of the hastily formed Montgomery Improvement Association, not particularly seeking acclaim or notoriety, he opened his mouth and altered history that night by the simple eloquence of his words and the trumpet sound of his voice. Bayard Rustin heard it and summoned Stanley Levison from New York to Montgomery. Levison heard it and decided on the spot that this young man and the cause he was creating were his own life's work, even as his old Communist impulses were fading in the glow of King's rhetoric.

By 1960, stabbed, bruised, stalked, arrested, confined, at once maligned and exalted, King had gained the callused confidence of a man clearly working in his own element. He was both a convicted felon and the subject for a fawning cover story in *Time* magazine. He was more than a parish minister; he was the self-critical, doubt-ridden, yet quietly valiant symbol of America's unrealized contrition with itself for the four-hundred-year crime of African bondage and degradation. Depending upon how one looked at it, everything had gone right—or wrong—for Martin King. His was a fateful arc and he submitted to it. But he never gave up his most basic role and opportunity as the man in the pulpit who could influence other people's lives.

And so it was with the California-based entertainment attorney named Clarence B. Jones. A dashing black man with a flair for good suits and fashion sunglasses, successful, erudite, and ambitious, Jones and his wife were doing well in the Pasadena area as the 1960s rolled across the continent. Jones was hardworking, smart, and lavish. He never lost touch with his roots in Cornwell Heights, Pennsylvania, and he carried the educational imprint of the boarding school nuns at the Order of the Sacred Heart who essentially raised him. But he didn't permit the color of his skin to interfere with his healthy American determination to thrive and prosper.

Worldly and savvy, Jones was probably aware of the frightful legal troubles being faced by Dr. Martin Luther King Jr. in Alabama in 1960. He likely knew some of the details: outlandish state claims of tax evasion and underreported income, contrived and illegal detention in a state penal facility, and a broad flouting of how the law is supposed to work in a republic. Jones knew, but he was not involved on any visceral level. He also did not know Dr. King. However, some of King's associates knew of Jones.

Jones remembered those days as we sat together in the boardroom of the Martin Luther King Jr. Research and Education Institute at Stanford University, where he is a professor, mentor, and living connection to the days when King was still alive and forging a sea change in the direction of this nation. "Initially, a mutual acquaintance of ours from Boston University called me. He said I'd be a valuable addition to the legal team defending Dr. King in Alabama. I declined at first. But then Martin happened to be speaking in Los Angeles that very week. Somebody from the SCLC called me and asked if he could stop by the house and visit. Just to say hello. Well, I could hardly say no."

Clarence did not think too much about the possible effect of his unusual and stately house upon the Gandhian Reverend King. The home had a retractable ceiling that accommodated a towering palm tree that grew out from within the structure. From inside, one could see feathery clouds during the day or a canopy of stars at night. An abundant, brimming spread of flowers and plants, from hyacinths to kangaroo paws to begonias, gave the mansion the appearance of a botanical garden. It obviously paid for Clarence Jones to interact professionally with and represent people in California such as Sidney Poitier and Nat King Cole.

"Yes, when Dr. King came by, he did look around very carefully and took note," Clarence told me.

A gleam of affection and bereavement was evident in Jones's eyes. Like so many people who are still around to personally recall King, Jones is unable to detach his emotional devotion—and his grief—for the preacher from his own historical recollections. He remembered King as "a man of medium stature, wearing a dark suit, white shirt, skinny tie, and fedora. He was gracious."

King came into the Joneses' home and commented wryly about its majesty of space and decor. He laughed with Clarence's white wife, cheerfully played with their one-year-old daughter, and breezily recounted his trip to India and the many things he learned through that and other journeys. He then proceeded to tell Jones about the pressing legal problem he was facing in Alabama; the two men didn't have to discuss what they both knew—that King was a black man of some repute who had simply been framed by the white hierarchy. Jones was interested and sympathetic but recalls telling King, "I'm sure you will beat it."

King would eventually describe Stanley Levison to Jones, conveying his own amazement and gratitude to this "white lawyer," selfless and loyal, who was giving so much of his time and expertise to the movement—and to this horrendous Alabama case. Jones was particularly fascinated by this account of the Jew from Queens that was mixing himself into the cause. Then King asked Jones to come to Alabama and join the legal team because, simply put, "more Negro professionals" were needed in this cause.

This was not something Clarence was prepared to do, at least not yet. He had labored hard for his status in Los Angeles, made an honest living, and was just enjoying the fruit of his efforts. He didn't picture himself suddenly transplanted indefinitely to Montgomery, Alabama, or some such place. He was a Pennsylvanian and a Californian and really had no affinity for the South, let alone its historic disposition toward African Americans. But he was about to find himself up against the moral persuasion of Martin Luther King Jr.

The preacher didn't get a positive response from Jones that evening; the latter, no matter how understanding, just couldn't be influenced to consider "the call." He'd be happy to offer research and advice by mail, but uprooting indefinitely to Alabama was not plausible.

The following Sunday, Jones attended a service at Friendship Baptist Church in nearby Baldwin Hills, where King was guest preaching. Clarence had never personally heard Martin, whom he termed "a rock star," and reported: "It was magic. What Frank Sinatra was renowned for doing with his singing voice, the Reverend Martin Luther King Jr. did with his speaking voice." Jones was moved, inspired, and—as he would soon realize—singled out. He wrote about King:

> He spoke of those Negroes who'd been fortunate to become doctors and lawyers and accountants and performing artists—and what they morally owed those black adults, especially in the Jim Crow South, who never had the chance to do what they did; and those black children who could never by themselves

rise above poverty and indignity. . . . What a shame it was, he said, that the kindness, generosity, and good will of [many] whites [who were helping], while dearly appreciated, was not dwarfed by the kindness, generosity, and good will of those Negroes most in a position to offer them to their own people.[1]

Jones began to feel a little uncomfortable and squirmed in his pew. He reported that King took a minor pause at this point and then resumed speaking:

"For example," he continued, "there is a young man with us in this church today who my respected friends and colleagues in New York tell me is a highly gifted attorney. They tell me that this young man's brain has been touched by God. He is so excellent, he can walk into any law library in this country and, in minutes, find cases and citations that an ordinary lawyer wouldn't find even after a full day of looking. . . . This gentleman lives in a suburb of Los Angeles in a fine, fine home—a home with a tree in the middle of the living room and a ceiling that opens up to the sky. I recently had a chance to meet this man. He has a convertible automobile parked in his driveway and a lovely family. . . . But I'm afraid that this gifted young man has forgotten from whence he came."

King cut into Jones's emotional being when he then proceeded to speak about the somewhat humiliated attorney's parents. "They were domestic servants," cried King, sharing that Clarence's father was a chauffeur and gardener and that his mother was a maid cook. Then the reverend read from a Langston Hughes poem entitled "Mother to Son." Jones recalled this crucible moment in a 2006 interview with *Vanity Fair.*

> Well, son, I'll tell you:
>> *Life for me ain't been no crystal stair.*
>> *. . . But all the time*
>> *I'se been a-climbin' on.*

In this magazine profile, Jones told reporter Douglas Brinkley: "His sermon had emotionally messed me up." And after this sly, powerful sermonic ruse, which profoundly affected Clarence Jones and shamed him to tears, he sought out Dr. King in the church parking lot and enlisted in the Alabama case. Jones would be at the helm of the legal team that got King acquitted by that all-white jury in Alabama and spared King from a career-ending conviction and imprisonment. And in the course of the proceedings, Jones met Stanley Levison—whom he took into his heart for life as "my beloved brother."

Jones went on to assist King and the SCLC in other legal quagmires, including the suit involving the *New York Times* and the controversial paid placement of "Heed Their Rising Voices." Jones described himself to me as "the quarterback" guiding a committee of lawyers. "I came to see that Martin was right when he maintained that the enemies of civil rights simply wanted to politically decapitate us. They wanted to intimidate us." Jones recalled that he perceived the movement as "quicksand from which I'd never escape. Nor did I want to." By 1961, he was completely captivated and, with his wife's encouragement, moved to New York in order to be more at the center of things. In short order, Jones's life and work became enmeshed with the persona of Stanley Levison. He said that he was completely in the orbit of Levison, Bayard Rustin, and A. Philip Randolph.

"I starting writing many of Martin's speeches, along with Stanley," Jones said. "But the speeches came out of Martin's mouth and because that's where they came from, they changed history." Jones recalled that he often offered his advice but that he wasn't always right. "We tried to desegregate Albany, Georgia, in late 1961. This was not a great success. But I was really overoptimistic about the role the Kennedys would play. I was certain that the administration would not let us down when we tried to do this. They did not help, certainly not with enthusiasm. Stanley was not surprised, and I began to really see and admire his steady mind and his careful approach to things."

King was fined and again arrested during the so-called Albany Movement. He was attempting to overcome the growing cynicism—even derision—of the younger, more aggressive Student Nonviolent Coordinating Committee, which even began applying the scornful name "Da Lawd" to King. The students deemed that King had not given his full support to the Freedom Rides of that era and that he maintained a safe distance from the often violent clashes that occurred between the riders and the indigenous, racist residents and law officials who brutally repelled the demonstrators attempting to desegregate the Greyhound busses and other interstate conveyances. Even women and youngsters, many of them white, were dragged off the buses and savagely beaten.

King and other black protestors came up against a crafty county sheriff in Albany named Laurie Pritchett. Pritchett, a segregationist at heart, actually mocked King by feigning respect for the campaign and publicly decrying any harsh police responses to sit-ins and lunch counter demonstrations but nonetheless arranging for quick, mass arrests to literally disable the efforts before there were any clashes in view of photographers and television cameras. He broke the back of King's "jail, not bail" mantra by releasing King after only three days in prison and disingenuously declaring his "respect" for the civil rights leader. "The man is clever," Stanley told Clarence as they increasingly confided in each other. "He's outwitted Martin at our own game."

Jones vividly and emotionally recalls King saying to him: "You and Stanley, you're like wintertime soldiers."

I asked Jones about the essential nature of the friendship between King and Levison. Was it comparable to King's with Ralph Abernathy?

"No, no. Dr. King's friendship with Ralph Abernathy was not like any other. But Stanley was absolutely, unequivocally his closest white friend. I would say that his relationship with Stanley was equivalent to mine with Dr. King." I understood, listening to the racial rhythm of this comment, that Stanley and Martin could not have been any closer. "They were like brothers," Jones summarized.

In fact, the brotherhood between Levison and King had a unique fence around it: the topic of sex. While Jones and King's other closest associates—the African Americans—helped cloak, rationalize, and defend King's rampant assignations and, often enough, put up with the preacher's obsessive self-flagellations about his habit, Stanley did not discuss this issue with Martin. There was, effectively, a color line here. Ralph Abernathy, who had his own share of run-ins with irate husbands and suspicious congregants over the years, was deeply bonded with King in the category of road trysts and sundry mistresses. Others, such as Andrew Young, Bernard Lee, and eventually Jones, winked at King's affairs and protected his privacy (or so they thought; the FBI was well aware and was wiretapping all of them) even while they forgave King his "humanizing" characteristics. Taylor Branch put it best in his King biography:

> They did not scorn him as a fallen preacher, nor lapse into paralyzing discomfort. These were people who tolerated or even applauded King's demon delights as a humanizing revelation that bonded them even closer to him and his public purpose. Often they accepted King more easily than he accepted himself. They saw sexual adventure as a natural condition of manhood, of great preachers, or of success, or of Negroes otherwise constrained by the white world, and they objected to King's mistresses no more than to the scores of concubines who had soothed King David during the composition of his Psalms. Some of them grew tired of King's insistence that it was a sin, and of his endless cycles from hedonism to self-recrimination and back. In any case, they adjusted—whether by sigh, sly wink, or eager imitation—and such adjustment defined an innermost circle around him.[2]

Stanley was everything to King but a member of this club. Clarence was a doorkeeper to it. Stanley did not comment about, nor join in the heady conspiracy of, accommodation or even indulgence. Clarence organized trysts for Martin and managed the whispers. He thought he was maintaining his leader's secrecy and providing dutiful cover but, in fact, the FBI eventually tapped into Jones's phone lines (partially due to his growing link to Levison) and methodically developed a surfeit of wired recordings that betrayed King's wildly carnal conversations, his decidedly un-minister-like vernacular, and his endless self-thrashing. J. Edgar Hoover reveled in it, dismissing King now as both a "tomcat" and a Communist. Hoover passed such inflammatory transcripts to Attorney General Robert Kennedy, who discreetly shared some of the documents with his brother, the president. About such wiretaps and others involving King's more public activities, Jones told me: "In the end, the joke was on us."

It was a cruel joke. Jones elaborated for me about the work he did with Levison, often punctuating his comments with the idiom "24/7." His eyes deep and expressive, his body still strapping at the age of eighty-two, Jones carries himself with the nobility of scholarship and experience. On television talk-shows and one-on-one interviews such as the one he and I shared, he talks to younger people with earnest conviction and just a whiff of impatience.

"The SCLC address may have been in Atlanta, but the actual fund-raising all those years, the mail-order operations we did to keep everything going, all that was done by us in New York. It was all supervised by Stanley. He was totally dedicated to it. Yes, the return address for the envelopes was to Atlanta, but we prepared all the solicitations and sent them out from New York."

Jones described a symbiotic relationship that inured to the benefit of the King campaigns. "Stanley did most of the personnel hiring for the SCLC," he said. "He sent me candidates for positions we needed and I did the screening, the interviews. But he did the actual hiring. He was responsible and he used exacting standards. He cared profoundly about who would be doing what. He also read Martin with great intuition and was very clear on Martin's strengths and weaknesses."

Jones and Levison fell into a mutually supportive pattern of writing speeches for the besieged and frenzied King—who was constantly torn between objectives and caught among his many acolytes, critics, would-be schedulers, the press, opportunists, and outright troublemakers that wanted him to fail. "Stanley kept it all together for him," Clarence reminisced. "I was there, I played a role, but he was really the one in charge of everything behind the scenes that had to happen for the movement to survive."

Then the lion in Clarence Jones began to roar. "I am extremely upset, and I am angry, 24/7, and have been for many years, about the glaring *omission* of the name and history of Stanley Levison in the civil rights chronicle." Jones, a tall man with a full bearing, leaned forward in his chair; one could feel the enragement coiling within him.

"There have been so many events recorded about all the things that happened. Nowhere do any of the major players give this faithful Jewish attorney, this saint who did it all pro bono and just because he felt it was right—nowhere is it acknowledged!" Jones's hands banged on the table and his always busy Blackberry slid back in fright. "What's the matter with them? I'm talking about all of them. Jesse Jackson, Andrew Young, John Lewis. They all have written memoirs and documented what happened. They barely say a word about Stanley. They treat him as though he was a *nonperson*. They know better! I'm afraid it's a racial issue, which makes it even more repugnant. It's as if he was never there."

I mentioned to Jones that, indeed, in Ralph Abernathy's 638-page memoir *And the Walls Came Tumbling Down*, there is but one mention, in passing, of Stanley Levison. "That's what I am talking about!" bellowed Jones. "Well, I'm not going to stand for it. That's why I dedicated my latest book [*What Would Martin Say?*] to Stanley. He is not going to be forgotten. Not on my watch."

· · · · ·

As the years rushed by, from 1960 to 1968, when Dr. King was struck down at the Lorraine Motel in Memphis, the bond between Jones and Levison deepened. Jones is the last survivor of the troika (Levison died in 1979 of asthma, diabetes, and cancer at the age of sixty-seven) and Jones is more demonstrative about his "white brother" than he is about King. "Stanley and I always knew that Martin would be assassinated," Jones told me. "It was not a question of if. It was a question of when."

Levison's own passing, alone in his New York apartment, decidedly unnoticed by the media or detailed in history, remains an unyielding wound in Jones's soul. "I go down to the civil rights museum in Memphis," he protests. "You know, on the site of the Lorraine. There's not one mention of Stanley, not a single document pertaining to him. It's a crime!"

Jones is not as much philosophical as he is plaintive; he does not do a lot of summing up, he prides himself on being current—working his Blackberry, updating his Facebook profile (things unimaginable when King and Levison were alive)—he keeps moving ahead. But a shadow looms over his head and it floats in from the past, and it hovers and forms old speeches, graying surveillance transcripts, fearsome headlines, and, especially, Martin Luther King's scrawled handwriting on scraps of newspaper and sheets of toilet paper.

It was Jones who was on the scene with King in Birmingham during the 1963 campaign in the nation's most notoriously segregated city (to be detailed in the next chapter). King was jailed on yet another trumped-up charge by Chief of Police Eugene "Bull" Connor, a rabid racist. Martin learned that the clergymen of Birmingham had released a proclamation imploring him to leave the city and let the people of Birmingham work out their own problems—implying that King was an outside agitator. He was livid and deeply hurt and expressed to Clarence and Stanley that he had to reply to the joint statement.

As King's attorney, Jones had access to the defendant—even if it was begrudged by the police. "Martin told me that he wanted to respond to his fellow ministers"—one of the signatories of the plea for King to leave was a leading rabbi—"but it wasn't easy to get him writing materials, and they would not have wanted him to be composing any kind of treatise while he was sitting in their jail."

Stanley suggested that Clarence smuggle scraps of paper into the reverend, hidden among his legal documents, inside the files of his briefcase, within the pockets and linings of his suits. "A sympathetic jailor would slip Martin a pencil or a pen so that I'd have less to sneak over to him," Clarence said. King worked for several days, occupying his mind, distilling his outrage. The result, rustled out in secret increments by Jones, and also edited by Jones, was King's classic "Letter from Birmingham Jail." The piece, a stirring call to human dignity and an astringent assault on the hypocrisy of some religious liberals, garnered King the 1964 Nobel Peace Prize.

Clarence and Stanley labored in tandem for years, two eastern-bred attorneys, erudite, progressive, color-blind, and both unflappably committed to the life and work of King and the SCLC. Their partnership was a fluid, instinctive, synchronized blend of brains and guts. Clarence saw in Stanley a clear-eyed, if understated, rejection of human submission. Stanley never declared that

Negroes were equal in humanity to whites, or that the fact of Bayard Rustin's homosexuality hardly disqualified him from full utilization in the movement, or that Native Americans were confined to reservations because of anything but historic national pathologies. He didn't say these things; he just acted to repair them. "He'd be as mad at Roy Wilkins for being so stubborn and obstructive to Martin as he was enraged at any southern sheriff for being a bigot," said Clarence. "It wasn't about color or ethnic background. For Stanley, it was about social justice."

Stanley and Clarence both saw and loved Martin for all his flaws, for rising again and again from his self-pitying funk, for his ability to somehow seize the moment—even when the moment seemed lost. They would occasionally find his fussiness and his timorous soul-searching about his flirtations and his "place in history" to be maddening. But they were unfailingly inspired, and always came back to Martin, because of the magic he made by not being afraid.

And so for Jones, who occasionally served as go-between between King and the extreme black separatist Malcolm X, who often ran interference between King and Robert Kennedy, who would discreetly pick up cash gifts from Nelson Rockefeller in banks and vaults in order to balance the SCLC treasury, and who spoke to King about delicate and personal things that Levison eschewed, there was—and remains—a mystique about the Jewish businessman and lawyer from Far Rockaway who gave his career to the civil rights movement.

Jones saw and welcomed Levison as a passionate pilgrim, a true zealot, and an out-and-out essential to the gripping, dangerous narrative. Combined with King, this unlikely threesome, a businessman Jew, a transplanted entertainment lawyer, and a preacher-scion, became an indomitable team of dreamers and seekers. They came from different places but what they agreed upon in that brief interlude between *Sputnik* and Vietnam, between Kennedy and the Beatles, between Montgomery and Memphis, was that freedom doesn't mean anything until you can no longer be arbitrarily shackled.

"I told my friends in the Congressional Black Caucus," Jones said to me, "that they ought to talk to President Obama about this *omission* of Stanley

Levison from the record. I see all these turkeys getting the Medal of Freedom. Stanley should receive this award posthumously for all that he did for the civil rights movement."

Jones received a Georgetown University decoration for his service to freedom at the Kennedy Center in Washington around the time we met at the King Institute. He pointed out that the previous recipient was General Colin Powell. But he emphasized even more that he intended to dedicate the prize to the memory of Stanley Levison exactly because it was a prime opportunity to help raise the legacy of the largely forgotten businessman. "It would be *blasphemy* for me to stand up and receive such an award and not use the chance to talk about Stanley. Of all the people met by Martin King, no one was even remotely more *reliable*, when it came to fund-raising, than Stanley."

I asked Jones, "Would you say that the movement would have been crippled financially, had there not been a Stanley Levison?"

"I can say that without hesitation. All of the fund-raising letters that appeared under Dr. King's signature, all of these letters were either drafted by Stanley, or drafted by Dr. King and then edited by Stanley. Occasionally, maybe 20 percent at the most, I had some input. But I had very small input. It was Stanley who kept the SCLC going. Remember, all the appeals, the mail-order operations, they were all done out of New York. They weren't done out of Atlanta, but they were postmarked from there. Stanley would send me some of the drafts, and I occasionally made some pitches more timely or topical. He didn't always know everything, every single nuance about what was going on in the black community. He'd write about something being in the past and I'd point out that it was still going on, that kind of thing. But it was all Stanley and it was produced in New York and then was posted out of Atlanta with Dr. King signing it just as if he himself had written it."

I posed the matter of Levison's indisputable, onetime association with the American Communist Party. Jones stated, "I didn't know Stanley yet in 1956 when he broke with the Party. But I can assert without question, because I came to know him and love him like a brother, that the Soviet invasion of

Hungary changed his feelings.[3] Here he was, already taking up the cause of freedom fighters in the United States, in Montgomery, Alabama, because of his strong feelings about such things. And at the same time, the Russians were killing freedom fighters in Hungary trying to achieve the same kind of thing over there that Stanley was so moved about here. It changed him completely and he was able to throw his complete being for the rest of his life into the work of Dr. King and the SCLC."

Stanley was energetic and demanding in this pursuit, especially from the small sanctuary of his simple desk and typewriter. The editors of *Time* magazine heard from him early in 1962. The newsweekly had published a major story called "Races" on January 12. Levison was incensed that some "anonymous students," African American radicals tied to SNCC, were quoted as disparaging Dr. King for his alleged lack of hands-on involvement in Freedom Rides, sit-ins, and even for not going to jail often enough. On the last score, Levison pointed out: "Dr. King is the only major civil rights leader in the country who has been in jail every year in the past five years and during the past year, more than once." Levison reminded the readers of the magazine that King had just spoken in Indianapolis in spite of the fact that the hall he was appearing in had been marked for bombing—and that this was not an atypical occurrence. "Again he defied the terrorists and completed his speech . . . it is still fresh in his memory that his home was twice bombed, once when his children and wife were asleep there."

Stanley also wrote:

> If this were not enough to establish his unique self-sacrifice, it should be remembered that at the height of the tension of the Freedom Rides, after bloodthirsty gangs had brutally beaten the first group of Riders, Dr. King went to Montgomery, Alabama and was besieged by a mob of more than a thousand, who attempted to burn down the church in which he was speaking. His coolness under fire was an inspiring example of leadership courage which should evoke admiration and respect from any fair minded person, uninfluenced by envy.[4]

The siege of the Montgomery church, formerly the pulpit of Ralph Abernathy, was a real thornbush, a no-holds-barred crisis, and a vexing issue for Robert Kennedy and his brother, the president. A group of Freedom Riders and local parishioners were perilously holed up in the church while malicious white rioters gathered and threatened to rush the building. Attorney General Robert Kennedy, though privately churning about what damage the Kennedy administration would suffer if it openly came to the aid of the Negroes, as well as the sensitivity of the state of Alabama if federal troops (which actually were being mobilized at Fort Benning, Georgia) overrode the jurisdiction of state and local troopers, was both wringing his hands and calling the shots.

Stanley could not locate Martin by phone and reached out to Clarence. Taking a particularly long drag from his Lucky Strike, enough to irritate his throat into another hacking cough, he practically shouted at Clarence through the phone receiver: "We've got to get him out of there or at least make sure the federal troops get in control! Whatever Kennedy does or doesn't do, it will take forever until he and his brother calculate the politically safe option."

In fact, Bobby Kennedy had established a radio command post at Maxwell Air Force Base near Montgomery. President John F. Kennedy had authorized the use of federal troops to protect Dr. King and the mixed group of protestors, sympathizers, and First Baptist Church congregants holding out in the church against an increasingly unruly and murderous mob of racists and opportunists gaining in both numbers and ferocity.

Robert Kennedy in Washington and his underlings on the scene were anxiously struggling with their humane considerations for the safety of King and the others in the church as against the brash declarations of Alabama state officials that this was their jurisdiction and their problem to resolve. The white mob had already overturned a car driven by a black man and then lit up the vehicle through its gas line. They threw rocks at the church building, and according to Taylor Branch's narrative of this episode, were chanting: "Let's clean the niggers out of there!" The insurgents outside added to their ranting with a smattering of Molotov cocktails and several independent assaults on innocent black bystanders. Inside the church, trying to stay despair and panic, a number of ministers, including King, rotated on the pulpit. Pleading for calm, they offered homilies and psalms and hymns while reassuring the group that everything would be all right. Men were being eaten up by the effort of maintaining composure.

A jumbled combination of federal marshals and National Guard troops ultimately dispersed the mobs outside with tear gas and pointed bayonets. At one point, Bobby Kennedy was able to speak directly to Martin King on a church phone line and offered support. But the Kennedy maneuvers, coupled with the Alabama contortions of aid and protection for the blockaded citizens inside that church, led to a stalemate that essentially sealed those citizens inside the building and in need of food, water, medicines, and relief. A second call between King and Kennedy deteriorated into rage and mutual recriminations.

The siege ended before dawn the next morning as national guardsmen—officially the provision of Alabama—led the people out of the church to safety. King had stood his ground and "delivered" the flock. The state, still in its Confederate throes, saved face. The federal government (that is, the Kennedy brothers) had intervened successfully without appearing to have done so. Martin Luther King and Robert F. Kennedy had more contempt for each other than any time before.

In New York, Stanley Levison put out his final cigarette of the long night and morning, letting his accumulated fatigue, tension, and wrath unwrap into an uneasy sleep and a sense of foreboding.

CHAPTER ELEVEN

I Am Not Now and Never Have Been a Member of the Communist Party

artin Luther King Jr. may have used the phrase "our friend," referring to Stanley Levison, for the first time on November 28, 1962.
He dictated a letter from Atlanta to Clarence Jones, in care of the
Gandhi Society for Human Rights on Fifth Avenue in New York
City. (The Gandhi Society was a somewhat short-lived institute
for nonviolence that Jones oversaw. It did not raise much money
and was overhauled by 1965 in order to acquire tax-exempt status.)

"Dear Clarence," wrote King. The editor of a publication called *The Nation* had solicited King to prepare a commentary, he reported. It was to be "something on what should be done on civil rights by the 88th Congress."

The typical working dynamic was now invoked. King wanted Jones to activate Levison to take on an assignment. "I would like to get the article in about the last of December so that it can come out in January. Please have our friend begin working on it and let me know when it can be sent to me. Thank you."[1]

This was still several months before the fateful Rose Garden encounter, during which President Kennedy demanded that King detach himself and his organization from Stanley Levison. The separation would require that Jones act as undercover intermediary between the men, filtering information and ideas from one to the other via telephone calls (which were being tapped, as it turned out), discreet letters, and occasional clandestine rendezvous. The code name for Stanley, one laced with affection and truth, was "our friend." Here it was already being used by King in the November 1962 letter, indicating that both King and Jones by this time knew that their association with Levison was fraught with some danger.

The Kennedys had not yet asked for Levison's discrediting, but the government had been hounding him for years. The FBI, driven by director Hoover's obsessions, made its first official report to the administration, asserting dangerous Communist-affiliate associations (specifically Levison) with King in January 1962. Robert Kennedy had some of his underlings speak with King, but the preacher was nonplussed. He was not aware of such a possibility and was not disposed to being judgmental about the people who helped him in his cause. He may have privately made some fun of Bayard Rustin's sexual orientation, but he believed in and trusted Rustin completely. His devotion to Levison was unshakable; he had no illusions about how financially bereft the movement would have been without this "winter soldier." He really had no direct familiarity with Levison's alleged Communist participation. And the record shows that, although King has no history of Communist leanings or activities, he did not consider the Party as something malignant or treasonous.

On the contrary: King declared from time to time that the egalitarian goals of the Communists were not inconsistent with the ideals of the civil rights movement. This would abet Hoover in his unending attempts to link King, as well as Jones and Belafonte, to Levison and left-wing enemies of the American republic. Hoover's exertions, backed by the voluminous FBI structure and his own longtime stranglehold on US presidents, pushed the already mistrustful Robert Kennedy, and his always calculating brother John, into a swirl of paranoia about King and company.

Levison was subpoenaed by the Senate Internal Security Subcommittee in April 1962. Hoover had sent secret memos to Robert Kennedy indicating that confidential sources (which were actually the wiretaps on Stanley's telephone) proved beyond doubt that King was manipulated by "the communist Levison." The memoranda reported that it was Levison who had created "in King's name" the new organization (shepherded by coconspirator Clarence Jones) known as the Gandhi Society for Human Rights. The organization was deemed highly suspect and likely subversive, even though it had a history of inviting noteworthy but decidedly non-Communist guests such as future secretary of state William P. Rogers and future senator Clifford Case (both Republicans) to its gatherings. Yet Hoover's communications implied that suspected radicals, including Harry Belafonte and A. Philip Randolph (who definitely harbored Communist sympathies) were in on the formation of this dubious agency.

Wiretaps, history, prejudice, and informants all combined into a web of foreboding and infamy: innocent or not, tainted or clean, a lot of hardworking freedom workers were being besmirched just by affiliations with the poker-faced and undeniably reticent Stanley D. Levison.

At the hearing, convened behind closed doors, Stanley neither implicated himself nor cleared up doubts. He certainly failed to salve the anxieties of Robert F. Kennedy and J. Edgar Hoover. Historian and Kennedy aide Arthur M. Schlesinger wrote:

If it was hard to regard inviting William P. Rogers and Clifford Case to a Gandhi Society luncheon as a major threat to the republic, Stanley Levison did present the Attorney General a more difficult problem. A few days later, the Senate Internal Security Subcommittee, no doubt tipped off by Hoover, subpoenaed Levison and interrogated him in executive session. "To dispose of a question causing current apprehension," Levison told the committee, "I am a loyal American and I am not now and never have been a member of the Communist Party." He went on, however, with the leftist attorney William

Kunstler at his side, to challenge the committee's right to inquire into political beliefs and thereafter took the Fifth Amendment. He did so, he later explained, because he feared the session would turn into an attack on King. Actually no one brought up King. Instead [Senator James] Eastland, who sounded as if he had been briefed by the Bureau, asked such questions as: "Isn't it true that you are a spy for the Communist apparatus in this country? . . . Isn't it true that you have gotten funds from the Soviet Union and given them to the Communist Party of the United States?" Levison declined to answer. Finally, after much exasperated quizzing and effective stonewalling, [Chairman John] McClellan terminated the hearing, calling it "one of the shabbiest performances I have ever heard before a Senate Committee by any witness."[2]

In fact, Levison was being duplicitous. Not only had he been a tireless leader, fund-raiser, and advocate for the CP-USA for decades, he remained a Marxist at heart. His departure from the Party by 1956 was a technical matter, though grounded in a conviction about the hypocrisy and violent duplicity of the Soviets.

Stanley sat with Martin a few days later. Levison smoked a cigarette while King nursed vodka with ice. Stanley chuckled to himself as he said: "Remember last year at the Mayflower Hotel?"

"What happened at the Mayflower Hotel?" asked King, uncommonly relaxed and enjoying a buzz from his cocktail. He pulled out and lit a Pall Mall from a pack in his pocket.

"We met with the Kennedy people. They wouldn't see us at the White House because it was too hot for them to see us—well, you—there. Classic Kennedy. They wanted to get a sense of who you are but not anywhere that people might think they are too close to you."

"Yes, I remember," said King. "Bobby was nervous. He's always nervous." King then proceeded to deliver a straight-on imitation of Robert Kennedy in discourse, the Boston accent clipping the words through teeth, attitude, and edgy authority. Stanley thought that Martin's mimicry was uncanny. He had occasionally been privy to King's hilarious impersonations of certain black preachers, capturing their histrionics and narcissism and, just for effect, their mispronunciations of certain words. These kind of theatrics were generally reserved for King's times alone with other people of his own race—along with the attendant devouring of soul food, beer, sweet ice tea, and, if time and circumstances permitted, women.

"Well, yes, and this was last year," said Stanley, mixing his own drink. "They had some Justice Department people, probably FBI connected. Burke Marshall did most of the talking."

"Yes, yes. I recall now. They were talking about how the way to go was with voting rights, not civil rights. Bobby always talks about voting rights. He doesn't even like to say civil rights. You were the only person with me at that meeting, Stanley, right?"

"That's my point. And nobody from their side ever really asked me, this white man, who I was or what I was doing there. I mean, it was a pretty good meeting—"

"How did you think I did?" King interjected.

"You were fine, Martin. I think they found your incredible calmness and courtesy disarming and pleasing. You were not a radical, threatening Negro and they really like that. But I overheard Harris Wofford talking to Bobby at the buffet table. He asked Bobby if he knew who I was, sitting there next to you."

King sat up straighter, the glow of the alcohol disappearing quickly. Stanley had something important to reveal.

"Yes, Harris asked him that. Bobby didn't know and hadn't asked. Harris told him, 'You know, that's Stanley Levison, the guy you've been asking so much about. The guy you've been investigating.' Bobby just looked at him. He really didn't know."

"Wait a minute, Stanley. Weren't you sitting right next to Bobby at that meeting the whole time?"

"Yes, absolutely, I was. And he never said a word to me. Guess I'm not such a threat or so bad for you to be associated with."[3]

This may have been wishful thinking on the part of Stanley Levison, even if Robert Kennedy, then attorney general, did not recognize him during a secret meeting in a Washington hotel in 1961. Within a few months of the meeting at the Mayflower, Kennedy signed an FBI authorization, personally requested by J. Edgar Hoover, to add to the wiretaps already placed on Levison's home.

Some of Levison's own comrades had questioned the wisdom of Stanley's relationship with King. When I spoke with Congressman Bob Filner in San Diego, he told me about concerns that his father, Joe Filner, had voiced more than once.

"Oh, yes, my dad told Stanley that he might be hurting King more than he was helping him. Dad and Stanley knew that their Communist backgrounds were risky for King, but they just believed so much in racial integration. They didn't know how not to get involved."

Taylor Branch writes in his *Parting the Waters* about a discussion that was active among American Communist leaders: "[Some] argued furiously that Levison was subjecting King to needless, unconscionable danger. If a spy or an FBI wiretap revealed such a call from a gathering of top national Communists, King might be destroyed."[4]

In his lifetime, Stanley Levison never made a definitive statement to anyone, including his closest friends, about what really moved him to do the things he did. "He was always just himself," Jones remembers. "He was confident and poised. I'd tease him about his paunch and he would simply chuckle. Very composed man, meticulous, and hardworking. I thought of him as a shield of steel. But he did know how to relax, always with that cigarette. He'd enjoy alcohol but moderately. I'd look at a restaurant menu for something different or exotic. Stanley liked a steak. He was deeply principled and when something upset him, especially something about justice or rather the lack of justice, he could not be intimidated."

In 1963, neither a Senate subcommittee nor the institutional racism of the city of Birmingham, Alabama, would intimidate Levison.

The principal opponent of Martin Luther King in Birmingham, the personification of dripping southern racism, was a stumpy, barrel-shaped man named Eugene "Bull" Connor. Born of another era in 1897, Connor had made his way through the ethnically cloistered world of Alabama politics, dodged charges of corruption, rampant promiscuity, and even murder during a career that began in the Klan and wound up with Connor positioned as the trigger-happy, savage commissioner of public safety in the city.

If there ever was a medieval, repressive southern police chief set to put fear into the hearts of Negroes—including King—it was Bull Connor. His jails were regularly filled to the brim with black folks, many dragged in by vigilantes, often on ethereal charges (traffic violations, alleged harassment of police officers, or just being in the wrong place at the wrong time in the wrong century).

Connor, who held a variety of state and local posts during his violent career, served as Birmingham's safety commissioner from 1937 till 1965, with one five-year interruption. Nobody succeeded Connor in the position: the events of 1963, during which he brutalized civil rights marchers, from schoolchildren to Martin King and Ralph Abernathy, employing billy clubs, paddy wagons, fire hoses, attack dogs, and bullets, left a vulgar legacy. The position itself was eliminated in 1965; even the white citizenry had had enough.

The leadership of the SCLC was looking for a decisive campaign in 1963. King and his entourage were disenchanted with President Kennedy's systemic dodging of the civil rights issue. Stanley Levison and Harry Belafonte worked to get King and the president together on the phone. Black entertainer Sammy Davis Jr., who had ties to the White House, was solicited as a conduit. (Kennedy liked Davis Jr., and was fascinated with Davis's "Rat Pack" buddies such as Frank Sinatra and Dean Martin, but was circumspect in having Davis perform at White House functions.)

Stanley told Martin: "You've got to remind Kennedy that he hasn't even tried to enact the civil rights legislation promised in the 1960 Democratic platform." Belafonte was disappointed as well, remembering that he had pushed King to meet JFK in 1960 and consider endorsing him.

The situation between King and the president was tenuous. King was constantly hurt by the Kennedys' failure to embrace him and to truly make the human rights campaign part of the New Frontier. King was often socially snubbed by the Kennedys—John and Jacqueline, host and hostess of the glamorous Washington culture that was later dubbed "Camelot"—preferred to limit their Negro guests at state dinners and other White House extravaganzas to black dignitaries not considered socially radical or as meddling in the administration's business. Besides, anytime King appeared somewhere, J. Edgar Hoover would fire off a damning, phobic memo to Bobby or John—especially if King was seen or heard in the presence of Stanley Levison.

Kennedy reportedly told King over the phone that any civil rights bill would be doomed in 1963. King was thoroughly rebuffed. He had asked Kennedy in person to consider decreeing a Second Emancipation Proclamation—a sweeping post-partisan executive statute to commemorate the one hundredth anniversary of President Abraham Lincoln's original act (January 1, 1863). Lincoln had officially freed the slaves of the Confederacy; Kennedy could reenact the landmark with a moral diktat that invoked the outright termination of segregation and slavery in America. Clarence Jones, working with Levison, had drafted the language of such a text. The answer came back from an electoral-sensitive administration looking ahead to 1964: No.

As King and the others were looking ahead apprehensively to the Birmingham campaign, John and Robert Kennedy were not listening to them. They heeded other voices: one of the president's top aides cheerfully assured him that all was peaceful with America's Negroes, and JFK liked hearing that. His advisers and his friends in the Congress made no bones about the fact that any attempt to pass a civil rights bill would forfeit the crucial South for the president in the next election.

But the Kennedys were also listening to Hoover. The FBI director and some of his closest colleagues had basically declared war on Stanley Levison. The invisible man who sat next to RFK at the Mayflower Hotel was becoming very apparent. Evidence was scant, however; the only thing Hoover had were the old and feeble testimonies of the unsavory Childs brothers. That didn't stop Hoover, however. Short on corroborating facts, he artfully developed an entirely new strategy and retained it as a screen with which to mislead the Kennedys: Hoover claimed that Levison's Communist connections were proving too difficult to document because his work was surreptitious even within the leftist hierarchy. And the files themselves that Hoover was accumulating on Levison—these were so sensitive, Hoover asserted, so dangerous to national security, that they had to remain sealed and could not be circulated!

In a once-concealed FBI transcript from 1963, Hoover sent instructions to his New York office. The document was marked both CONFIDENTIAL and DO NOT DISSEMINATE. The subject was STANLEY DAVID LEVISON, INTERNAL SECURITY—C.

> The Bureau desires that you conduct a thorough and searching review of your file on Levison. Direct your efforts towards ascertaining the following:
>
> (1) Communist Party (CP) and CP front activities.
> (2) Affiliation of Levison with organizations connected in any manner with Martin Luther King, Jr., and organizations under King's control and sponsorship.
> (3) Specific instances where King has been influenced by Levison, including any pressures or suggestions by Levison to influence King or his organizations.
>
> Your review in this case must not be confined to your main case file on Levison but should also include a check of all cases where the desired information may be available and a thorough search of your references. It should be done in a painstaking and searching manner so as to insure that all information in your office which will reveal the above desired information is brought to the attention of the Bureau.
>
> During the review, be constantly alert for sources and/or informants who are or have been in a position to know of Levison and of his past and present activities.[5]

In his effort to stigmatize Stanley Levison and thereby destroy Martin Luther King, J. Edgar Hoover co-opted all presidential authority and flouted his constitutional responsibilities to keep the administration judiciously informed and properly in touch with the realities of what is now termed "homeland security." Hoover, revealing his racial pathology, routinely termed King "a notorious liar," while applying several other degrading epithets to the beleaguered civil rights leader. His exertions succeeded: In May 1963, as Birmingham began to swelter in the coming confrontation between King and Bull Connor, John Kennedy told brother Bobby that he'd prefer not to have the minister anywhere near him. In a long-shrouded White House tape recording, the president says: "King is so hot that it's like Marx coming to the White House."[6]

Now Birmingham and Bull Connor lay waiting, and it can be fairly construed that neither King nor Levison nor any of other principals in the still-struggling civil rights movement had anything else on their minds. There was peril; the city did not come to be known by its gruesome nickname, "Bombingham," for nothing. Though he was outwardly brave and serene, Martin Luther King did struggle with fear, a sense of physical vulnerability, and the oppressive intuition about his inevitable murder. Stanley knew of these burdens that wore Martin down and exacerbated his mood swings and that, yes, even explained his sexual escapades about which Stanley certainly knew though he remained circumspect.

C. T. Vivian, the Baptist minister and author, onetime Freedom Rider, staff member to King, and a leader of the Nashville sit-in movement, told me: "We called it 'Project C.' The C stood for confrontation. There was no other way to describe our attempt to desegregate Birmingham and get the civil rights story into the nation's consciousness. The only way to deal with someone like Bull Connor was to confront him. Martin knew this would be a threshold campaign and that he would likely have to go to jail. He was prepared for that. But he was scared, too. He was always putting his fears away someplace when we were going into something like this because he knew he was the prime target, a sort of prize for the people who just hated us."[7]

Stanley Levison took a grim, realistic view of the prospects in Birmingham. "Look, we may not like Bull Connor," he told King, "but we better respect his record." Levison did his homework and reported to King that in the 1930s, before and during Connor's original tenure as commissioner of public safety, Connor had masterfully written out suspected leftists from the local labor unions. "His methods were ruthless but he won the people's allegiance.

They love him. He made sure there have never been any interracial unions. The movement he started then, with a pure white leadership and no blacks anywhere was stronger than our civil rights movement is now."

The FBI knew of this conversation, which took place at an SCLC leadership summit in Savannah just before Project C, because the FBI was recording and/or filming every discussion in which Levison was a participant.

Demonstrations against the segregated downtown stores, lunch counter sit-ins, and street marches began in early April. King and his colleagues recruited people who were willing to be arrested and spend time in jail—this was a key strategy of the civil rights movement designed to elicit national sympathy and to break the backs of the police authorities. Results were mixed at the outset; not many local black residents were willing to volunteer for jail time, and some of the local black media did not welcome the intrusion of King and his circle into an already tense local situation.

Bull Connor quickly and confidently went to his K-9 corps. The first waves of demonstrators were met with helmeted police that propelled their dogs into the crowds, and the results were bloody, fierce, and drove terror into the hearts of many protestors. King knew that he himself would have to submit to jail—which he did, with Ralph Abernathy. But in the early going, with the crowds summarily beaten back, bitten, clubbed, and sprayed with fire hoses, King was overwhelmed with panic and guilt.

Over the telephone, Levison told one of King's staffers, "A little violence is good. It might help Kennedy wake up to his image around the world." The comment was captured on tape by Hoover's eavesdroppers. King, in a rare moment of deviation from Levison, spurned the assessment. He was deeply concerned about the prevailing commitment of his movement to nonviolent civil disobedience. He turned to the White House for some expression of support.

President Kennedy declined to make any statement on the Birmingham situation. Instead, Burke Marshall was directed to call King and ask that the protests be delayed. Robert Kennedy called the campaign "ill-timed."

In the ensuing weeks, the Birmingham campaign gained traction. While abhorring the aggression of the police, King began to see the dark wisdom of

Levison's comment—that violence can be "good." The preacher's melancholy realigned toward expectation. Network television crews began to transmit reels of what was blatant police brutality against citizens, the thrashings, beatings, head-banging, and, perhaps most memorably, the use of high-pressure fire-hosing against even schoolchildren who marched in protest of segregation.

Like John Kennedy, Martin Luther King Jr. understood the utilization of television in order to influence and galvanize the public. By summer, the SCLC and the city of Birmingham signed an agreement that would incrementally eliminate segregation in the city's schools and public places. Bull Connor, who had been seduced by the protestors, and succumbed to his own rage, lost the moral battle by indulging in far too much savagery and inhumaneness against unarmed American citizens.

The television images of kids being hosed in the streets—some of them plummeting against the sidewalks or retaining walls of the neighborhoods—finally affected an important citizen of Washington, DC.

On June 11, 1963, having watched the evening news the night before, Kennedy declared in a national television address: "We are confronted primarily with a moral issue. It is as old as the Scriptures and is as clear as the American Constitution." For the first time, JFK directly addressed the social inequity of American Negroes, urging that black students be admitted to universities without qualification, that segregationist laws be repealed in all states, and that Americans realize the disparities in education, career hopes, health care, and longevity that existed between the two races:

> We preach freedom around the world, and we mean it, and we cherish our freedom here at home, but are we to say to the world, and much more importantly, to each other that this is the land of the free except for the Negroes; that we have no second-class citizens except Negroes; that we have no class or caste system, no ghettoes, no master race except with respect to Negroes?[8]

In bold strokes, Kennedy challenged the Congress to finally consider and pass the civil rights bill that was sitting in a legislative muddle on Capitol

Hill. In a limited nod to King's longtime request for a Second Emancipation Proclamation, Kennedy said:

> One hundred years of delay have passed since President Lincoln freed the slaves, yet their heirs, their grandsons, are not fully free. They are not yet freed from the bonds of injustice. They are not yet freed from social and economic oppression. And this Nation, for all its hopes and all its boasts, will not be fully free until all its citizens are free.

The president emphasized, in eloquent, if staccato Bostonian tones:

> Now the time has come for this Nation to fulfill its promise. The events in Birmingham and elsewhere have so increased the cries for equality that no city or State or legislative body can prudently choose to ignore them.

Martin Luther King had gone to jail—and written a classic letter that has become enshrined in American history. Countless anonymous citizens had been beaten, hosed, pummeled, and incarcerated. The most notoriously racist city administration in America was brought to its knees in an agreement made with the Southern Christian Leadership Conference. A president repeatedly criticized by Stanley Levison for his "aloofness" had been moved enough by the television images to step up and demand moral redress. Stanley lit a cigarette in his New York apartment and thought to himself, again, "A little violence is good and Kennedy lived up to his image."

CHAPTER TWELVE

I Have a Dream Today

T he year 1963 was one that both lifted and trounced human souls. With prophetic irony, the heralded musical *Camelot* closed at New York's Majestic Theater on January 5 after 873 performances. The term "Camelot," implying a short-lived dream, would come to pertain to the Kennedy presidency just months after his assassination in Dallas in November. George C. Wallace was sworn in as governor of Alabama. Taking the oath of office on January 14, he declared, "Segregation now; segregation tomorrow; segregation forever!"

Nikita S. Khrushchev, who shook the Marxist world at the 1956 Twentieth Party Congress, and now often dismissed John F. Kennedy as an unformed amateur, claimed that the Soviet Union had a major megaton nuclear bomb in its arsenal. Americans smoked cigarettes freely, watched *The Andy Griffith Show* on television and the new, triple-screen "Cinerama" comedy *It's a Mad,*

Mad, Mad, Mad World, starring Milton Berle, Jack Benny, Ethel Merman, and Edie Adams, in movie theaters—while conducting bomb shelter exercises at home, work, and school. The Dallas Texans of the American Football League relocated to Kansas City and renamed themselves the Chiefs.

A new quartet known as "The Beatles" came out of Liverpool and began their first tour in Britain. Birmingham, Alabama, experienced a particularly bloody race riot in May. A few weeks later, the Ayatollah Khomeini was arrested by the state regime in Iran; in June, the American Heart Association released a first-ever statement that cigarette smoking is harmful. Cardinal Giovanni Battista Montini succeeded the much-loved John XXIII as Pope Paul VI. President Kennedy made a triumphal journey to West Berlin and to his ancestral Ireland.

In September, both CBS and NBC News expanded their evening networks from fifteen to thirty minutes. The Sixteenth Street Baptist Church in Birmingham was bombed by Klansmen during Sunday school, killing four little African American girls, including a childhood friend of future secretary of state Condoleezza Rice. *The Outer Limits* premiered on ABC television; *The Judy Garland Show* premiered on CBS; a massive hurricane devastated Haiti, killing 6,000 and injuring 100,000.

Nelson Mandela went on trial in South Africa in the fall; he would ultimately serve a twenty-seven-year sentence for trying to end apartheid. The Los Angeles Dodgers, led by pitcher Sandy Koufax, swept the New York Yankees in the World Series. President Kennedy, uncharacteristically working closely with Vice President Lyndon B. Johnson, began planning a November trip to Texas in order to heal a Democratic Party feud that threatened his chances in that critical state for the 1964 election.

Millions of Americans witnessed the first-ever live murder on television when, on Sunday morning, November 24, Jack Ruby, a Dallas thug and nightclub owner, killed JFK's alleged assassin, Lee Harvey Oswald, as Oswald was being transferred from the downtown police jail to another facility. Frank Sinatra Jr. was kidnapped for a week starting on December 9; President Lyndon B. Johnson was already pressing the flesh of Washington legislators to ratify

President Kennedy's proposed civil rights bill; the young Beach Boys made their first appearance on *Shindig*.

Throughout 1963, a small cluster of men that surrounded Martin Luther King Jr. was developing ideas for a dramatic, national rally in Washington, DC, to push Congress to enact jobs and human rights legislation. The group, which included Ralph Abernathy, Andrew Young, Bayard Rustin, Wyatt Tee Walker, and Clarence Jones, among others, also featured two white men: Harry Wachtel and Stanley Levison. The ruminating and planning for a watershed march on the nation's capital continued through the ups and downs of the Birmingham campaign. The men were buoyed by the SCLC's solid victory in Birmingham—the pact that essentially ended segregation there and brought down the police regime of Eugene "Bull" Connor. The strategizing for Washington was not even upended by the horrific events of September 15, 1963, when those white terrorists bombed the Sixteenth Street Baptist Church and again forced King into his painful role as the chief eulogizer of black anguish and anger.

Proposed marches on Washington did not have a particularly rewarding history. Stanley told Martin: "It's a good idea and we should attempt it. But even FDR fought Randolph on such a thing."

The reference was to A. Philip Randolph's original effort to generate a mass citizens' protest for jobs for blacks during the presidency of Franklin Delano Roosevelt. FDR oversaw a new national industrialization as the nation entered into the fray of World War II. Randolph was president of the Brotherhood of Sleeping Car Porters in 1941 and petitioned the president—who was after all the father of the New Deal—to support the proposed march.

Roosevelt did not want the march (as Kennedy would not in 1963) but made a deal with Randolph in 1941: cancel the march in exchange for a presidential executive order upholding the basic rights of African Americans. Though this was essentially a paper decree, Clarence Jones told me that it was significant given that it was the sole such pronouncement from a sitting president since Lincoln's Emancipation Proclamation in 1863.

Randolph, an aging but vital icon in 1963, took note of Martin King's efforts to finally launch a "March on Washington for Jobs and Freedom." Randolph had a long relationship with Bayard Rustin, who was a living link between the two premier civil rights leaders of the successive generations. "Talk to Martin," Randolph told Rustin. "I've never given up on the idea of such a march right on the capitol."

Rustin first spoke with Levison. Stanley said: "Well, it can't just be a march. The demonstrations must be carefully organized and peaceful. That's the biggest challenge, that everything be peaceful. The Kennedys will try and prevent it but they can't knock it down if it is really peaceful. There need to be nonviolent sit-ins outside congressional offices and rallies and other strategic sessions with congressmen and senators. And we can't do this by ourselves. We need to bring in all the big labor unions to make it work as a message for jobs. Kennedy doesn't relate to 'civil rights.' He does relate to jobs."

Clarence Jones shared with me: "Of course, Martin was very enthused. He had a lot of people to talk with all around the country by then, many of them in labor, in the clergy, and some in politics. We had the momentum of the big victory in Birmingham. But the two people that he consulted with at that time almost daily were Stanley and me. So when Bayard presented him with the idea, Stanley and I were among his closest advisers on fund-raising, political strategy, and the media. Yes, we were both key members of the inner circle. But unknown to us at the time, the FBI turned out to be a silent partner in that inner circle as well."

Jones explained that both his home and office phones had been tapped for years by the government. "Martin always thought that my caution bordered on paranoia but I knew how things were from my time in the military. The people who made the rules were always the first not to play by them. We were right in the middle of the Cold War and if a government organization such as the FBI slapped a Communist label on you, regardless of the facts, all the rules went out the window."

Jones certainly knew about intrigue and secrecy. In 1963, while King was jailed in Birmingham, the nagging issue of bail for the leader again fell to

Jones—even while Jones was slipping paper and pens to King for the ongoing composition of the "Letter from Birmingham Jail."

A call came to Jones from the offices of New York's liberal Republican governor, Nelson Rockefeller. Apparently, Harry Belafonte had mentioned to the governor's people that Dr. King was having some trouble down in Birmingham. Jones was to fly out to New York City forthwith and follow a series of cryptic instructions that would lead to a resolution. Jones was to meet Governor Rockefeller and an aide that Saturday at a Chase Manhattan Bank in midtown Manhattan.

Clarence called ahead to Stanley and described the invitation—knowing this would probably be about Rockefeller quietly handing over some big money to help get King out of the Birmingham jail. "I'm not sure what to say or do," he told his friend. "We are in no position to reimburse Rockefeller for any generosity."

"Just do what they say," replied Stanley. "The reimbursement will take care of itself."

So Clarence appeared at the bank (it was closed to the public on Saturdays) and found "a skeleton crew . . . a security guard, a banker, Hugh Morrow [an aide], Nelson Rockefeller, and me." Though anxious and grateful, Jones was nonetheless nonplussed. "There I was in the role of the hat-in-hand Negro, trying hard to appear as if this were not the strangest situation I had ever encountered."

It was indeed surreal. Jones walked with the others, no one making much conversation, into a cavernous vault. "Money was stacked floor to ceiling," he said. A guard removed one hundred thousand dollars in crisp bills, banded them, and placed them into a shiny leather briefcase. This was handed to Jones—along with a promissory note that he was asked to sign. Jones knew that neither he nor the SCLC could make good on a loan of such magnitude. He recalls that Rockefeller read the look of concern on his face and that the philanthropic governor said to him: "Just sign for it, Mr. Jones. You don't need to worry about it."

And he didn't. The note would be returned to Jones's Manhattan law office by messenger on the following Tuesday marked PAID.

That promissory note eventually found its way into the formal text of Dr. King's "I Have a Dream" speech delivered during the March on Washington, August 28, 1963. The transaction in the vault left Clarence Jones with both a recollection and an inspiration as he and Stanley Levison began preparing drafts for King's preachment in the hot midsummer days of that year. "I kept thinking about all the money in the vaults of the wealthy, the privileged, and the government," he told me. "The government was so rich with the power to help us but so miserly in doing so. The promissory note we had been given by virtue of us being citizens like everyone else was never redeemed."

The image worked its way into the early part of King's speech (the second half—about "The Dream"—was suddenly and unforgettably extemporized). In his book, *Behind the Dream: The Making of the Speech That Transformed a Nation*, Jones documents the section of the legendary oration that directly migrated from his interlude in the Manhattan bank vault:

> In a sense we've come to our nation's capital to cash a check. When the architects of our republic wrote the magnificent words of the Constitution and the Declaration of Independence, they were signing a promissory note to which every American was to fall heir. This note was the promise that men, yes, black men as well as white men, would be guaranteed the unalienable rights of life, liberty and the pursuit of happiness.
>
> It is obvious today that America has defaulted on this promissory note in so far as her citizens of color are concerned. Instead of honoring this sacred obligation, America has given the Negro people a bad check; a check which has come back marked "insufficient funds."[1]

Clarence Jones, fiercely intellectual, well traveled, now both a professor of the civil rights saga and the key fund-raiser associated with the Martin Luther King Jr. Education and Research Institute at Stanford University, has deep memories. Even while carrying a memorial psalm in his heart for his friend

Stanley Levison, and respect for the Jewish community in general for its historic fidelity to the cause of African Americans, Clarence has other recollections of white people he has met and with whom he has sometimes grappled.

Bobby Kennedy was difficult for Jones to grasp. Jones would literally observe the occasionally bipolar attitude that the thin, intense, take-no-prisoners attorney general, future senator, and ultimately martyred presidential candidate exhibited. Kennedy seemed to be conflicted about African Americans—sometimes displaying compassion, other times indifference, and occasionally, contempt. Kennedy was at war with himself on the topic, vacillating from hard-boiled investigator and wiretapper to sympathetic interventionist and federal adjudicator when it came to southern sheriffs, magistrates, and governors. Did Bobby make critical telephone calls that saved the day for King and others because he actually cared or because it was the politically opportune thing to do?

How to explain Kennedy's coldhearted surveillance of King, Jones, Levison, Belafonte, and others, and his fanatical need to alternately appease or control J. Edgar Hoover in this track? How does this stack up against Kennedy's historic emergence as the perceived steward of the civil rights movement, the struggle for Native American redresses, and the opposition to the Vietnam conflict begun by his brother John as part of the president's overall Cold War mind-set?

Stanley had his own ideas. "Neither Kennedy has ever really taken this issue to heart," he'd tell Clarence and he'd also remind Martin. Levison, while grateful that Robert had convinced John to make the call to Coretta King while Martin was jailed, and while heartened in June 1963 by the president's apparent burst of conscience after viewing the television newsreels of police brutality against black adults and children in Birmingham, nonetheless remained cynical. Levison's feeling was that the Kennedys even did "the nice things" because they viewed the black constituency as an easy harvest for votes. "They need Negro votes to offset the troubles they're going to have in the South in 1964," he muttered. "So they take these cautious steps now and then, knowing it will rally Negroes to the polls."

Indeed, Stanley perceived what others did not always pick up—that for

Robert and John Kennedy, civil rights were not of great significance. On the other hand, the two men did take a serious interest in *voting* rights. This was an issue they could discuss and evaluate rationally (much like foreign policy or the economy), and this was an opportunity. In other words, civil rights would not deliver Texas or Florida in 1964; voting rights could.

But because Clarence is black, he remembers something more visceral about Robert F. Kennedy. John was distant, aloof; he feigned contemplativeness when he was actually calculating. Bobby was present—for better or worse. He felt things; one could see and hear that, and his flare-ups of spleen were scalding and mythical. (Robert Caro, the prolific biographer of Lyndon B. Johnson, asserts that Jack Kennedy actually turned the rivets of Bobby's wrath to his own advantage and cunning; in this the younger brother was dutifully complicit.) And so it was that, more than once, Clarence Jones became the object of Robert Kennedy's peculiar, harsh swipes.

Only three months before the 1963 march, a private meeting was convened in Manhattan, an attempt to bridge the gap, and to cool the fires that flared between the Kennedy cabal and the King circle. Oddly, Robert Kennedy bypassed King himself and made the author James Baldwin the linchpin of the gathering. Harry Belafonte and Lena Horne were present—both puzzled why, if RFK wanted to get a feel for the mood of America's Negroes, he didn't call in the obvious civil rights leaders themselves. Clarence Jones was there because he was Baldwin's attorney.

The meeting began politely but deteriorated rapidly into mutual charges of neglect and irreverence. If Kennedy preferred to invite artists rather than personnel, he got drama. And he got angry. Bobby could not tolerate even an inference that his brother's administration was not doing the right thing. He lectured the assemblage on how solid was the president's record on human rights and how calamitous it was that some Negroes were being influenced by extremists such as the Nation of Islam and Malcolm X. He called for patience, which only exacerbated the frustration and poor temper of his invited listeners. Bitterness pervaded the hotel suite; both sides reportedly showered mocking laughter upon each other.

Jones tried to save the day as the session ground to its forlorn conclusion. He approached Kennedy in a cloying manner that irritated the attorney general. When Jones spoke to Kennedy, trying to conciliate with faint praise regarding the administration's track record, Kennedy just scoffed and complained that Jones was a hypocrite who hadn't spoken up to that effect during the embroilment. Jones left deeply hurt and went to share his pain with Levison—who reportedly droned that the Kennedys operated with "mad illusions."[2]

When Jones described this episode with Robert Kennedy to me, his eyes narrowed and his mouth became a wound.

Jones also recalls the manner in which the Kennedy administration—and the Washington police—anticipated the March on Washington. The White House opposed it and wished it wouldn't happen for fear of violence and for the possibility of being tacitly associated with such a large-scale Negro invasion of the capital. As for the district police, says Jones, "They approached it like an army approaches a battle."

Ironically, every rehearsal, every planning session, every statement of March policy brimmed with declarations and affirmations of nonviolence, order, dignity, peacefulness, and civility. In fairness, such a demonstration, with so many people, against the canvas of national racial tensions and a number of high-profile altercations, riots, and murders, had never been planned before. The record shows that 250,000 citizens came and left the District of Columbia and not a single incident occurred. With that hindsight, it is understandable that Clarence Jones has since lamented the government's "bunker mentality" and that he has written sorrowfully about the troop deployments that occurred, the blanket canceling of all police leaves, the ban on liquor sales, the thousands of paratroopers lurking on standby, and the FBI's swarming surveillance of all the many Hollywood celebrities who were on hand to lend their support and spirit.

Stanley was not in Washington that day. It had been two months since King's previous visit to the city, when President Kennedy had warned him in the Rose Garden that he must separate himself from Levison. So Stanley watched the grainy television images of the successful, rousing march, and

King's pinnacle speech, from his New York apartment. Jones was well into his role as the stealthy interlocutor between King and Levison, although he eventually learned that his role was hardly undisclosed to the FBI.

Harry Belafonte also claims to have been a link between King and Levison. Both he and Jones attest to Levison being distraught and irate with the dictate from Kennedy but immediately offering his resignation. The movement, Levison stated, was more important than his own role in it. In his memoir, Belafonte writes:

> Stan did stop talking to Martin—for a while. The truth was, though, we needed Stan too much to let him go, especially with the March on Washington looming. He was just too powerful a chess player. So risking the Kennedys' rage, and perhaps with the civil rights bill hanging in the balance, Clarence and I became Stan's secret conduits to Martin. I didn't call Stan at his office; he didn't call Clarence or me directly, either. Instead, I'd go to a friend's house and call a third party, who would relay the message that Stan should call their mutual friend. Stan would then go out to a pay phone and call me at that friend's house. Both parties were then on "safe phones," as we called them, and the FBI was, we hoped, left out of the loop.[3]

The FBI was hardly out of the loop, keeping scrupulous track of King—and falling onto the trace of his sexual adventures—via the trail left by Jones, Belafonte, and others. Nevertheless, the rectangular, if provisional, phone pattern maintained by King/Jones/Belafonte/Levison was, in Belafonte's words, "enough to guide us as we organized the March on Washington . . . enough, too, to help Martin write one of the most famous speeches in American history."

John F. Kennedy, awash with his foreign policy triumphs (his thunderously effective speech in Berlin that summer just four days after admonishing MLK in the Rose Garden; his landmark commencement address at American University calling for a ban on nuclear testing just days earlier), was actually feeling a bit more magnanimous toward the gathering March by the time it opened. He let brother Bobby continue to hold the reigns of caution and preparation, and he offered no public welcome to the gathering throngs who came from across the nation into the steaming heat of late August 1963. But apparently he was impressed, as the rally unfolded, with one particular thing: the startling collection of Hollywood celebrities that were appearing "with the Negroes."

Belafonte had done most of the inviting but in the end, these luminaries joined in because they wanted to. They included personalities mentioned earlier but also Burt Lancaster, Leonard Bernstein, James Garner, Shelley Winters, Paul Newman, Joanne Woodward, Tony Curtis, Diahann Carroll, Sammy Davis Jr., Woody Guthrie, Joan Baez, Robert Ryan, and Sidney Poitier. Jack Kennedy could not resist star power and he understood glamour. (J. Edgar Hoover saw all this and cried that Communists were besieging the nation's capital.)

After King's stirring and rhythmical speech, after he repeatedly declared, "I have a dream today," after it sunk in, with the humidity, that the day had been extraordinarily positive and peaceful, after 250,000 people began to happily disperse, the president sent messages to King: come to the White House for a reception. John and Robert received the buoyant preacher, along with the leaders of the NAACP, and other Negro agencies that had effectively set aside their own differences and rivalries and little scorns and had pulled off an unheralded triumph. Sandwiches were served, cool drinks poured, hand-shaking and back-slapping ensued, and the Kennedys congratulated themselves for being vigilant and maintaining the peace. For one halcyon afternoon that extended into a sublime dusk, the American government frolicked in interracial mirth and relief.

In New York, Stanley Levison, alone, sidelined, happy enough, lit another cigarette. He knew better.

CHAPTER THIRTEEN

The Same Thing Is Going to Happen to Me

The euphoria of the Birmingham victory, the "I Have a Dream" coup, and the Kennedys' warm and fancy reception for King and the others at the White House was short-lived. August gave way to September, and Klansmen were making plans in Alabama to retaliate and break the hearts of innocent families.

September 15, 1963: just three weeks after the March on Washington, the nation was rocked by the ghoulish bombing of Birmingham's Sixteenth Street Baptist Church—one of the original acts of domestic terrorism perpetrated by Americans against Americans. Known members of the Ku Klux Klan planted nineteen sticks of time-release dynamite in the basement of one of Alabama's most venerable houses of God.

The names of the young victims were Denise McNair, Cynthia Wesley, Carole Robertson, and Addie Mae Collins. The dynamite had been planted by the Klansmen precisely underneath a certain corner of the church. It was just below the anteroom where the children would be donning their white robes for Sunday choir. Denise was eleven years old, the other three were fourteen. Their interests ranged from sewing to reading to softball to Girl Scouting. Denise was friends with another youngster named Condoleezza Rice. Twenty-two people were injured in the brutal explosion that sprayed stained glass, pews, prayerbooks, blood, and hope across Sixteenth Street and the heart of the country.

Dr. King came to eulogize the little girls as well as innocence itself: All that they were guilty of, declared the shaken preacher, and all they possessed, was a yearning for love.

Two more black teenagers were killed in the aftermath of the bombing. Johnny Robinson and Virgil Ware were shot wantonly in separate incidents, one by police, and one by white passersby.

Strangers of all colors spontaneously visited the bereavement houses of their parents. Eight thousand mourners attended the funeral, which, besides King, was conducted by clergymen of three denominations. President Kennedy, fresh from receiving the leaders of the March on Washington, now began to earnestly talk about the urgent need for a civil rights bill. He was after all, a young father himself. In his final few weeks on earth, Kennedy seemed at last to emotionally connect with the grievous and perilous trouble of the nation's Negroes.

There had been other incidents of savagery against black citizens of Birmingham in the weeks prior to the church blast, including a random shooting of a man who, to his misfortune, resembled the outspoken Reverend Fred Shuttlesworth. The atmosphere in town was poisonous with intimidation and hate. King fired off telegrams to the White House imploring President Kennedy to take a public stand against the unabashedly racial haranguing of Governor George C. Wallace.

King had many issues that he wished to discuss with Stanley Levison, including a range of vexing internal personnel matters simmering within the sclc. He spoke often by phone with Jones in New York. One of the agenda items was the possible appointment of Bayard Rustin to the directorship of the SCLC's New York office. The FBI was listening with great interest, given Rustin's known homosexuality and Communist inclinations. In *Bearing the Cross*, David Garrow summarizes the psychological and political labyrinth in which King and his associates were trapped:

> King wanted to discuss that and other questions with Levison, but Jones reminded King that his promise to the Kennedys barred SCLC's president from making contact with his old friend. "I'll discuss it with our friend and get his feelings about it," Jones reassured King. "He'll understand why I haven't called him," King asked. "Yes, absolutely. In fact, he'd be a little upset if you did," Jones responded. "I'm trying to wait until things cool off—until this civil rights debate is over—as long as they may be tapping these phones, you know—but you can discuss that with him," King explained. Jones made contact with Levison, and the FBI promptly informed Robert Kennedy that the King-Levison connection remained intact despite King's promise."[1]

Using the once-removed telephone encryption, King relayed another inquiry to his friend via Jones: What should King do in light of the violence in Birmingham and the increasingly strident calls by more militant groups—particularly by the Student Nonviolent Coordinating Committee (SNCC)—to confront white Birmingham with riots and guns? Jones told King that "our friend" suggested he and a few others take advantage of the situation and try to meet personally with the president. King was honestly concerned that the church bombing could trigger a serious conflagration among the bitterly frustrated and deeply aggrieved black community and that all of this, though understandable and correct, would wipe out the gains created, or at least perceived, by the March on Washington.

King was unquestionably bereft, alarmed, bewildered, and deeply dejected by the tragedy that engulfed the church on Sixteenth Street. He told Ralph Abernathy—on the scene with him in Birmingham—that he fully empathized in his heart with those who wanted blood in return for the blood of the little girls. The image of "those angels," dressed in white, practicing their hymns, filled with the hope of a Sunday morning, dogged and plagued King—along with the guilt he constantly fought about his movement creating innocent victims in its wake. Sore with grief and wrath, King warned of "a racial holocaust" if the federal government did not intervene in the South, and he began blaming "complacent Negroes" for the tragedy.

But these cascading emotions did not prevent King from trying to capitalize on the moment in favor of gaining a deeper national sympathy for the black crusade. In the aftermath of the blown bodies, the shrieks, the ambulances, the subsequent street shootings, the horrifying morgue visits, King called for a shared funeral ceremony. He knew—and Stanley conveyed through Clarence—that such a setting, before a massive television audience, would offer unprecedented effect and would prey on the nation's conscience. Levison also cautioned King to discontinue his public venting that the calamity was caused by Negroes who remained on the sidelines of the revolution. Through the telephone matrix, he admonished King to stay focused on the malevolence of Alabama's Governor Wallace and the passivity of President Kennedy.

King appealed to the families of the four martyrs that they join in a combined funeral. One family demurred; they appreciated King's intent but wanted to grieve privately. A published report indicated that they regarded a group ceremony as "grandstanding." King did get three shiny caskets, lined up side by side, draped by hundreds of flowers, for the service that took place at the church on September 18. Reverend C. T. Vivian was among the sea of mourners. He told me: "I'd never seen Martin so broken, so angry." No Birmingham city officials were in attendance.

King fulfilled his role as the national pastor for black pain but kept his mind on President Kennedy as well. He had to move with dramatic consequence; younger, more militant leaders of SNCC and other more radical black groups were bristling with rage and lusting for vengeance. Individuals such as the widely respected Diane Nash, along with figures like Julian Bond and James Farmer, had had enough of King's sort of intellectual tussling with state and national figures. Some openly despised what they viewed as King's "Uncle

Tom" appeasement, his (in their view) vacuous calls for momentary boycotts, futile marches, and hollow talks with politicos.

Stanley Levison conveyed to King that perhaps it was time to move the campaign beyond Birmingham and to better prospects. "Martin wasn't ready for that," Clarence Jones told me. King wanted to confront the president face-to-face and demand federal troops to protect Birmingham's blacks.

Within days of the church bombing, King was received at the White House with a small delegation of Birmingham's top Negro figures. Even Jones (who was not present) was concerned that King went into the Oval Office with no plan but to demand federal troops. Jones told me: "The trouble with the Kennedys was that they were strictly opportunists."

Robert Kennedy upended the day before it even began by publicly declaring that there was no legitimate basis to commit national guardsmen to Alabama. The Kennedys were exhibiting their reflexive cautiousness, though both men did feel anguished for the families of the murdered children.[2]

The Kennedys instead announced the appointment of two presidential emissaries (both establishment-type white men) to go down and investigate the Birmingham situation. One of the men was a former secretary of the army; the other a retired West Point football coach. The envoys had been contacted and formally recruited even before King and his companions arrived at the White House. Levison later expressed disgust when he learned the sequence, and even Jones was privately dismayed that King did not protest such a co-opting of the crisis and the pain.

Jones told me that his dear friend Martin had been outmaneuvered and that it did not look good. No doubt many of King's supporters were taken aback when the preacher told the press outside the White House that day that "this is the kind of federal concern needed."

A few days later, several of Birmingham's white elite appeared in Washington to speak with President Kennedy. (Eugene "Bull" Connor was not among them; he had already been replaced—a fact that these white leaders presented as evidence of their goodwill and magnanimity.) Kennedy had no feelings for or about Connor and, in fact, challenged the men to arrange for the hiring of the first black policeman in Birmingham. (That did not happen until 1966.) The president admonished them just do a few things to cool off the situation in their besieged city. Gingerly linking himself more closely with King than ever, he warned the Birmingham group not to expect that they could run King out of Birmingham so quickly. He defended King's uncompromising belief in nonviolence and perceptively drew a line between the SCLC's approach and that of the adversarial SNCC group. Kennedy cautioned the gathering not to create an opening for SNCC, at one point declaring, "They're sons of bitches."[3]

Though members of the student group were more extreme than King in tactics, JFK may have been proprietarily lumping serious men and women such as Julian Bond and Diane Nash with hard-core extremists from the so-called Black Power movement. Nonetheless, Kennedy's reproach had some effect: before 1963 was out, a few downtown stores in Birmingham hired their first-ever black sales clerks. Progress was minimal and begrudged. Clarence Jones told me that "Martin knew, at the end of '63, that some kind of big, new dramatic push had to take place somewhere soon to get the movement rolling again. Stanley's viewpoint that we had to go on from Birmingham eventually prevailed, but Martin seemed haunted and obsessed by and with that city."

And then the president was shot to death in Dallas, Texas.

The movement was quaked by the events of November 22, 1963. John Kennedy, riding in an open vehicle, accompanied for the first time on a political trip by his wife Jacqueline, was murdered in the blazing sunlight of Dealey Plaza. The trauma to the nation—and to the civilized world—was indescribable and visceral. African Americans, who had been almost giddy with hope after the March on Washington, then gutted by despair by the church bombing, now grieved with the impression (deserved or not) that the first American president who really cared about them since Lincoln had been taken from the scene.

No one really knew what posture the new president, Lyndon B. Johnson, would assume with respect to civil rights. What was known was that Johnson hailed from Texas, had traditionally been associated with the "Blue Dog

Democrats" who remained segregationist, and that Johnson, as Senate majority leader, had weakened the already feeble Civil Rights Act of 1957.

Clarence Jones and Stanley Levison both knew something else: their friend Martin King would have a pathological personal reaction to the assassination.[4]

In New York, Stanley tried to reach Martin but to no avail. He didn't know that Martin had, rather impulsively, booked himself a ticket from Atlanta and was headed to Idlewild Airport (soon to be renamed "JFK")—where Clarence was waiting for him. Stanley tapped his fingers nervously and said to his wife Beatrice, "I know that he's taking this very personally. I know that he's even more scared for himself than ever. He'll be given to more doomsday prophecies."

The 1958 Harlem stabbing incident ran through Stanley's mind as he began to chain-smoke furiously. He remembered a visit he had earlier in 1958 in Atlanta with Martin's parents. It seemed like centuries ago, long before the jail cells, the threats, the wiretaps, the sudden, dangerous fame that put Martin in his excruciating high profile, and before this—the public execution of the young president who only months earlier had banned Stanley from even speaking with Martin. Stanley remembered sitting with Daddy King and Alberta, the delicious smell of coffee filling the house, the brisk conversation about the developing civil rights movement, and the mixture of pride and concern the parents shared about their suddenly prominent son.

Stanley wrote a letter to Martin the very next day just after he returned to his apartment on Thirty-Ninth Street. "I was in Atlanta yesterday for the Consultative Conference on Desegregation and saw your Dad," he laboriously typed. "He took me home and your mother fed me chicken and home-made lemon pie which was presented as a favorite dish of yours. They were lovely hosts."[5]

One must wonder if Stanley might have thought *If only Martin could be sitting here right now*. He would have asked Bea to somehow re-create the savory dishes and they'd sit by and enjoy watching Martin eating and relaxing and maybe even breaking out with his jokes and merriment and the world that pressed against him and frightened him would suddenly vanish and people would stop hurting each other and Martin Luther King Jr. could just fulfill his wishes and go teach philosophy somewhere and stop running, running, running from all that afflicted him.

It's easy to imagine that Stanley must have chuckled to himself as he remembered more about that letter he composed on February 28, 1958. He recalled writing Martin primarily about an invitation he had garnered for the civil rights leader to address a convention of the American Jewish Congress in Miami (one of several such speaking engagements Levison arranged with the Jewish agency over the years). But even as Stanley referenced the chicken and lemon pie delicacies, he also waxed about the convention accommodations that Martin would appreciate: "This hotel is Miami's newest and has an ice skating rink, so if you can come bring some skates as well as your bathing suit. Imagine ice skating in Miami Beach!"

It was one of few playful phrases, marked with an exclamation point that Stanley ever used in communicating with Martin. Now, five years later, with the young president dead, his civil rights bill in doubt, and the country deeply bereft and apprehensive, Stanley longed for thoughts of Martin free and skating across a rink of leisure—only to return home safely to his mother's lemon pie.

Clarence Jones filled me in about where Martin was on that day of JFK's assassination.

"He had been watching the events on television, at home, just like so many of us," said Jones. "He leaned over and said to Coretta, 'This is going to happen to me.' He was overcome with fear and trepidation. He called me and said, 'I have to come to New York right away and talk with you. We have to think out all of our strategies in light of this terrible thing.' So he did."

Jones relayed that King got on a flight and arrived relatively late that night of November 22. As they had agreed, Jones waited for King in the Eastern Airlines lounge.

"I saw him running in, his hat in his hand, his overcoat flapping, his face full of anguish. He practically fell into my arms. Before he even said hello, he burst out with the statement, 'You see, if they can get Kennedy, they can certainly get me. Clarence, the same thing is going to happen to me.' He was paralyzed with that terror." The two men sat in the dim, empty lounge, sipping cocktails and talking of the great hate that was sweeping the country and that precipitated the horror in Dallas. King smoked incessantly during the session, uncharacteristically removed his tie, and sometimes just disappeared into his profoundly dark thoughts and melancholies.

The forced disjunction between King and Levison, mandated by the murdered president, was now partially responsible for the unlikely geographic mishap that occurred involving the two close friends. Both of them wound up in Washington for the funeral, but neither knew of the other's presence. Levison took a train down to the capital, preferring anonymity and churning with his conflicted thoughts about JFK though deeply distressed for the president's family and the nation. King was again feeling hurt—he had not been officially invited by the family to be a part of the ceremonies, and the snub injured his pride and generally heightened his feelings of insecurity and vulnerability.

So there among the throngs was the rather short, somewhat stubby black man in a blue suit and thin tie, privately mourning the youthful president that he both censured and admired, even as King pined in his own frustrations, fears, and loneliness. The muffled drums of the cortege and the tender wail of "Taps" at Arlington National Cemetery bore down on both Martin and Stanley, in isolated positions, unaware of each other, locked in the same nightmare.

King did appear at the White House briefly to meet, with others, with the new President Lyndon B. Johnson, but Johnson, who would ultimately pass the greatest civil rights legislation in history, nevertheless took pains—less than a year from the 1964 election—not to be photographed with King.[6]

Meanwhile, the antediluvian Hoover and his FBI did not take pause from the slaying of President Kennedy. On the very day of the assassination, November 22, 1963, a secret memo was prepared by Hoover to Attorney General Robert Kennedy. Perhaps the letter was dictated prior to 1:30 P.M. Eastern time—the moment of the shooting—but the dispatch was sent and filed regardless.

The missive was entitled:

COMMUNIST PARTY, USA

NEGRO QUESTION

COMMUNIST INFLUENCE IN RACIAL MATTERS

INTERNAL SECURITY —C

It went on to detail alleged recent meetings involving the triumvirate of "Reverend Martin Luther King Jr., Stanley David Levison, and Clarence Jones."

> Levison has been described as a secret member of the Communist Party, USA. Jones is the General Counsel of the Gandhi Society for Human Rights, an organization formed by King to promote his aims. Jones has been a frequent intermediary in contacts between King and Levison. . . .
>
> As further evidence of a continuing King-Levison relationship, the following is noted concerning a speech delivered by King on October 23, 1963, at Madison Square Garden, New York City, before the 30th anniversary meeting of District 65, Retail, Wholesale and Department Store Union, American Federation of Labor-Congress of Industrial Organizations. In the speech, King, among other things, urged that the Union work for strong civil rights legislation. He said that a year ago President Kennedy gave "the finest speech on civil rights any Chief Executive has ever delivered." King, however, criticized you [referring to Robert Kennedy] by claiming you had retreated from a strong civil rights bill.[7]

Hence on the very day that John F. Kennedy was shot down in Dallas, J. Edgar Hoover was trying to create more havoc for Martin Luther King by goading Robert F. Kennedy into believing that King thought well of Jack and poorly of Bobby.

The same memo of November 22, 1963, continued:

> The foregoing ties in with other information this Bureau obtained indicating that Levison and Jones may well have prepared the King speech of October

23, 1963. The above-mentioned source advised on October 16, 1963, that King was in contact with Jones relative to King's speech scheduled for October 23, 1963, at which time King requested Jones to get some material together with their mutual friend. This Bureau has learned from many references made by King and Jones to "mutual friend" that their reference is to Levison.

So, even as Stanley and Martin, individually, stood in Washington rain and sunshine sorrowing for the freshly slain president, Hoover was compulsively scheming to undermine the bridge between them with the infestation of Communism. Almost fifty years later, Clarence Jones reflected with me on the incongruity of Hoover's (and the Kennedy brothers') obsession with Levison's supposed Soviet sympathies. "Stanley a Communist? *Then*, when he was working with Martin? When would Stanley have had *the time* to be a Communist? All he did, 24/7, was work on the civil rights movement. Absolutely *nuts*."[8]

It's not hard to sympathize with Jones's deeply felt frustration. It's just that Levison had been decidedly busy with and among Communists for many years before embracing King and partnering with Jones. Even his son Andrew, while cataloging his father's gradual disillusionment with the Party, and quoting Stanley branding of the Communists as "stale" long before 1956, notes Levison's vigorous crusade against the Smith Act, McCarthyism, and the "naming of names" right up to the time of the Montgomery bus boycott. "As long as men Stanley deeply respected as friends and union militants were being thrown in jail, Stanley saw the ranks of those who were disavowing their past and even denouncing their former friends as acts that would be cowardly rather than admirable."[9]

Clarence Jones may not have seen it by the time he personally met Stanley Levison, but Levison's transition from radical leftism to civil rights insider, certainly completed by 1956, was thorny and incremental. He did finally crush his Soviet cigarette firmly into the ashtray, but the smoke lingered for a while.

Did that make either Levison or King any less valiant in their alliance and quest, especially given the government's unflagging and often illicit pursuit of them?

No one has answered this better than Taylor Branch, who wrote: "The hidden spectacle was the more grotesque because King and Levison both in fact were the rarest heroes of freedom, but the undercover state persecution would have violated democratic principles even if they had been common thieves."

CHAPTER FOURTEEN

Lyndon Johnson, Ping-Pong, and Bobby's Transformation

L yndon Johnson had both disdained the Kennedys and wished desperately to please them. The unremitting social snubbing they afforded the vice president was incalculably more pronounced than what the Kennedys saved for Martin Luther King Jr. King, a Negro leader and an inconvenient outsider whose agenda kept confounding the administration, was nonetheless not part of the administration. John Kennedy had chosen Johnson as his running mate in 1960 after a bitter fight with him for the presidential nomination—specifically to secure the electoral votes of Texas and help deliver other parts of the South. Then, in office, he and Robert and the other members of the Kennedy inner circle alternately ignored or parodied him as a Dixie buffoon.

King liked Johnson personally but was probably unaware that the strapping, former Senate majority leader was decidedly more insecure than King and that whatever indignities King endured at the hands of the Kennedys, they never caricatured or lampooned him as some sort of outlandish southern hick. This level of cruel mockery, routinely invoked by the cool, imposingly slim, and cosmically successful Kennedys, was reserved for the man who had very likely made the difference in JFK's 1960 razor-thin victory over Richard M. Nixon.

Stanley Levison was aware that Johnson had been a stumbling block in the feeble attempts at civil rights legislation of the 1950s, but he also understood that LBJ depended upon his network of "old boys"—like a person depends on oxygen—to maintain his unparalleled and historic management of the US Senate during that era. Martin was occasionally naive when it came to political realities, Stanley knew. He even complained to Clarence, from time to time, that "it would be nice if Martin paid closer attentions to some of the details of this work."

Nonetheless, even though Johnson had avoided a photograph with King at the White House on November 23, 1963—sending King back out into the gloomy Washington showers following the assassination—the new president had made an important statement that day. In one of scores of pressured, sometimes hushed but crucial sessions that developed while JFK's body lay in the East Room, LBJ said that the finest way to memorialize John Kennedy was to pass the civil rights bill that Kennedy had tried to get through Congress. Stanley calculated correctly that the movement urgently needed to decisively tie economic justice and labor rights to the freedom campaign. "Johnson has this in his heart," he conveyed to Clarence. "He's going to make this issue the centerpiece of his presidency. He knows he has to work from Kennedy's legacy but he wants to make his own history."

King, emotionally distraught, fretted for the future of the movement after the gunshots in Dallas, trying to swallow back his fresh fears for his own safety, was gushing about Kennedy. Levison winced when King labeled JFK "a martyr." King persisted with the praise, declaring that the fallen president was "a friend of civil rights and a stalwart advocate of peace." In the end, whether grieving for four little girls in Birmingham or for a youthful president struck down in the open, Martin Luther King Jr. simply abhorred violence and deliberated to his depths about the human proclivity for evil.

But Stanley tended to skip over such philosophical ponderings and cut to the real-life possibilities. He carefully noted President Johnson's soothing address to the nation on November 27, just two days after Kennedy was laid to rest at Arlington National Cemetery. In a masterful stroke that truly helped heal the nation, Johnson opened the speech in the House chambers by stating, softly, mournfully, "All I have I would have gladly given not to be standing here today."[1] Even Stanley was gratified and reassured that the nation had a president in touch with things, seemingly gracious and real, intuitive about the national soul.

But Stanley also heard a new president, his Texas intonation having now replaced the imperial Bostonian timbres of his predecessor, shrewdly getting down to business. Johnson announced that "No memorial oration or eulogy could more eloquently honor President Kennedy's memory than the earliest possible passage of the civil rights bill for which he fought so long."

King and Levison and Jones and Belafonte all knew, deep down, that John Kennedy had not "fought so long" for the bill. But they all, particularly Levison and Jones, understood the engineering of politics. They all also knew—or at least they had developed the sense—that the doomed president had actually experienced something of an epiphany during that summer of 1963—a summer during which he and Mrs. Kennedy experienced the anguish of losing a preterm child in birth.

The attempt on the part of Governor George C. Wallace to prevent Negro students who had earned matriculation into the University of Alabama from registering for classes on the campus, which led to Kennedy federalizing troops and ensuring their entry; the deployment of dogs and fire hoses and police sticks on black schoolchildren who stood with their parents and clergy in the streets of Birmingham in order to bring segregation to an end; and, of course, the murder of the four girls at the Sixteenth Street Baptist Church—collectively, had pricked the gentry-level conscience of John Kennedy. In spite of his Cold War emphases, his attentions to the budget, his overriding focus on being reelected in 1964, he began to visualize black Americans as real people, as mothers and fathers with a right to raise their children with the same advantages as whites, as human beings who were systemically downtrodden in an inequitable social structure that finally required the federal government to override the state legislatures that fossilized the bias.

In death, Kennedy became the spiritual liberator of the blacks; in life, Johnson would get the legislative votes to make the legend true.

Stanley Levison generally couldn't talk directly to Martin King about it because the FBI was still tracking everything, Robert Kennedy's signature on the surveillance orders was still in ink, and Johnson was thinking about poor and disadvantaged people much more than he was personally interested in King. But when Stanley did convey ideas to Martin through Clarence, he began proposing that King let himself become more than just a spokesman for African Americans.

Levison intuited two things: (*a*) that King genuinely possessed a philosophical bent toward labor and its natural link with human rights for minorities and the disenfranchised and (*b*) the way to help Lyndon Johnson win a cloture vote in Congress end the filibuster of the Civil Rights Act was to help nourish the bond among this cluster of Americans for whom Johnson almost immediately became a beacon.

Johnson had deep roots in the impoverishment and droughts and meager prospects of the Texas hill country that was his provenance. Stanley knew that Johnson had resented the Kennedys' New England aristocracy, their posh state dinners and elegant White House art and musical revelries (to which Johnson was rarely invited while he was vice president) and their overall Ivy League superciliousness. LBJ did not graduate from Harvard; he was an alumnus of the decidedly humble Texas State Teachers' College. The Kennedys and their colleagues were all alumni of stellar schools—and Johnson understood that they were brilliant and gifted. But they did not understand that Johnson was, in his heart of hearts, a schoolteacher who had been exposed to poor children who were hungry, needy, brown, and black. If JFK was champagne, LBJ was beer.

"You are both Southerners," Stanley told Martin. "This could really account for something." Even Roy Wilkins, so long a nagging adversary of King's, surmised that Johnson, though a Texan and technically a "good ol' boy," was actually—based on a variety of LBJ statements though his career—a person as connected to the impoverished folks of the South as he was to the region's red soil and scorching wind. One published report indicates that Wilkins told King: "Johnson's speeches could have been written by a Negro ghostwriter."[2]

Stanley wasn't so sure about Wilkins's rather kowtowing declaration and, while he had more confidence in Johnson than in Kennedy, he was not prepared to become a sycophant. He listened with great interest to LBJ's initial State of the Union Address on January 8, 1964. The president announced something daringly new: "This administration, here and now, declares unconditional War on Poverty." It was sincere, but it was also a masterful device through which to link himself to the supposed Kennedy legacy while creating an agenda, an aura that would be his own.

King was ecstatic—and not without some reason. JFK had, at best, made cautionary statements and spoken tentative words that were too often as obscured by politics as they were honest. This new president, an old hand in Washington who knew the infrastructure of Capitol Hill and could convince almost anybody to change his or mind on any issue—or could and would cajole, arm-twist, or threaten his listener into compliance—was saying something that Kennedy never even intimated. Kennedy was charming and witty; Johnson was forceful, in-your-face, unrelenting, and he had big hands that he grabbed you with and a big body that he literally pressed against you until you simply acceded to his implorations. And something that had always been in Johnson's hill country blood, his many years in a blistering classroom, posting words and ideas in front of little brown kids on rough-edged chalkboards, was now as full-blown in his breast as the immense power of the office he had always coveted and now held. If FDR had crafted the New Deal, LBJ was now going to create the Great Society on the short-lived tenure of JFK's New Frontier.

And yet Stanley was skeptical. He told Clarence: "It's great, but Johnson never actually spoke about the Negroes. Not specifically at all. And he's got to get the big tax cut Kennedy was trying to push through Congress. So it's a start, but he's only putting down a billion dollars for the poverty program and he sure is couching it in general terms. It's not that any poor person doesn't deserve to be rescued from poverty. It's just that Johnson didn't ask for any help or even mention a single one of the Negro agencies that have already been trying to do this all these years and who could really lead the government through this thicket."

Indeed, the money for Johnson's "war" was both meager and would be funneled principally into social welfare agencies that were operated by white, middle-class bureaucrats, school superintendents, social workers, and politicos with most of the spending discretion. "Johnson is carefully not putting the financial power to arrest poverty directly into Negro hands," said Stanley, "because he knows better than to scare the Southern politicians who need this help for their states but don't want poor Negroes to get their hands on too much money and then be empowered to protest or start more riots."

Clarence understood what Stanley was thinking. Johnson's efforts were noble, maybe even historic. But Johnson was not (as Martin likely imagined) making any new pact with the civil rights movement. King, of course, would come to a rude awakening within a relatively short time when, as early as 1965, Johnson's War on Poverty would be consumed in the flames and napalm of the war in Vietnam.

Lyndon Johnson was as complex a person as Martin Luther King was sentimental. The historian Thomas F. Jackson has revealed the startling contradictions in Johnson's public moral stands—upon which he followed through with real legislation—and his sometimes crude "deference to local elites and his [own] paternalism." Jackson quotes (from a telephone recording) a statement Johnson made to a journalist early in 1964:

> I'm going to try to teach those niggers, that don't know anything, how to work for themselves instead of just breeding, and I'm going to try and teach these Mexicans that can't talk English to learn it, so they can work for themselves,

and I'm going to try and build a road in eastern Kentucky . . . so they can get down and up to school, get off our taxpayers' back.[3]

Stanley Levison likely was never aware of these comments, but he would have understood them. Though never given to surrendering his trust to any government official, Levison detected the layers of ambiguity within the once very poor and socially disdained Johnson—the product of a destitute family and progeny of a father who had never amounted to anything and whose indigence humiliated and haunted the young man. Though Johnson often talked about "breeding niggers" and "lowlife Mexicans," the irony was that he actually carried a substantial streak of identification with them. Kennedy never said much about them and didn't do anything in particular for them. Johnson talked about them, bawdily, Texas-like, sometimes implausibly. But he did more for American minorities than any president since Lincoln.

Robert Caro offers the account of a Hispanic custodian named Thomas Coronado. It was 1928; Johnson was twenty years old and a teacher at the so-called Mexican school in the remote and bleak hamlet of Cotulla, Texas. Caro writes in *The Passage of Power* that "no teacher had ever really cared if the Mexican children learned or not—until Lyndon Johnson came along."

> And it was not only the children whom Lyndon Johnson taught; to help the school's janitor, Thomas Coronado, learn English, he bought him a textbook, and before and after classes each day, sat tutoring him on the school steps. . . . Whether it was because he had had to do "nigger work" as a youth—picking cotton, chopping cedar in the Hill Country—or because as "a Johnson" he had felt the sting of unjust discrimination, there had always existed within Lyndon Johnson genuine empathy and compassion for Americans of color.[4]

Whatever President Johnson might have said privately and out of old habits, he was likely gratified when *Time* named Martin Luther King Jr. as "Man of the Year" in January 1964. LBJ regarded King as a true trailblazer; he did not need to be instructed, as Kennedy had been initiated years earlier by

Harry Belafonte, to seek out and work with King if he wanted to comprehend the black community.

The changing of administrations, along with the varying sensibilities of successive presidents, had no effect upon the deeply entrenched FBI culture of reconnaissance and deploring of King, Levison, and Jones. Stanley was feeling cut off; Robert Kennedy, though traumatized and crippled by his grief, was still attorney general. In fact, any constraints that RFK might have had at his disposal to check J. Edgar Hoover's tyrannical, fixated surveillance campaigns were gone without the executive intermediation of John Kennedy. In short, Robert Kennedy had no buffer with Hoover, and King had no buffer with Kennedy. And Levison was still marooned from King even as the civil rights movement was, post-Birmingham, floundering financially and suffering with the exhaustion and angst of its leader—who now openly declared to others: "It's just a matter of time till somebody gets me."

The SCLC leadership, wounded emotionally, confused and divided about strategy, would be further confounded by FBI activity regarding King as 1964 unfolded. "Be careful in Washington," Clarence told Martin as the latter headed to the capital for some legal discussions. Jones was increasingly worried about what the persistent FBI taps on King—ostensibly because of Levison—would actually reveal about King's personal life. All these perilous factors became intertwined with tape reels when King lodged at Washington's Willard Hotel several weeks after the JFK assassination.

Agents got advance notice of the King visit and gleefully placed a full gamut of listening devices in the room to which he'd be assigned. David Garrow succinctly reports: "The bugs picked up a lively, drunken party involving King, several SCLC colleagues, and two women from Philadelphia."[5] The FBI had a new windfall of damaging intelligence about King's moral shortcomings and began focusing more on his libido than on the original subject of Levison. The tapes were passed along to Robert F. Kennedy and to President Johnson.

Just days later, FBI agents saw King meeting in person outside a New York hotel with both Levison and Jones. Perhaps due to his still-crushing sorrow over the murder of his brother, Kennedy noted all this but had lost some of his zeal. Jack Kennedy was no longer around to run for reelection in 1964; what difference did it really make anymore to Bobby if King was, or had associations with, Communists? And LBJ, interested in passing the civil rights legislation and creating a Great Society, actually needed King and never got too distracted by Hoover's fixation. At one point in 1964, as King made a swing through Mississippi under open threats from the Klan to assassinate him, Johnson sternly ordered J. Edgar Hoover to have FBI agents protect the civil rights leader. The director grudgingly acceded to the command.

King endured a bomb threat as his plane was departing Asheville, North Carolina, for Atlanta after a fractious retreat of SCLC staff in the nearby mountains. Everyone aboard the flight, which was evacuated, stared resentfully at Martin and Coretta, along with staff executive Dorothy Cotton, while the group walked away from the plane—which was not in danger. But the moment once again got the better of the exhausted preacher. He was quoted as saying out loud to his two companions: "I've told you that I don't expect to survive this revolution, this society is too sick."

I asked Reverend C. T. Vivian, who attended that 1964 SCLC retreat, if King ever really relaxed. "Well, he did sometimes during those there days in the mountains, believe it or not. We were trying to figure out Johnson and we had financial problems—I mean, the direct-mail fund raising wasn't going too well. It was harder to do without Stanley Levison really being in the picture. In fact, Clarence and the others were having some tough discussions at that retreat about whether it was safe anymore for Martin to work with Stanley. They didn't decide. It was hard. Martin just loved Stanley so much. But there was still some relaxin' time and jokes and fun. We took breaks and played softball and Ping-Pong, cards, and Martin just seemed to let out a lot of steam during those times."[6]

"Did you ever see him unwind at any other time in your years together?" I asked.

"I never actually saw it, but I knew of two times when he apparently let go of all the tensions. Once he took a trip to Jamaica with Ralph and he just disappeared from the planet, so to speak. I don't think he ever wanted to come back from that trip. They swam and drank and ate and nobody told them they couldn't sit here or enter there. And another time, Roberto Clemente, you know, the great Pittsburgh Pirates player who died in a plane crash, took Martin out to his stables on a farm in Pennsylvania. Martin just loved that. He and Roberto had a mutual admiration society and Martin so enjoyed riding the horses and just being around them. I imagine he just felt so far away from all the trouble and the pressures and the fears. He just felt safe, I suppose, around those beautiful horses."

There had always been stiffness for King when it came to Robert F. Kennedy. The murder of John Kennedy did serve to end most of the exertions between the two men, both doomed for assassin's bullets themselves in 1968. As one historian has written, "The two of them had stumbled through relations from camaraderie to contempt." The mountain of correspondence between them, for many years sealed, ranging from frantic pleas via Western Union to dismissive missives to polite invitations, reveals the collective transcript of an involuntarily symbiotic relationship. They were both sad men, pulled by the gravity of their times, largely thwarted by fate and the toxic mixture of other men's ambitions, both destined to die young in their own blood.

In March 1963, for example, King had found himself once again inexorably tangled in danger—this time during a campaign in Virginia, not far from Washington. He sent a telegram to Robert Kennedy, received by telephone, and essentially ignored, in Washington:

> Request immediate investigation on inadequate police protection at Peterburg Virginia the use of police dogs on peaceful demonstrators in clear violation of civil liberties has provoked wide spread discontent unlawful application of trespass ordinance in violation of civil rights has resulted in 22 arrests to date
> Very truly yours Martin Luther King Jr[7]

The seasons changed. On January 22, 1964, exactly two months after Dallas, the lame-duck attorney general sent an official communiqué to Dr. King at the Ebenezer Baptist Church in Atlanta. Robert Kennedy wrote: "As you know, we are planning an oral history program on the Kennedy Administration—i.e., a systematic effort to interview President Kennedy's colleagues and contemporaries about the issues and decisions of the Administration."

RFK described the effort as "unprecedented" and noted that was no such collection for earlier presidents such as "Jefferson or Lincoln or Wilson or F.D.R."

> You are obviously one of the persons who ought to be interviewed in order
> to get a full record of the Administration, its policies and its achievements.
> . . . I well know the demands on your time, and, assuming your willingness
> to join in this effort, would hope that the process can be made as efficient
> and expeditious as possible.[8]

Kennedy was leaving for Japan; he explained courteously to King at the end of the letter and requested a response by January 25, if it were possible. Levison and Jones urged King to participate (both of them knowing that it was politically expedient for the Kennedys to include such a prominent Negro voice in such a compilation). Martin needed no pressing and was only too eager to be included.

Yet something was happening within the broken soul and slight body of Robert F. Kennedy. Harry Belafonte has been among those close to the scene of all this history, so much of it driven by the personal vicissitudes of life, who has written about the discernible change in Robert Kennedy that began in the shadow of his brother's assassination. Although it was not immediate, and some people close to Bobby had observed it in unexpected patches even while Jack was alive, Robert Kennedy, the vivacious father of eleven children (though one was born after Kennedy's death on June 6, 1968), did have a well of compassion within him. Belafonte declares that, in the wake of Kennedy's accelerated and emotional visits among the nation's poor and outcast, from the urban ghettos of the North to the hunger-ridden towns of Mississippi—all of which became the tapestry of Kennedy's short-lived run for the presidency in 1968—"Bobby had been transformed." Belafonte was one of the people who prompted Kennedy to run in 1968, and he notes that "the days of wondering how we might find access to his moral center were long gone."

Many historians have expounded upon the deepening of Robert Kennedy that occurred after he lost his brother. There are innumerable accounts of his midnight jaunts over the fence at Arlington National Cemetery, sometimes alone, sometimes with a trusted friend, where he would spend hours in prayer over the president's grave. The eternal flame would capture the unspeakable woe etched permanently into the gaunt face, tears poured out of his hollow eyes, and even his thick, wavy shock of hair would appear wracked and hopeless.

Kennedy, always thin, became agonizingly gaunt, a despondent reed of a man once obsessed with details who now sat staring out the window at meetings and conferences. He was known to disappear on solitary walks through Washington at all hours of the day or night; he donned his late brother's jackets and cufflinks and even transferred his papers into one of John's favored carry cases. Robert Kennedy was suffering; no one or anything could reach him—so profound and extreme was his bereavement. The two brothers had been physically and spiritually inseparable, each other's sealed confidantes and absolute protectors. Bobby was Jack's supreme adviser, a kind of guru who nonetheless willingly and dutifully subsumed his own ambitions and even his career in favor of the exalted older sibling who had fulfilled the family mission of the presidency.

Once coldly gripped with facts, figures, specifics, and certainly with vendettas, Kennedy became the soft-spoken reciter of the Greek tragedian, Aeschylus. Time and again, reflecting on his brother's death and then later upon other catastrophic situations (including the murder of Martin Luther King), Kennedy would mournfully invoke the ancient playwright's famous axiom: "Even in our sleep, pain which cannot forget falls drop by drop upon the heart, until in our own despair, against our will, comes wisdom through the awful grace of God."

But the business of human rights in America did not bow to Bobby's hard-earned tenderness. By the spring of 1964, a virtual race war had broken out in St. Augustine, Florida, and Martin Luther King was again petitioning the weary attorney general.

CHAPTER FIFTEEN

Selma, Vietnam, and the Gathering Shadows

K ing and the SCLC leadership were churning about two very different settings as Lyndon Johnson settled into the White House and the cherry blossoms bloomed in Washington. On one hand, a civil rights bill, truly historic, was to be signed at some time soon and King was invited to be present at the White House for the occasion. On the other hand, Klansmen and their adherents, including members of the local police force, were assaulting and terrifying African Americans in the city of St. Augustine, Florida, at an unprecedented and appalling level.

King decided he had to go there—certainly as long as there was no fixed date for the signing of the much-anticipated legislation.

He began with a telegram to Robert Kennedy, its language approved by Stanley Levison via Clarence Jones, sent on March 30, 1964.

St. Augustine, Florida is America's oldest city. Yet the city continues in brutalising Negro citizens. The St. Augustine, Florida situation highlights the need for the protection of minorities provided by the Civil Rights Bill. In St. Augustine, Four Hundred years of local control and States Rights has not lead [sic] to a betterment of relationships but a denial of basic human rights.

The moral weight of America should come to bear on St. Augustine. Shootings, housing, burnings and Klu [sic] Klux Klan beatings have continuously occurred in the Florida town. Nothing has been done. Law and order has been successfully opposed by naked violence.

If our National government supports, morally or financially, the 400th Centennial in St. Augustine, it will be endorsing 400 years of segregation, hate and brutality. In St. Augustine, Florida America remains a single shuffling step away from slavery. Local leaders, political and religious, have not spoken out or helped change the conditions in St. Augustine.

Dr. Martin Luther King, Jr., President

Southern Christian Leadership Conference[1]

A handwritten annotation at the bottom of the original draft of this telegram (this jotting not seen by RFK) noted: "Sent to Associated Press, United Press, 3-30-64 1:00 PM." Kennedy, marked and humanized by both the death of his brother and their father's illness (Ambassador Joseph P. Kennedy had been fallen and severely weakened by a stroke; Bobby now agonized over the two key men of his lifetime), did not dismiss the text or the implications of King's dispatch. Kennedy had come to understand human vulnerability.

The protests against the extraordinarily harsh treatment of blacks in St. Augustine had actually begun in 1963, while President Kennedy was still alive. C. T. Vivian, noting that there was no SCLC presence in the old city, had urged involvement. Stanley Levison agreed that a response to the appalling situation was necessary but cautioned King not to get too distracted from the pending March on Washington and the never-ending push for the Civil Rights Act.

Reverend Vivian told me: "St. Augustine was very hard, very hard. We got some students from the North to help us stage demonstrations against the segregated restaurants and schools and stores. The Klan people had no problem shooting at us and burning things down. People were getting hurt real badly. When Martin came down the first time, they shot up the house where he was going to be staying. Luckily, he wasn't there at the time."[2]

In fact, a few hundred activists, black and white, from many regions, came together in St. Augustine. The collective police response was ruthless. Taking advantage of the sweltering spring and summer weather, officers forced protestors to stand erect in a confined coop in daylight. Others, deemed particularly felonious, were sealed into a brick "sweatbox" overnight. The city arbitrarily raised bail from $100 to $1,000 for each individual. "It's like the Nazis," Stanley said bitterly when he heard about all this.

The Senate was settling into a filibuster on the civil rights legislation by Easter of 1964, but the news from St. Augustine may have helped to break the impasse. The history also shows that President Johnson was relentless in his pursuit of votes for passage. Providentially, a Florida judge named Bryan Simpson made several decrees in favor of the protestors and even encouraged the SCLC to bring more lawsuits against the local Klan. A few businesses began to grudgingly desegregate. A second visit by King helped to further lift the spirits of the beleaguered—and battered—black residents.

Sadly, these small triumphs did not turn the tide of hatred and terrorization away from the historic city. The Klansmen could not have their racism and their firearms legislated out from them, and the SCLC, consistently lacking in funds and personnel, was unable to maintain more than a short-term presence in the region.

In the midst of all this, on July 2, President Johnson signed the Civil Rights Act of 1964 into law at the White House. There are a number of celebrated photographs of the occasion, more than one showing Johnson looking up at King, who stood at the president's shoulder, Johnson unquestionably sharing pride and triumph with the elated preacher. It was only six and a half years since the Montgomery bus boycott that had catapulted King into the national consciousness and that had also brought Stanley Levison, and then Clarence Jones, into his life. King was thirty-five years old, though in his perennial dark blue minister's suit, with his trademark moustache, and his weary smile, he did not look much younger than the fifty-six-year-old Johnson.

But again, Stanley knew better than to view the photographs as an unalloyed achievement that came without conditions or even entrapments. He believed that Johnson expected something in return for the enactment of the landmark legislation—something big and something directly to do with Johnson's bid in just a few months to be legitimately elected to the office he had inherited by the calamity that befell President Kennedy.

"He will want Martin to keep the Negroes out of the streets now that they got the bill," Stanley told Clarence. And indeed, Johnson more or less expressed this in a closed conference following the signing ceremony with the several black leaders present, including King of the SCLC and Roy Wilkins of the NAACP. The president was not vague about his sentiments. The way for Negroes to continue making advances, he expressed in paternalistic tones, was to keep on working with him on legislation—and not create rioting and gunplay in the cities. King and the others got it: LBJ had given them something huge, and in return he wanted the civil rights struggle to basically remain off the radar till he could defeat Senator Barry Goldwater in the November presidential election.

Stanley was pleased to discern that Martin had grown enough in his own wariness to recognize the political football that was endemic to Johnson's method of play. King, stopped in his tracks more regularly by exhaustion and depression (to the point of intermittent hospital stays), took good measure of Johnson's complex relationship to the freedom campaign. King got a degree of satisfaction, in terms of Johnson's caginess, when he received the stunning news that he was awarded the Nobel Peace Prize for 1964. This was within the same year of his being named *Time's* "Man of the Year"—which he had oddly minimized. At the time, he actually remarked to Stanley that the magazine award was not that big of a deal (and the article had contained some distortions that peeved King). "I have all these plaques already on my walls, so what's one more?" He had asked Stanley.[3]

But the constant maneuverings with John Kennedy, the sometimes outright confrontations with Robert Kennedy, and now the wriggling with Lyndon Johnson—not to mention the real and harrowing prison stays and police cruelties—had grown in Martin King's loins a certain set of emotional calluses. Reverend Samuel "Billy" Kyles, a longtime friend of King's from Memphis, who was standing next to King on the balcony of the Lorraine Motel at the moment of the assassination of April 4, 1968, told me: "Martin was overwhelmed by the Nobel prize because he felt it was not really about him. It was about validating the whole movement and making our struggle an internationally revered cause."[4] Andrew Young remembers that when King got the news from Stockholm, King was in a hospital bed in Atlanta, recouping from fatigue and pronounced hypertension. Young was among a few trusted aides close by; King seemed at once lifted by the news but also deeply earnest about the implications. King asked all of them to join him in a moment of prayer. If his life hadn't already been unalterably changed by the civil rights movement that he now truly personified, the path of his existence was now sealed.

What Stanley noted was that while congratulatory telegrams and celebratory messages poured in from all corners of the globe, not a word of acknowledgment came from the White House. The same president who, out of sincere recollections of brown kids he had taught in the Texas hill country, and who truly coveted the civil rights bill he got passed, was just as focused now on winning the election. That prohibited a word of praise to the Negro preacher who had earned the highest award in the world for the pursuit of peace and justice in the nation that Johnson wanted to lead.

The distance between King and Johnson was just beginning to be drawn, briefly mitigated when LBJ invited King and his closest associates to the White House after the Nobel honors. But the president might have been forgiven for some ambivalence about King, given what the FBI assiduously recorded and reported during the brief, but wild, sojourn in Stockholm.

Stanley was not privy to the goings-on but would have his patience tested by the ensuing revelations. Various sources let it be known that members of the King entourage pushed the limits of carnal sprees in the luxury accommodations given to them—particularly Martin's brother, A. D. Lewd women and security officials and complaining lodgers in other rooms all found themselves interacting unhappily during the night.

According to one historian, King was emotionally upset by the behavior of Ralph Abernathy and his wife Juanita, who, characteristically, grumbled that they were not afforded the kind of privileged treatment given to Martin and Coretta. David Garrow has written: "Among SCLC's staff, many had grown to dislike Abernathy's self-importance and superior attitude toward others, especially women."[5] Bayard Rustin did his best to control and manage the libidinous escapades under way and the mood swings of King. But he chattered a lot about these travails while in his hotel room, and all of his talk was being carefully tapped by the FBI and then reported to President Johnson.

King was in a free fall of depression because he again was self-flagellating about the indulgences of this journey, heavily ruminating about the new level of responsibilities that came with the Nobel award, bickering significantly with Coretta, and already brooding and worrying about the next—and supremely dangerous—campaign target: Selma, Alabama.

Alabama was chosen because of its very nature as the broiling epicenter of southern racism and also because an alliance of freedom agencies had weathered the so-called Freedom Summer in Mississippi during 1964. That campaign was led by CORE (the Congress of Racial Equality) with assistance from SNCC and the NAACP. It was a grueling and treacherous endeavor to help blacks register to vote, and it was met by bloody and murderous resistance—including, most infamously, the nighttime execution by Klansmen and police officers of three student volunteers. They were pulled over on a remote highway in Nashoba County: a twenty-one-year-old black Mississippian, James Chaney, and two white Jewish New Yorkers, Andrew Goodman, twenty, and Michael Schwerner, twenty-four.

Stanley Levison mourned for every person, private citizen or widely known, from housewives to students to clergy, who was martyred in the battle for civil rights. But it was impossible for him and his friends, the Filners in New York, and other Jewish activists, not to feel a particular anguish for and connection with Goodman and Schwerner. They also were aware of and concerned about a prominent rabbi from Cleveland, Arthur Lelyveld, who had his skull cracked open by white supremacists and suffered severe injuries while marching with voting rights activists in Mississippi during that summer of 1964.[6] Clarence Jones has said repeatedly: "Even though Stanley was not an observant Jew, he was very proud of his heritage and its traditional involvement with social justice causes."

By 1965, Stanley was meeting more frequently again with Martin, and they were less optimistic about Lyndon Johnson's War on Poverty and his commitment to what they deemed "the ultimate civil right"—the access to a voting booth. The "war" was, ultimately, a trickle-down effort, distilled through bureaucratic sieves, its miserly funds generally withheld directly from black recipients that were increasingly lumped together as radicals and social criminals.

The fiery burst of annual summer riots that turned urban centers, from Watts to Detroit to Newark, into war zones between 1964 and 1967 turned many white Americans into committed racists, raised the profile of unabashedly belligerent black activists such as H. Rap Brown and Stokely Carmichael who believed that violence was the only response to white indifference and discrimination, and began the declining repute of Martin Luther King Jr. More white people saw him as weak and ineffective, unable to tame the ferocious gangs of black insurgents, looters, and firebrands; more black people (many of whom were now rejecting the very term "Negro"—though King never did) decried the increasingly despondent "Dreamer" as the ultimate "Uncle Tom" and appeaser of the white establishment.

Even before the breakthrough Selma campaign and marches, which did succeed in pushing LBJ into implementing and enacting the Voting Rights Act of 1965, another war was bleeding into the King-Johnson relationship and egregiously diverting resources and motivation away from the lofty aims of Johnson's Great Society and into the killing fields and jungles of Vietnam. Just as sure as King marched the fifty-five miles from Selma to Montgomery in March 1965, leading hundreds of marchers across the Edmund Pettus Bridge to the state capitol (a trek during which King was certain he'd be ambushed),[7] the weary preacher was also having his soul ripped apart by his increasing inability to tolerate the quickly escalating conflict in Indochina—which he viewed as immoral, imperialist, and a deadly diversion of funds away from American children who needed bread and education even while American mortars and bombs were killing innocent Vietnamese children.

In a conference call recorded by government agents in 1965, King spoke despairingly to both Andrew Young and Stanley Levison. He said: "I don't really have the strength to fight this issue and keep my civil rights fight going. The deeper you get involved the deeper you have to go, and I am already overloaded and almost emotionally fatigued."[8] Stanley heard his friend's bone-breaking exhaustion and hoped that King would give in to his dilemma and not take on the war issue. Levison deplored the war but was more concerned that King could be making a crucial political mistake by linking Vietnam to the civil rights agenda and thereby risking any collaboration with and from the very imperious and stubborn Lyndon Johnson.

There were three attempts to make the march from Selma to Montgomery. The first, on March 7, was to have taken place in response to the police killing of twenty-six-year-old Jimmie Lee Jackson, who was shot by a state trooper while trying to shield his mother from the officer's nightstick. King was not present for the attempted march that became known as "Bloody Sunday." It was launched primarily by a young John Lewis, the SNCC commandant who, decades later, continues to serve in a long and distinguished career in Congress. Over a quiet lunch in Washington, Lewis told me: "The police and [Sheriff] Jim Clark came at us with clubs and dogs and tear gas pellets. They knocked people unconscious, bludgeoning them from their horses. It was pure terror. We never got across the bridge, of course. Martin was in Atlanta and he was just sickened. People were lying all around, beaten and choking and just screaming. We just wanted to demonstrate that we wanted the right to vote like anybody else."[9]

Lewis did not mention to me that he himself was struck repeatedly by troopers and sustained serious head and body injuries. But he did remember that the marchers pleaded for federal protection so that they could proceed in safety. After the attack, Lewis, bandaged and bloodied, had declared: "'I don't see how President Johnson can send troops to Vietnam, I don't see how he can send troops to the Congo, I don't see how he can send troops to Africa and can't send troops to Selma."

Newsreels captured the outright police assault on the peaceful marchers trying to walk across a bridge. The televised carnage affected the nation and moved President Johnson. In an unprecedented declaration of empathy for African Americans, Johnson spoke to Congress a few nights later and announced: "Their cause must be our cause too. Because it is not just Negroes, but really it is all of us, who must overcome the crippling legacy of bigotry and injustice. And we *shall* overcome."

King had curtailed a second march attempt from Selma (he led people who knelt in prayer at the edge of the bridge) two days after Bloody Sunday. He was criticized for the "retreat" by some and even termed a coward. In fact, he had made a deal with Johnson to delay the protest so that Johnson could both deploy federal troops along the fifty-five-mile route and begin rousing up votes in Congress for what would become the Voting Rights Act of 1965.

The actual march began on March 21 and was heavily guarded by federalized troops and, ironically, FBI agents. Camping at night, the demonstrators were cheered and entertained by the singing of Harry Belafonte, Lena Horne, and other notable entertainers. Levison—still officially banned from King's presence—worried and smoked and paced in his New York apartment. After King's safe arrival in Montgomery and his defiant speech adjacent to the state capitol building (Governor Wallace rebuffed any attempts at a meeting), Stanley, intuiting that the Selma-Montgomery trek was a turning point in the whole struggle, sat down at his old typewriter and prepared a letter to his friend: "For the first time whites and Negroes from all over the nation physically joined the struggle in a pilgrimage to the Deep South. [This] made you one of the most powerful figures in the country—a leader now not merely of Negroes, but of millions of whites."[10]

Levison believed that Martin had shown new maturity, restraint, and political savvy—let alone courage—in pulling off the treacherous campaign. King had put himself physically at risk, had again capitalized on news media coverage that betrayed the savagery of white officials, had effectively recruited his celebrity friends to also be present, and had worked craftily with the president. "Masterful," Levison told Clarence Jones over the telephone. They also spoke, with bitter sorrowfulness, about the murders of two white volunteers in the Selma campaign, housewife and driver Viola Liuzzo from Detroit and Unitarian minister James Reeb from Boston. The two had both been termed "white niggers" and were killed in separate incidents by racist marauders.

Robert F. Kennedy was also affected by the Selma story. Now a US senator from New York, Kennedy was free to discover and share his greater identification when it came to suffering and injustice. On March 26, Kennedy signed a letter to the "Selma Student Delegation" that had joined the Alabama campaign from Buffalo. Kennedy hailed "the need for immediate action on strong, new voting legislation to cope with the continued denial of voting rights in the South, which was dramatized by the shocking and distressing events of the past few days in Selma, including the death of the Rev. Reeb."

The senator continued:

> I am sure I need not dwell on my commitment to achieving the opportunity of free exercise of constitutional rights for all of our fellow citizens. The President has submitted to the Congress a bill which will go far toward eliminating the problem insofar as voting is concerned. I have been in close touch with the Justice Department since the bill was drafted, and I shall be actively involved in the effort to get it passed. I have also urged that evidence of violating of federal laws in the recent brutality be submitted to a federal grand jury, and the Justice Department has indicated it intends to do this.[11]

The costly triumph in Selma-Montgomery also marked the beginning of a significant transition in the entire dynamic of the civil rights movement. In a sense, this had been the last great staging area that was geographically centered in the South. Even as Stanley Levison, an old socialist after all, had long calculated that real social liberation would require an alliance of blacks and the labor movement, and King had always agreed, the movement now spread—with fire and gore—to places such as Chicago and Los Angeles. Within days of the passage of the Voting Rights Act, the Los Angeles ghetto of Watts exploded in rebellion and bloodshed.

Not unlike the case of the brutally clubbed motorist Rodney King in 1992, the violence in Los Angeles was provoked by an undisciplined, reactionary Los Angeles police force. Clarence Jones ruefully used the circumstance of the Watts eruption, during which thirty-four people died and some nine hundred were injured, to point out something to Martin King: black helplessness was economically based and national. If the police were often Klansmen in the South, they were "occupying forces" in America's big cities. King understood and became crestfallen. He comprehended that the civil rights gains made, even the large legislative victories, had little to do with the day-to-day reality of life for the poor black masses of Los Angeles, Detroit, Chicago, Cleveland, or Boston. America was teetering on the brink of a racial war; King became ever more hostile toward the administration's mounting deployments of troops to Vietnam and the attendant waste of human lives, hope, and treasury. He became something of a ghost longing for life.

He maintained his public statements and private commitment to nonviolence. His critics—and they were growing in number and volume—mocked and dismissed his diffidence and courtesies toward white mayors and other officials. At one point, Stanley had to endure a telephone conversation with his longtime friend that practically embarrassed Levison. King had just addressed a large gathering of angry African Americans in Los Angeles, admonishing them to link together with their brethren across the land and practice peaceful civil disobedience. "I think they responded well to the message of nonviolence," Martin said to Stanley over the telephone. Stanley had already learned that some people had shouted "Let's burn!" at King while others actually laughed at him. His heart breaking for King, for America, and for humanity itself, Stanley told Martin to make sure and get some rest. He anguished that more and more people were dismissing King's statements as the bromides of a man passed by time.

When King took his antipoverty and fair housing campaign to Chicago in the summer of 1966, he was met with an extraordinary level of hostility, threats, jeering, as well as the disingenuous gestures and skilled deviousness of Mayor Richard Daley Sr. King took up temporary quarters in a city housing project; the city government promised housing reform but delivered on nothing. King was talking much more about jobs and education than he was about race. But the reaction to him in this northern city was completely racial and toxic. "I've never encountered anything like this," said King, "anywhere in the South."

A reporter named Frank James filed a story in the *Chicago Tribune* on August 5, 1966.

The headline was "Martin Luther King Jr. in Chicago." The subheadline read: "During his stay in the city, the civil-rights leader faced a 'hateful' crowd." The dispatch then summarized what King encountered during the steamy and frightful days of his so-called Chicago Campaign.

> On this muggy Friday afternoon, Martin Luther King Jr. stepped out of the car that had ferried him to Marquette Park on Chicago's Southwest Side to lead a march of about 700 people. The civil-rights leader and his supporters were in the white ethnic enclave to protest housing segregation. Thousands of jeering, taunting whites had gathered. The mood was ominous. One placard read: "King would look good with a knife in his back."[12]

As King marched, someone hurled a stone. It struck King on the head. Stunned, he fell to one knee. He stayed on the ground for several seconds. As he rose, aides and bodyguards surrounded him to protect him from the rocks, bottles, and firecrackers that rained down on the demonstrators. King was one of thirty people who were injured; the disturbance resulted in forty arrests. He later explained why he put himself at risk: "I have to do this—to expose myself—to bring this hate into the open." He had done that before, but Chicago was different. "I have seen many demonstrations in the South, but I have never seen anything so hostile and so hateful as I've seen here today," he said.

In a way, King and Levison and Jones—along with King's indisputably faithful and staunch SCLC clan—including Andrew Young, Bernard Lee, Hosea Williams, and others—were running out of options and relevancy. The Vietnam War curdled into the debate and the domestic angst and was contaminating the political climate, creating a pernicious distrust of the advancing military establishment, consuming any hope of a Great Society as well as Lyndon Johnson's presidency, exacerbating the so-called generation gap, deepening the umbrage of black Americans who were being drafted and shipped to Vietnam out of proportion to their demographic numbers because they could not garner deferments like many whites, and poisoning any chance for a national racial conciliation.

The raised fists and the raucous, Black Power declarations of *Burn, baby, burn!* were all turning Martin Luther King's dream into a standing nightmare. Stanley, coughing up phlegm and despondency, still a confidante by phone, letter, and occasional stealth meetings, knew it: Martin was becoming extraneous, almost a parody of himself. Yet it only made Stanley admire and love Martin even more deeply; their relationship, though constrained by the government ban, as well as King's unrelenting travel schedule and his need to remain relevant—which only drove him to more speaking engagements, more crowds to bolster his spirits and to possibly hear his entreating message of nonviolence—their mutual need for one another was never diminished.

They were both men who believed in personal loyalty (King's marriage excepted) and in the ultimate need to repair a nation being torn apart by the advancing trudge of war and the growing chasm between classes. King publicly bemoaned that America was "sick"; Levison privately agonized that King was in danger.

In the end, it had a lot to do with what Stanley read and ingested as a young man back in Far Rockaway, as he scanned the Yiddish-Bolshevik newspapers and quietly began to fund the leftist parties that were staples of that era: people needed to work and families had to share in a system of social parity.

That was what Stanley was thinking about as far back as the 1920s and 1930s. In 1966, his protégé and idol, Martin King, declared in Chicago: "When you deprive a man of a job, you deprive him of his manhood, deprive him of the authority of fatherhood. Place him in a situation which controls his political life and denies his children an adequate education and health services while forcing his wife to live on welfare in a dilapidated dwelling and you have a systematic pattern of humiliation which is as immoral as slavery and a lot more crippling than southern segregation."[13]

When King said these kinds of things, Levison knew he was right—though Johnson and the nation were generally not listening anymore. When King bewailed the manned space program before a Senate committee that included Robert F. Kennedy, calling it a "striking absurdity" to reach the moon while millions of people were hungry on the earth, Levison knew that the preacher was imprudently again antagonizing Kennedy. It was President Kennedy, after all, who had rekindled the nation's hope and confidence when he challenged America to send an astronaut to the moon and return him safely before 1970. Stanley might have wondered how Martin could be so brilliant a prophet yet so clumsy a politician.

Martin, mused Stanley, was either too good for this world, or the world was too depraved for Martin. The two friends continued to work together, as best they could, and tirelessly, on economic proposals; a dignified minimum wage, "freedom budgets," labor-management alliances, and the establishment of corporate foundations dedicated to alleviating poverty. But even King once muttered to Clarence Jones that the sporadic White House conferences on such issues were fairly meaningless and lacking in authentic passion. Though King was, to the core, a man of faith and a teacher of the Gospel, his naiveté gradually evolved into cynicism even as his migraines intensified, his drinking and smoking compounded, and his waistline thickened.

Finally, he could no longer restrain his fury about Vietnam. He might have reached his threshold when, during a rare vacation in Jamaica in January 1967, he came across the horrifying photographs of burned and killed Vietnamese children who had suffered from American napalm and strafing attacks. His longtime aide and bodyguard Bernard Lee was with King at that moment and recorded that the preacher became physically ill and overcome with rage. As quoted by David Garrow, Lee said: "That's when the decision was made. Martin had known about the war before then, of course, and had spoken out against it. But it was then that he decided to commit himself to stop it."[14]

Ironically, Robert F. Kennedy, chastened by grief, and increasingly sensitized to the disgracefully high number of American children starving and suffering and without hope in a land that was not winning any war on poverty yet wasting its resources in Vietnam, would become King's symmetrical partner on the question—and eventually run for president against Johnson on that very plank. But RFK was a politician and King was a minister; very, very few of his own acolytes, including Stanley Levison, thought it wise for King to take on this issue.

On April 4, 1967—exactly one year before his assassination—King delivered his most unrestricted and wide-ranging statement against the Vietnam War. Addressing a crowd of three thousand people in New York City's Riverside Church, King delivered a speech entitled "Beyond Vietnam." Unabashedly equating America's actions with war crimes, King asserted that the conflict was "taking the young black men who have been crippled by our society and sending them 13,000 miles away to guarantee liberties in Southeast Asia which they had not found in southwest Georgia and East Harlem."

He had consulted with a few of his closest advisers that morning, including Stanley. It was clear that King's position about going public, and effectively linking his civil rights leadership to the antiwar movement—was nonnegotiable. Levison understood King's conscience, but he was deeply worried about the political fallout that would, and did, ensue. Levison also knew that the stance taken by King would cost the SCLC and the civil rights movement devastating philanthropic damage. Stanley's face, withered by smoke and worry, was a road map of dread and mystification.

Dr. King was viscerally unable to separate his concern for the poor, segregated, and reviled in America from what he saw as a mad rampage of power and violence in a futile war that specifically and tragically usurped concern, relief, and funds away from antipoverty and fair housing and equal opportunity efforts on the home front. Having once believed in Lyndon Johnson, he now felt a complete disillusionment with the president—which would quickly become mutual.

New York Times Bob Herbert columnist reflected on the speech in 2010. Herbert wrote: "This was on the evening of April 4, 1967, almost exactly 43 years ago. Dr. King told the more than 3,000 people who had crowded into Riverside Church that silence in the face of the horror that was taking place in Vietnam amounted to a 'betrayal.'"[15]

King pleaded that he could no longer keep Vietnam out of "the field of my moral vision."

For his inspiring and courageous preachment, proven right by history, and which foretold our preoccupations today in Iraq, Afghanistan, and elsewhere, King suffered the estrangement of President Lyndon B. Johnson and earned the excoriation of many patronizing black leaders such as Senator Edward Brooke.

Dr. King, alone with his conscience and unable to keep silent, declared on April 4, 1967:

> We can no longer afford to worship the god of hate or bow before the altar of retaliation. The oceans of history are made turbulent by the ever-rising tides of hate. History is cluttered with the wreckage of nations and individuals that pursued this self-defeating path of hate. We are now faced with the fact that tomorrow is today.

And then, in one of his most famous of aphorisms, King declared: "We are confronted with the fierce urgency of now."

Things were never the same for King after this bold and cathartic oration of despair, disquiet, and hopelessness over America's lost way. He was never welcome at the White House again. As Stanley feared, many benefactors of the civil rights movement withdrew their patronage. Other black leaders, fiercely covetous of King's eminence, pounced on him as being, at best, foolish; at worst, a traitor. Roy Wilkins of the NAACP, persistently envious of King's prominence and eager to bring him down, immediately dissociated from the Riverside speech.

It goes without saying that history proved King right. But at the time, in the moment, several years before the 1975 cessation of hostilities that sealed America's defeat in Vietnam, the deaths of one million Vietnamese and 57,000 American troops, precious few people could see the moral and prophetic audacity of Rev. King. Even Levison told King he had problems with the speech, admonishing Martin, gently, that it was uneven and not really developed with enough thought and contemplation. Martin was somewhat defensive about Stanley's comments but nonetheless agreed to become a cochairman of a new group called Clergy and Laymen Concerned About Vietnam.

In 2010, I spoke with Rev. James Lawson, the ascetic, Methodist minister who eventually invited his friend King to Memphis in the midst of the 1968 sanitation workers' strike that would cost King his life. Lawson reflected on King's painful decision to speak out on Vietnam. He told me, over the phone, barely audible: "It was a heavy cross to bear."

King never let up on Vietnam. Nor did his spirits ever truly rise again in the remaining year of his life. The only way to save the soul of the nation, he came fervently to believe, was to finally forge an alliance between the labor and freedom movements, and to make *poor* people—not black people or white people or brown people—the centerpiece of his moral crusade.

His last idea was to gather thousands of the nation's outcast and under-privileged in a Poor People's Campaign that would literally camp out in the shadow of the capitol in Washington—and whose teeming presence would force the government to redress two centuries of economic and social injustice. But then he was diverted by the wildcat strike of predominately black garbage workers in Memphis, Tennessee, and the twigs were finally bent under his feet.

CHAPTER SIXTEEN

Bobby Prays in Indianapolis; Stanley Weeps in Atlanta

" s it certain that he was killed?" asked presidential candidate Robert F. Kennedy, as a misty dusk settled over the predominantly black section of Indianapolis on April 4, 1968.[1] Kennedy had proclaimed his entry for the Democratic presidential nomination just a few weeks earlier—as an antiwar candidate, as an advocate for the economic liberation of the nation's destitute, as another alternative to the incumbent and besieged President Johnson. If Martin Luther King had a disagreement with Johnson about social policy and the Vietnam War, Robert Kennedy loathed Johnson personally and always had. The state of the world, the plight of the poor, and the dark serendipity of violence had brought MLK and RFK, from completely disparate backgrounds, into the same moral field of vision.

But now Kennedy was told by devastated and hard-breathing aides that King had been shot, and yes, fatally, while standing on the balcony of the Lorraine

Motel in Memphis. A sniper had tracked the preacher, who was enjoying a light moment outside the door of his customary Room 306, preparing to gather with some of his friends and go to a festive dinner at the home of Reverend Samuel "Billy" Kyles. A single blast from a Remington .30-06 rifle, traveling at a velocity of 2,670 feet per second, shattered King's jaw and face, and then imploded within his chest.

Bobby Kennedy, unscripted, no doubt reliving the permanently unhealed lesion of his brother's murder just four and a half years earlier, made a decision. Word would spread fast of King's martyrdom and the country, its cities already ravaged by annual summer rioting, its national psyche embedded in the incinerator of Vietnam, might explode. Kennedy, thin, so vulnerable-looking, his mop of hair flying in different directions, stood up on the back of a flatbed truck. There was anticipation in the air, and a strong bond between him and these unadorned citizens—Bobby had become a kind of frail white hope for black folks who knew that no one from their race could even dream about running for president, let alone advocate for their sores and wants and deprivations. And then Kennedy told them what had just happened.

I'm only going to talk to you just for a minute or so this evening, because I have some—some very sad news for all of you—Could you lower those signs, please?—I have some very sad news for all of you, and, I think, sad news for all of our fellow citizens, and people who love peace all over the world; and that is that Martin Luther King was shot and was killed tonight in Memphis, Tennessee. [Audible shrieks of horror and disbelief in background.]

Martin Luther King dedicated his life to love and to justice between fellow human beings. He died in the cause of that effort. In this difficult day, in this difficult time for the United States, it's perhaps well to ask what kind of a nation we are and what direction we want to move in. For those of you who are black—considering the evidence evidently is that there were white people who were responsible—you can be filled with bitterness, and with hatred, and a desire for revenge.

We can move in that direction as a country, in greater polarization—black people amongst blacks, and white amongst whites, filled with hatred toward one another. Or we can make an effort, as Martin Luther King did, to understand, and to comprehend, and replace that violence, that stain of bloodshed that has spread across our land, with an effort to understand, compassion, and love.

For those of you who are black and are tempted to fill with—be filled with hatred and mistrust of the injustice of such an act, against all white people, I would only say that I can also feel in my own heart the same kind of feeling. I had a member of my family killed, but he was killed by a white man.

But we have to make an effort in the United States. We have to make an effort to understand, to get beyond, or go beyond these rather difficult times.

My favorite poem, my—my favorite poet was Aeschylus. And he once wrote:

> *Even in our sleep, pain which cannot forget*
> *falls drop by drop upon the heart,*
> *until, in our own despair,*
> *against our will,*
> *comes wisdom*
> *through the awful grace of God.*

What we need in the United States is not division; what we need in the United States is not hatred; what we need in the United States is not violence and lawlessness, but is love, and wisdom, and compassion toward one another, and a feeling of justice toward those who still suffer within our country, whether they be white or whether they be black.

So I ask you tonight to return home, to say a prayer for the family of Martin Luther King—yeah, it's true—but more importantly to say a prayer for our own country, which all of us love—a prayer for understanding and that compassion of which I spoke.

We can do well in this country. We will have difficult times. We've had difficult times in the past, but we—and we will have difficult times in the future. It is not the end of violence; it is not the end of lawlessness; and it's not the end of disorder.

But the vast majority of white people and the vast majority of black people in this country want to live together, want to improve the quality of our life, and want justice for all human beings that abide in our land.

And let's dedicate ourselves to what the Greeks wrote so many years ago: to tame the savageness of man and make gentle the life of this world. Let us dedicate ourselves to that, and say a prayer for our country and for our people.

Thank you very much.[2]

Beyond the power and consoling effect of Kennedy's words, which helped keep violence at a minimum that night in Indianapolis while so many American cities detonated in riots and fire, the people closest to RFK were astonished with his poise and almost pastoral composure.[3] The essentially spontaneous homily has been recorded as one of the finest moments of American rhetoric. Kennedy's staff noted, with a collective jolt, that he had just also made his first public reference ever to the murder of his own brother, John. Purportedly, a journalist standing next to Kennedy at the moment Bobby heard about the shooting of King would recall: Kennedy "seemed to shrink back as though struck physically and put his hands to his face, saying 'Oh, God. When is this violence going to stop?'"[4]

There was no ambivalence anymore, no obsession with FBI wiretaps, with the possible political ramifications of being associated with King. Kennedy had made two campaign stops that very day in Indiana and had spoken out forcefully against the war, about the unfair draft laws that were sending less-privileged youngsters to Vietnam, about American poverty, and about the escalating national level of violence and racism. Pulling himself up on that flatbed, in spite of the warnings from local police that they could not protect him, and the worries of his staff that what he would announce could spark an uprising right then and there, Kennedy became instantly the spiritual heir to King.

Kennedy was assassinated just eight weeks later in the kitchen of the

Ambassador Hotel in Los Angeles, moments after winning the California Democratic presidential primary. He was forty-two years old and was buried next to his brother at Arlington National Cemetery. In one of the darkest moments of his eighty-two-day campaign, he had confided to an aide that "there are guns between me and the White House."[5]

$$\cdot \ \cdot \ \cdot \ \cdot \ \cdot$$

The entire SCLC staff was hell bent against Martin Luther King Jr. becoming personally involved in the Memphis situation that began unraveling in the winter of 1968. Clarence Jones emphasized to me that "Stanley and I were solidly opposed to it. It was a distraction from the bigger picture, which was, at that time, trying to galvanize and raise money for the Poor People's Campaign we were planning for that summer."

Stanley got an earful of Martin's deep despair that enveloped his entire being in those final days; it likely helped Stanley comprehend why his friend needed the possible lift of Memphis and that his valuableness in the strike situation was a necessary balm for him.

In a telephone conversation that took place just one week before the assassination, King opened his soul to Levison and spoke bluntly about his awareness that other black leaders were overtaking or spurning him:

> All I'm saying is that the Roy Wilkinses, the Bayard Rustins, and that stripe—and there are many of them—and the Negroes that are influenced by what they read in the newspapers, and Adam Clayton Powell [the Harlem congressman who always disdained King], for another reason, you know, their point is: "I'm right, Martin Luther King is dead, he's finished, his nonviolence is nothing. No one is listening to it."[6]

All Stanley could do was to remove his thick glasses and cover his eyes in pain.

But neither Levison nor Jones was physically present in those tense, even rancorous sessions of the SCLC leadership that took place in those closing weeks of King's life. While conducting a seminar that I attended in Memphis in 2011, Andrew Young responded to a question I asked him: did Young feel that King should have come to Memphis at that time in 1968?

"I wasn't for it at first," he told me. "You knew that Martin couldn't just go down there and just give a speech and then disconnect from the thing. Jim Lawson was calling him and Lawson was a true friend and had taken his share of bumps and prison over a long career. He was here leading the garbage workers and he's always been the real thing. So I knew that it was going to be very hard for Martin to refuse. He really almost needed something specific to help with somewhere, something that might validate him at that point in his life."

But like Jones and Levison in New York, the majority of King's aides in Atlanta were truly worried that Memphis would dilute the bigger Poor People's Campaign and, more ominously, create new personal danger for King. Young has written that some of the inner circle (whom he criticized for their "egomania") expressed resentment toward King for possibly dragging them toward Memphis when they were all trying to get to Washington for the national crusade on behalf of the poor. Young reports that King, who sensed that Memphis presented the perfect moral fusion of civil rights and the labor movement, declared, indignantly: "Memphis is the Washington campaign in miniature."

"He really believed that," Clarence Jones said. "He got a rousing response when he first went down there in March and spoke at a rally that Lawson organized. He calculated that, besides representing a heroic response to an outrageous human rights violation, the Memphis sanitation workers' strike was an exact paradigm of the Poor People's Campaign."

By the time King had returned to Memphis for the third time, on April 3, the entire SCLC leadership was with him, in person and in spirit. That is why so many of them, including Young, Ralph Abernathy, Bernard Lee, Jesse Jackson, James Bevel, and others were on the scene at the Lorraine Motel at 6:01 P.M., April 4, 1968.

Young phoned Levison in New York within an hour of the murder. Levison surely knew about it and had always expected that, "sooner or later," it would happen. But Young felt that Levison deserved the courtesy of the call. Young later said: "Of all the unknown supporters of the civil rights movement, he was perhaps the most important." Stanley was unable to talk; his heart was broken and he could only distill his deeply embedded emotions by going into action. He organized an air ticket for himself and prepared to get down to the King home in Atlanta by the next day. Like so many other people whose lives had been galvanized and shaped by the young preacher, he just found himself needing to be present—he moved into a pattern of preparation that was at once terrifying and yet hauntingly anticipated to happen at some time. "We always knew that someone would get Martin," Clarence reflected with me. "Stanley and I would talk about it. It really wasn't a question of if. It was just a question of when."

Their old nemesis Robert F. Kennedy was phoning Coretta Scott King well past midnight after the assassination. Was he reliving his brother's murder? Was he remembering the manner in which J. Edgar Hoover had called him at his Virginia home during that dreadful afternoon of November 22, 1963, and mechanically informed him that John Kennedy had been murdered in Dallas? Was he, Bobby, keenly aware that King's death created a vacuum into which so many people, including distraught and grieving African Americans, were now placing the New York senator and did that not, understandably, make Bobby a little more afraid for his own safety?

Kennedy, soft-spoken on the phone, hurting in his core, reached Coretta after numerous attempts. Nervous, struggling for words, he first conveyed to the new widow that her home required additional phone lines and he was taking care of it. Perhaps Coretta, though grateful, thought about the irony of receiving this gift from the man who had authorized so many wiretaps on King and his family and associates over the years.

According to a number of people present in the chaos and disarray of the King household that awful night, Kennedy asked Mrs. King if there was anything else he could do for her. Kennedy mentioned that he understood Mrs. King wanted to fly to Memphis to retrieve her husband's body.

"Yes, I would like to do that." Coretta spoke up. No provision had been made for the task; King's death was not a state or national matter, and no one in any government agency at any level had made any gesture. Kennedy informed her that he was already corralling a private plane to be at the disposal of the King family and staff. The senator, speaking then to a King aide in Coretta's house, also indicated that he was having entire sections of several Atlanta hotels reserved for all the thousands of envoys and notables that would undoubtedly be arriving in the city for Dr. King's funeral. According to one journalist, Kennedy said: "My family has experience in dealing with this kind of thing."[7]

Harry Belafonte called several times during the night and reassured Coretta that he was on his way to be with her and the King children. He wanted to come there and just "do menial things . . . and share the sorrow with you." He would ultimately help Coretta pick out the ministerial suit that Martin would be buried in. He served, along with Stanley Levison and Harry Wachtel, as one of the coexecutors of King's exceedingly modest estate. In his memoirs, Belafonte described King's worth as "meager." There were some $5,000 in a checking account and a payout coming from a life insurance that Belafonte himself had secured for the family years before.

To Coretta's long-running consternation, Martin had always given away his book royalties, speaker's fees, and the Nobel Peace Prize cash award to the movement, to his alma mater, Morehouse College, and to the Ebenezer Baptist Church. Without fanfare, both Levison and Belafonte would send checks to Coretta for years following King's death. She remained financially solvent as a result and was able to establish the King Center in Atlanta—where she is now buried next to her husband.

People who came to the King home all through the night and day of April 4–5 remember a number of things: the self-possession of Mrs. King (how many times did she imagine or foresee exactly these circumstances?), the suppressed din of so many hushed voices, the cakes and sandwiches and salad bowls sealed in cellophane that kept appearing, the smell of coffee and the accumulation of cups and saucers and dishes in the small kitchen that were repeatedly washed and rewashed by rotating sets of hands, the muffled cries, the emptying boxes of tissue paper, and the two men—one black, one white—who stood by the front doorway ceaselessly and just greeted and hugged people.

Harry Belafonte and Stanley Levison were both there by the morning. Belafonte took it upon himself to welcome people, breaking their pain a bit with his disarming celebrity and sincerity. Levison was more reticent, his own anguish filling his body and keeping his heavy shoulders stiff—being white and mostly unknown to the visiting throng, he fulfilled his own needs more by just being there than by taking on the carriage of an ambassador.

Both men would, from time to time, look in on Coretta and the children, who were largely ensconced in the bedroom that she and Martin had shared during his rare interludes at home. It was herein that Coretta allowed herself to occasionally break down and then quickly retreat into discussions of logistics and practicalities. Where should Martin's body lie in state to accommodate the deep need of so many people to pass by and pay tribute? Where and when should the funeral take place? The burial? Who should speak and how not to offend the countless colleagues and disciples of King that expected to share in the spotlight of the memorial rituals? How to accommodate the proceedings in terms of the vast national television audience that Stanley reminded her would surely be watching? Coretta spoke from time to time about how she might emulate the courage and dignity of Jacqueline Kennedy. What should she wear to the service? She realized that she may not have the proper mourning gown and hat.

A number of individuals who were in the house on April 5 have corroborated the story of the credit cards. According to author Rebecca Burns, Coretta King had an assistant named Xernona Clayton, who was exceptionally devoted and attentive. In *Burial for A King,* Burns recounts Clayton's discussions with Coretta King about the need for a headdress or a veil that would be suitable yet not resemble or appear to mimic the long-veiled hat worn by Mrs. Kennedy during JFK's funeral observances. Clayton drove to a department store (one that had until just prior to this time refused to serve black people) and ordered outfits for Mrs. King, which were promised for delivery by the next day.

When Clayton returned to the hectic, tearful house, she encountered Levison and Belafonte at the doorway, still welcoming and mixing with people. She told them, straightforwardly, that she had just ordered bereavement clothes for Mrs. King but really had no idea how to pay for them. Almost at the same time, Levison and Belafonte both pulled out their wallets and handed Clayton credit cards. Levison reportedly said, "Don't worry." Belafonte was quoted as stating, "Take this one, too. Get whatever is needed."

Over the next several months, Levison as well as Belafonte helped Coretta King negotiate a series of lucrative book deals and interviewing opportunities. She emerged as her own spiritual successor to her husband even as Ralph Abernathy officially followed King as president of the SCLC. Belafonte remained dutiful and charitable for many years but has explained in his own memoirs that he grew somewhat disenchanted with Coretta and particularly with the King children—who have fought legal and personal battles with one another over the years and have not particularly triumphed in making the King Center in Atlanta a truly illustrious or innovative facility. There have been distasteful clashes with the National Park Service over landownership at the complex in Atlanta's "Sweet Auburn" district and a number of laborious scuffles with scholarly agencies and individuals over the issue of "intellectual property" as it might apply to Dr. King's words and papers.

But the manner in which Stanley Levison immediately transferred his loyalty and service to Coretta after Martin's death was of great relevance to J. Edgar Hoover and the FBI. Dr. King was barely in the ground when, later in April, FBI operatives in Atlanta and elsewhere were tracking Levison and recording his interactions with Mrs. King. Transcripts reveal that agents were scurrying to report to Hoover that "Stanley Levison, long-time secret Communist Party member, has been in contact with Coretta King twice and counseled her relative to public appearances and finances."[8]

Hoover could hardly contain himself. In what was once a sealed directive, he instructed:

> The Atlanta Office should immediately open a case on Mrs. King and conduct a discreet investigation to follow her activities through established

informants and sources. You should furnish the Bureau with the results of a file review concerning Mrs. King's background and activities in a form suitable for dissemination.

But it was all really over—the King movement, the Levison intrigue, the Kennedy fixation with the whole civil rights narrative that King had embodied and Levison had funded. Coretta King and Ralph Abernathy did not work well together. He—and his wife Juanita—once part of an affectionate foursome who had marched, mingled, dined, and worried together as the first and second couple of the movement, now had different objectives than the widow.

Abernathy, lacking King's magnetism and humility, fell flat. The Poor People's Campaign, though also cursed by heavy rains, mud, and the general indifference of the Washington political establishment it had meant to shame into action, was a dismal failure. Jesse Jackson, already on his own compass of ambition, proved to be a rather inept "Mayor" of the so-called Resurrection City that basically dissolved on the National Mall. The other former lieutenants of the movement were scattering into their own peculiar interests and motivations; they were bereft, broken, and uninspired by Abernathy. He wanted Coretta to help him raise money for the movement, but she became focused on developing various projects dedicated to her husband's memory.

Bobby Kennedy's death on June 6, and the coincidental arrest, in Great Britain, on June 8, of King's assassin, combined to suck the air out of the struggling movement. People were engrossed and distracted by other things: the turbulence and street riots of the Chicago Democratic National Convention of that summer, when Senator Edward M. Kennedy wisely declined a draft movement that would have crowned him with the nomination that his brother Robert had basically won (Vice President Hubert H. Humphrey garnered the nod without having run in any primaries); the coiling, raging, impossibly divisive Vietnam War; the significant third-party presidential bid of the unapologetically racist Alabama governor George C. Wallace; the solar racial conflagrations that splattered American streets with blood and rage.

J. Edgar Hoover (who died in 1972) had outlasted both Kennedy brothers and King. Only Stanley outlived all these principals—but not by much. The subject and nucleus of 11,000 pages of government enquiry and surveillance, he limped through his final years fighting off diabetes, asthma, and the general effects of his incessant smoking. He died in his New York apartment, alone, on September 12, 1979. His obituary appeared on page B8 of the *New York Times*; Stanley David Levison was sixty-seven years old. Cousin Leon Schwartz showed me the obituary that was printed in the *Los Angeles Times* on September 17, 1979. It was headlined: "Civil Rights Strategist S.D. Levison Dies: FBI Claimed He Was Communist Link to Martin Luther King."

Levison had remained in the shadows following the murder of his hero King, but he did not disappear into the night. He transferred some of his potent fund-raising skills to Andrew Young, the thoughtful knight that Levison had hoped would succeed King as the leader of the movement. He helped to organize and finance Young's first congressional campaign in 1972. This was very gratifying for Stanley, perpetually bereft for his friend Martin: Young became the first African American since Reconstruction to be elected to Congress from Georgia. Levison assisted Young with money, advice, and direction through his subsequent terms in the House of Representatives and on through Young's tenure as the UN ambassador appointed by President Jimmy Carter.

Levison remained comfortably in the company of African Americans, their causes and aspirations. His commitment to them was larger than his personal fealty to Martin Luther King. As long as his health permitted, he continued to create dollars and donors for King's Southern Christian Leadership Conference; his development efforts helped spawn the new Congressional Black Caucus.

Levison took a robust interest in and helped Coretta Scott King create the Martin Luther King Center for Nonviolent Social Change in Atlanta. He quietly wrote checks for Coretta when she needed money for herself and her children. He also turned his attention to several labor movement issues; according to his son Andrew, he helped recruit Leonard Woodcock of the United Auto Workers into a combined effort to form the National Committee for Full Employment and the Full Employment Action Council. Levison liked

Woodcock and remembered the many times the union chief had marched with King. He also enjoyed the fact that Woodcock ranked number 9 on the notorious "Enemies List" compiled by President Richard M. Nixon.

Levison's name is enshrined nowhere on a plaque or in an exhibit.

There are some in the Jewish community who remain perplexed, even chagrined about Levison's inconspicuousness across the record of Jewish involvement in social justice—particularly the civil rights movement. The impressive chronicle of commitment by rabbis, lay activists, students, professors, well-known and anonymous, simply has never included very much about Stanley. One professor and journalist has asserted that Levison wore "a spiritual yarmulke" during the King years. The notion of Stanley wearing a skullcap, real or spiritual, is scoffed at by his son Andrew, the only direct survivor of Levison. It may be that Stanley knew of the creed of human rights, "to feed the hungry, clothe the naked, and plead for the widow," that is the hallmark of the Hebrew prophetic tradition. But if he knew it, it was likely not the reason he chose to do what he did.

Nonetheless, Samuel G. Freedman, who proffered the phrase "spiritual yarmulke," persuasively wrote:

> The truth is that Levison typified an American Jewish leftie of his era—very much including the fact that he made his money as a capitalist, practicing law, investing in real estate, and operating a Ford dealership. The truth also is that, so far as the historical record reveals, Levison was not a communist agent or party member while closely tied to King.[9]

It was never clear if or how Stanley's Jewishness directly influenced his path. But one thing is irrevocably clear: there never appeared, in any statement or assertion by the US government, a shred of conclusive evidence that Levison had been involved with, or given a single dollar, to the Communist Party after 1956—when he met and embraced the young Baptist preacher who fatefully stood up to lead a bus boycott in Montgomery, Alabama, and thereby sealed his own fate in Memphis, Tennessee, just thirteen years later.

Negroes Will Not
Return to Passivity

n May 1967, just a month after Martin Luther King Jr. delivered his now-acclaimed but at that time scorned speech against the Vietnam War, Stanley Levison sat down at his old Olivetti typewriter, lit a cigarette, adjusted his glasses, and began a personal exposition about his compassion for black Americans. He lamented their very place in the American narrative and the lack of black history that could be found in books and literature.

He began: "A recurring criticism Negroes justifiably make of the publishing industry is the paucity of books on Negro history and the appalling distortions that mar most general histories." He typed several more paragraphs about how "the education of Negroes and their self-pride have deeply suffered by the contrived myth created by omission and commission in books, that Negroes are a people without a significant history."

He typed additional paragraphs, paused, removed his glasses, and automatically lit up his next smoke. An erudite and thoughtful man, he recalled a testimonial once made by a favorite author of his, John Steinbeck. Since this was 1967, and there were no home computers, he grabbed a separate clean page from the stack next to him and began, in his own block handwriting, to print what he labeled as "INSERT A."

> More harmful than the absence of books is the existence of books that defame and denigrate the Negro on a scale that is scarcely short of national brainwashing. To understand how grave are the consequences of lies and distortions emanating from books that purport to be scholarly it is well to remember a very profound observation of John Steinbeck. He said:
>
> "A book is somehow sacred. A dictator can kill and maim people, can sink to any kind of tyranny and only be hated, but when books are burned the ultimate in tyranny has happened. This we cannot forgive. People automatically believe in books. This is strange but it is so. Messages come from behind the controlled and censored areas of the world and they do not ask for papers and pamphlets. They invariably ask for books. They believe books when they believe nothing else."[1]

And then Stanley typed: "I think that what is happening now is a most profound phase of progress for Negroes. They are experiencing an inner transformation that is liberating them from ideological dependence on the white majority."

He paused and put his hands on his chin. He saw Martin sitting calmly in the Harlem bookstore, a letter opener lodged in his chest. He flashed back to his own very early days in Far Rockaway. He and Roy were sitting around the kitchen table eating steaming soup and discussing worker politics. Stanley was looking out the window, listening to the rackets of cable cars and street vendors and kids running past, shrieking with delight and taunting each other with dares, even as he knew that the world and its profound social deficiencies would weigh heavily upon him.

"What Negroes did not learn from books," he continued to type, "they learned from the bitterness of experience . . . the slashing blows of backlash and front lash have hurt the Negro but they have also awakened him and revealed the nature of the oppressor. . . . It may appear to the white establishment that they can with impunity still manipulate and delay, but the tragic consequences will not be long in appearing."

Again he paused—a wordsmith ruminating within his own bluish smoke. Although he had only known Martin Luther King for some twelve years, he could not remember a time when Martin was not at the epicenter of his thinking, his planning, his angst, and his anxieties. Yes, Clarence, his dear friend and confidante, often his only human link to Martin, was articulate and organized (which Martin was not, he chuckled), but Clarence would dabble in alliances, and even visit, with Malcolm X when Malcolm was still alive (he was assassinated in 1965) and Clarence sometimes tried too hard to placate Robert Kennedy, and Clarence was, after all, an attorney and not a prophet. And Bayard, poor Bayard, trapped in both his radicalism and sexual complexities, was brilliant but could never lead a movement. No, not like Martin. Martin, so shy sometimes, so ribald at other times, so incredibly vulnerable and often enough insecure—Martin was the only one who captured and embodied the slow, painful, heaving, unwelcome, but simply inevitable transformation of black people in this America. Stanley shook his head, satisfyingly discovering the key phrase of his private dissertation: "Negroes will not return to passivity."

He finished off his missive and put in neatly in a file folder within the desk drawer. *Where was Martin right now?* He thought. *Let me call Clarence and find out . . .*

· · · · ·

I n 1970, two years after the assassination in Memphis, Levison gave a rare, extended interview to a journalist named James Mosby of the Civil Rights Documentation Project. Mosby asked Levison about the origins of his friendship with King. Stanley shared the narrative of Bayard Rustin linking him with King at the time of the Montgomery bus boycott in 1956, which he described to his visitor as "the dawn of the day of mass action."

He relived the founding of "In Friendship" with Rustin and Ella Baker, the original fund-raising rally at Madison Square Garden featuring Harry Belafonte. He reminisced about King's milestone journey to India and how he, Levison, had worked with Libby Holman's Christopher Reynolds Foundation to create underwriting for the trip. There were so many personalities, perils, voices, marches, meetings, jail cells, churches, suitcases, letters, telegrams, secrets, funerals, triumphs, defeats, jubilations, and the expected requiem. Stanley drifted off in thought and smoke for a moment; the writer interrupted his rumination.

"Do you recall your first impressions of Dr. King?"

Stanley became alert and focused.

Yes. I recall them vividly. The reason why I recall them vividly is that I think Dr. King that night made a very significant statement about himself, personally. We were driving in [a] car, and someone said that a subpoena had been issued for Dr. King in Montgomery and he'd probably be served with it when he got back there.

Somebody else, in a jocular vein, said they'll be making a big mistake if they do that because it's only going to give the movement in Montgomery more publicity. And a joke kind of passed around the car about how—how stupid and foolish they can be when they try to be repressive.

Mrs. King stopped the frivolity by saying, you—you know a Southern jail is nothing to joke about. If Martin has to go to jail in the South, we don't take the view that that's just a—a trivial occurrence because people go to jail and never come out. Or someone comes to the jail and takes them out and they never see them again. This is a serious matter.

Then those who were joking tried to explain that they weren't making light of it, but there was a certain tension in the air. And then Dr. King broke it by starting to talk. And he said, if anybody had asked me a year ago to head this movement, I tell you honestly that I would have run a mile to get away from it. I have no intention of being involved in this way. He said that as I became involved, and as people began to derive inspiration from their involvement, I realized that the choice leaves your own hands. The people expect you to give them leadership. You see them growing as they move into action and then you no longer have a choice, you can't decide whether to stay in it or get out of it, you must stay in it.[2]

But Stanley had more to say about his admiration for Martin, for whom he still grieved with fresh urgency. "In a personal discussion," Stanley told the reporter, "he didn't seem to be the type to be a mass leader. There was nothing flamboyant, nothing even charismatic about him as he sat in an ordinary discussion. He was . . . very thoughtful, quiet, shy—very shy. The shyness was accented with white people."

Stanley even remembered, with a certain ache, and a vague sense of unintended guilt, that the shyness around white people was even discernible when King sat with Levison in their early days together. "There was a certain politeness, a certain arm's length approach, and you could feel the absence of relaxation."

But the shyness evaporated, Levison indicated, when King found himself caught in the winds of the freedom movement that pushed him into the limelight he did not covet. "The essential difference in the movement that Dr. King developed was a mass, as distinguished from a small group. Dr. King, for the first time united a total community—forty-eight thousand black people who were almost 100 percent united in Montgomery. That was new. That, nobody had ever done before."

There is a running mistake, a spelling error in the transcript of this generally unknown, if singular, interview of Stanley conducted in early 1970. The name of the interviewee appears consistently as "Levinson." Even in the brief introductory paragraph, the journalist had typed: "I am James Mosby, representing the Civil Rights Documentation project in an interview with Mr. Stanley Levinson."

Someday, broods Clarence Jones, the last survivor of quiet heroes that gathered around Martin Luther King Jr. for a painfully short number of years and that changed America, someday people will learn how to say and even to spell the name of Stanley David Levison.

Notes

Chapter One. Cousin Stanley

1. Leon Schwartz, *A Scion of the Times* (Altadena: Consortium House, 2010), 301.

2. Communist Party–USA, website statement, http://www.cpusa.org/the-party/.

3. Ben Peck, "The Stalin-Hitler Pact," *In Defense of Marxism*, August 24, 2009, http://www.marxist.com/the-stalin-hitler-pact.htm. The Comintern was created in Moscow in 1919 during the so-called Third International. It was dissolved by Joseph Stalin in 1943, a move that added to the growing hostility toward the Soviets shared by American Marxists such as Stanley Levison.

4. Contained in "Martin Luther King: We Are Not Interested in Being

Integrated into This Value Structure" by writer Raj Patel, in an Internet column dated January 18, 2010, posted on http://rajpatel.org/.

Chapter Two. A Walk in the Rose Garden

1. New York office of FBI, from King Papers Collection, archived, Martin Luther King, Jr. Research and Education Institute, Stanford University (hereafter referred to as "King Papers"). Papers edited by Professor Clayborne Carson.

2. Conversation with Rabbi Joachim Prinz (now deceased), recorded by the author at an American Jewish Congress meeting in 1979. Prinz spoke just prior to Dr. King at the 1963 March on Washington.

3. Several conversations with Reverend Vivian are included in this book, taking place in Memphis, Atlanta, and a number of phone conferences. Vivian, a Birmingham-based preacher, was prominent in the civil rights campaigns, and was famously punched in the face by Sheriff Jim Clark in Selma, Alabama, while trying to help African Americans register to vote.

4. Otherwise unattributed quotations in this text reflect the recollections of Clarence Jones and Leon Schwartz, as well as Eugene Schwartz, members of the Joseph Filner family, Samuel "Billy" Kyles, Harry Belafonte, Maxine Smith, C. T. Vivian, and other eyewitnesses to these events.

5. Letter, King Papers.

6. From conversation with Andrew Young, Memphis, April 2011. Young was lecturing at the University of Memphis Cecil C. Humphreys School of Law on the occasion of the forty-third anniversary of the assassination of Dr. King. Event sponsored by the National Civil Rights Museum.

7. Andrew Young, *An Easy Burden* (Waco, TX: Baylor University Press, 2008), 200–201.

8. Telephone conversation with Harry Belafonte, 2012.

9. Orlando Figes, *The Whisperers: Private Life in Stalin's Russia* (London: Picador, 2008), 96.

10. Yaacov Ro'i, *Jews and Jewish Life in Russia and the Soviet Union* (Abingdon, UK: Routledge, 1995), 21.

11. David Garrow, *Bearing the Cross: Martin Luther King, Jr., and the Southern Christian Leadership Conference* (New York: William Morrow, 1986), 200.

12. From among several interviews in person with Clarence Jones. Most were held at the Martin Luther King, Jr. Research and Education Institute, Stanford University, where Jones is scholar-in-residence.

13. Taylor Branch, *Pillar of Fire: America in the King Years 1963–65* (New York: Touchstone, 1998), 114.

14. From "Famous Leadership Quotes," *The Happy Manager*, www.the-happy-manager.com.

15. Gary Thomas, *Sacred Influence: How God Uses Wives to Shape the Souls of Their Husbands* (Grand Rapids: Zondervan, 2007), 113.

Chapter Three. From Far Rockaway to Montgomery

1. Based on interviews by author with members of the Joseph Filner family, close friends of Beatrice and Stanley Levison. These include former congressman Bob Filner and Levison cousins Eugene and Leon Schwartz.

2. Derived from the files of *The Jewish Daily Forward* and yearbooks as well as alumni publications of Far Rockaway High School, Queens, New York.

3. Hilene Flanzbuam, ed., *Jewish American Literature: A Norton Anthology* (Amherst: University of Massachusetts Press, 2001), 245–46.

4. Garrow, *Bearing the Cross*, 66.

5. Letter, King Papers.

6. Author conversation with Reverend Moss, Cleveland, May 2011.

7. Letter archived in the King Papers.

8. From ongoing e-mail correspondence with Andrew Levison, 2011–13.

9. This and several other points garnered from Federal Bureau of Investigation, *Stanley Levison—the FBI Files*, 5 vols. (Lexington, KY: Filiquarian Publishing/Qontro, 2009).

10. Transcript files: Matthew Schuerman, ed., WNYC Radio, New York, January 17, 2011, http://www.wnyc.org/story/108985-martin-luther-kings-hidden-friend-and-advisor/.

Chapter Four. The Communist

1. W. E. B. DuBois, *The Souls of Black Folks* (New York: Bantam Classic, 1989), 30.

2. Niagara Declaration of Principles, 1905.

3. Robert Harvey, *A Short History of Communism* (New York: Thomas Dunne Books, 2004), 197.

4. Robert Service, *Comrades! A History of World Communism* (Cambridge: Harvard University Press, 2007), 144.

5. Notes compiled from the series "Execution of the Rosenbergs," *The Guardian*, June 20, 1953.

6. This is among several quotes and accounts derived from David Garrow, *The FBI and Martin Luther King, Jr.: From "Solo" to Memphis* (New York: Norton, 1981), 37.

7. Garrow, *The FBI and Martin Luther King, Jr.*, 43.

8. E-mail to author from Andrew Levison, February 2013.

Chapter Five. In Friendship

1. Jeanne Scheper, "Libby Holman," in Jewish Women's Archive, *Jewish Women: A Comprehensive Historical Encyclopedia*, March 1, 2009, http://jwa.org/encyclopedia/article/holman-libby.

2. Taylor Branch, *Parting the Waters: America in the King Years, 1954–63* (New York: Simon and Schuster, 1988), 861.

3. Correspondence between the author and Andrew Levison, 2012, 2013.

4. Conveyed to the author by Reverend C. T. Vivian.

5. Branch, *Parting the Waters*, 209.
6. Letter archived in the King Papers.

Chapter Six. Harry Belafonte, Janet Levison, and a Totally Different "Kennedy"

1. Author conversations with Reverend Lawson, 2010 and 2011.
2. Harry Belafonte, *My Song: A Memoir* (New York: Alfred A. Knopf, 2011), 149.
3. Belafonte, *My Song*, 282.
4. Archived in the King Papers.
5. Clarence J. Karier, *The Individual, Society, and Education: A History of American Educational Ideas* (Champaign: University of Illinois Press, 1986), 308.
6. Interview with Belafonte recorded in 2005 and archived by JFK Presidential Library and Museum.
7. Information gathered in this narrative from article in *SpyTalk*, November 2, 2011; HBO 2011 documentary *Sing Your Song* about Harry Belafonte, and from files accessed via the Freedom of Information Act.
8. Garrow, *The FBI and Martin Luther King, Jr.*, 31.
9. Based upon research and interviews done by the author for his previous *Room 306: The National Story of the Lorraine Motel* (East Lansing: Michigan State University Press, 2012).
10. Ralph David Abernathy, *And the Walls Came Tumbling Down* (Chicago: Lawrence Hill Books, 1989), 477.
11. Author interview with Georgia Davis Powers, Louisville, 2011.
12. FBI transcript archived in the King Papers.

Chapter Seven. A Stabbing in Harlem

1. Branch, *Parting the Waters*, 243.
2. Gabe Pressman, "The Day Martin Luther King Jr. Was Stabbed in Harlem," NBC New York, January 16, 2012, http://www.nbcnewyork.com/news/local/The-Day-Martin-Luther-King-Jr-Was-Stabbed-in-Harlem-81964952.html.

3. Garnered from letters and notes archived in the King Papers.

4. Louis Uchitelle, "For Blacks, a Dream in Decline," *New York Times,* October 23, 2005.

5. Garrow, *Bearing the Cross,* 299.

6. Letter archived in the King Papers.

Chapter Eight. Stanley Knew Better

1. Among several quotes transmitted by Clarence Jones.

2. FBI file via the Freedom of Information Act.

3. From David Garrow, "The FBI and Martin Luther King," *Atlantic Monthly,* July–August 2002, 80–88.

4. Letter archived in the King Papers.

5. Letter archived in the King Papers.

6. Letter archived in the King Papers.

7. Letter archived in the King Papers.

8. Letter archived in the King Papers.

9. Service, *Comrades!* 204.

10. From "Jacqueline Kennedy: In Her Own Words, Historic Conversations on Life with JFK" (ABC News, 2011), DVD.

11. Phone conversation with Reverend Lawson, 2011.

12. Phone conversation with Diane Nash, 2011.

13. Garrow, *Bearing the Cross*, 130.

Chapter Nine. Senator Kennedy Is Calling

1. Branch, *Parting the Waters*, 277.

2. Archival video footage from WSB-TV Newsfilm Collection, The Walter J. Brown Media Archives & Peabody Awards Collection, University of Georgia Special Collections Libraries, Atlanta, 1960.

3. *New York Times* advertisement, March 29, 1960.

4. Relayed in a conversation with Clarence Jones.

5. Belafonte, *My Song*, 215.

6. Conversation with Julian Bond, Washington, DC, 2010.

7. Branch, *Parting the Waters*, 357.

8. Branch, *Parting the Waters*, 362.

Chapter Ten. Martin, Stanley, and Clarence

1. Clarence Jones, *What Would Martin Say?* (New York: Harper, 2008), 12.

2. Branch, *Parting the Waters,* 860.

3. It is true that Jones did not meet Levison until after the latter had quit the CP-USA. The record shows, however, that Levison's departure from the Party, his cessation of fund-raising and public relations for it, did not revolve around the singular event in Hungary in 1956. This, for Levison, was at best the culminating and definitive perfidy by the Soviets, but it was preceded by a long trail of disappointments and betrayals that Levison and others felt had been perpetrated by Moscow. Leon Schwartz told the author that many years prior to 1956, for example, "Stanley had misgivings about the fact that the Marxists in Eastern Europe were training students in their party schools using both physical exercise and guns. Not a single one of us in this country who were part of the leftist movement ever held a gun. It was troubling for Stanley."

4. Original letter archived in the King Papers.

Chapter Eleven. I Am Not Now and Never Have Been a Member of the Communist Party

1. Letter archived in the King Papers.

2. Arthur Schlesinger, *Robert Kennedy and His Times* (Boston: Houghton Mifflin Harcourt, 1978), 588.

3. Conversation based upon recollections shared with author, separately, by Clarence Jones and Georgia Maxine Powers.

4. Branch, *Parting the Waters*, 697.

5. King Papers, "Secret" Memorandum, FBI, New York, NY, dated 12/31/63, Bureau File #100-3-116, "Re: Communist Party, United States of America—Negro Influence In Racial Matters Internal Security."

6. Transcript from JFK Library files involving MLK, Levison, and Harry Belafonte.

7. Telephone conversation with Reverend Vivian, from Atlanta, 2011.

8. From archived transcript, JFK Presidential Library, Boston.

Chapter Twelve. I Have a Dream Today

1. Clarence Jones and Stuart Connelly, *Behind the Dream: The Making of the Speech That Transformed the Nation* (New York: Palgrave Macmillan, 2011), 76ff. The author has also learned that the copyright for the "I Have a Dream" speech was purchased decades ago by Clarence Jones.

2. This meeting and its atmosphere are also corroborated by Arthur Schlesinger Jr. in his *Robert Kennedy and His Times*, 567ff.

3. Belafonte, *My Song*, 275.

Chapter Thirteen. The Same Thing Is Going to Happen to Me

1. Garrow, *Bearing the Cross*, 291.

2. In an informal conversation, Clarence Jones indeed muttered that the Kennedys were "just opportunists." But in recalling the Birmingham bombing, Jones stated that the president's and attorney general's pain was unquestionably evident.

3. Garrow, *Bearing the Cross*, 296.

4. "It was the first thing Stanley and I spoke about after Kennedy was killed," Jones told me.

5. Letter archived in the King Papers.

6. Robert Caro, *The Years of Lyndon Johnson: The Passage of Power* (New York: Alfred A. Knopf, 2012), 407.

7. From Clarence J. Karier's piece, "The Reassassination of Martin Luther King Jr.," *Educational Theory* 38, no. 4 (1987): 463–75.

8. Again, it is important to note that Jones did not meet Levison until after the latter's severing of ties with the CP.

9. E-mail from Andrew Levison to author, February 2013.

Chapter Fourteen. Lyndon Johnson, Ping-Pong, and Bobby's Transformation

1. Recorded in many sources, including Caro's *The Passage of Power*.
2. Robert Caro, *The Passage of Power: The Years of Lyndon Johnson* (New York: Knopf, 2012), 491.
3. Thomas F. Jackson, *From Civil Rights to Human Rights: Martin Luther King, Jr. and the Struggle for Economic Justice* (Philadelphia: University of Pennsylvania Press, 2007), 192–93.
4. Caro, *Passage of Power*, 257.
5. Garrow, *Bearing the Cross*, 310.
6. Telephone conversation with Reverend Vivian, 2012.
7. Archived in the King Papers.
8. Letter archived in the King Papers.

Chapter Fifteen. Selma, Vietnam, and the Gathering Shadows

1. Telegram archived in the King Papers.
2. Phone conversation with Reverend Vivian, 2012.
3. Reported to the author by MLK friend and former Memphis NAACP chairperson Maxine Smith, 2010.
4. Conversation with Reverend Kyles in Memphis, 2011.
5. Garrow, *Bearing the Cross*, 417.
6. The author spoke frequently with the now deceased Rabbi Lelyveld in Cleveland during the late 1980s and mid-1990s. Lelyveld was physically present in the South during a number of civil rights campaigns.
7. Confirmed to the author by Andrew Young during a conversation in Memphis, 2011.
8. From Federal Bureau of Investigation, *Stanley Levison—the FBI Files*, vol. 2:v.
9. Author meeting with Congressman Lewis and Congressman Louis Stokes in Washington, 1996.
10. Letter archived in the King Papers.
11. Letter archived in the King Papers.

12. Frank James story in the *Tribune*, August 5, 1966.
13. Jackson, *From Civil Rights to Human Rights*, 256.
14. Garrow, *Bearing the Cross,* 543.
15. Bob Herbert, "We Still Don't Hear Him," *New York Times*, April 2, 2010.

Chapter Sixteen. Bobby Prays in Indianapolis; Stanley Weeps in Atlanta

1. Viewed and heard on press pool film available on YouTube, April 4, 1968.
2. Text widely available; this edition from "American Rhetoric: Top 100 Speeches" website, http://www.americanrhetoric.com/top100speechesall.html.
3. Reported to me by Robert Klein, a 1968 Kennedy staffer, in a 2009 conversation.
4. Reporter John Lindsay as quoted by Arthur J. Schlesinger in *Robert Kennedy and His Times*.
5. RFK said this to civil rights activist Walter Fauntroy in April 1968, as quoted in Thurston Clarke, *The Last Campaign: Robert F. Kennedy and 82 Days That Inspired America* (New York: Henry Holt, 2008), 115.
6. FBI surveillance transcript archived in the King Papers.
7. Rebecca Burns, *Burial for a King: Martin Luther King Jr.'s Funeral and the Week That Transformed Atlanta and Rocked the Nation* (New York: Scribner, 2011), 39.
8. This and the subsequent excerpt archived in the King Papers.
9. From the essay, "An Inconvenient Man," by Samuel G. Freedman, published in the *Jerusalem Post*, January 26, 2006.

Afterword. Negroes Will Not Return to Passivity

1. Levison document, typed and handwritten, including Steinbeck quotation, archived in the King Papers.
2. Levison interview with James Mosby, February 1970, Ralph J. Bunche Oral History Collection, Moorland-Spingarn Research Center, Howard University.

Sources

Abernathy, Ralph David. *And the Walls Came Tumbling Down*. Chicago: Lawrence Hill Books, 1989.

Belafonte, Harry. *My Song: A Memoir*. New York: Alfred A. Knopf, 2011.

Branch, Taylor. *Parting the Waters: America in the King Years*. New York: Simon and Schuster, 1988.

———. *Pillar of Fire: America in the King Years 1963–65*. New York: Touchstone, 1998.

———. *At Canaan's Edge: America in the King Years 1965–68*. New York: Simon and Schuster, 2006.

Burns, Rebecca. *Burial for a King: Martin Luther King Jr.'s Funeral and the Week That Transformed Atlanta and Rocked the Nation*. New York: Scribner, 2011.

Caro, Robert. *The Passage of Power: The Years of Lyndon Johnson*. New York: Alfred A. Knopf, 2012.

Carson, Clayborne, ed. *The Autobiography of Martin Luther King*. New York: Warner Books, 1998.

———. *Martin's Dream: My Journey and the Legacy of Martin Luther King Jr.* New York: Palgrave Macmillan, 2013.

Christman, Henry M., ed. *Essential Works of Lenin*. New York: Dover Publications, 1966.

Clarke, Thurston. *The Last Campaign: Robert F. Kennedy and 82 Days That Inspired America*. New York: Henry Holt, 2008.

DuBois, W. E. B. *The Souls of Black Folks*. New York: Bantam Classic, 1989.

Dyson, Michael Eric. *I May Not Get There with You: The True Martin Luther King, Jr*. New York: Touchstone, 2000.

———. *April 4, 1968*: *Martin Luther King's Death and How It Changed America*. New York: Basic Civitas Books, 2008.

Figes, Orlando. *The Whisperers: Private Life in Stalin's Russia*. London: Picador, 2008.

Flanzbuam, Hilene, ed. *Jewish American Literature: A Norton Anthology*. Amherst: University of Massachusetts Press, 2001.

Frady, Marshall. *Martin Luther King, Jr*. New York: Viking, 2002.

Frank, Gerold. *An American Death: The True Story of the Assassination of Martin Luther King, Jr., and the Greatest Manhunt of Our Time.* Garden City, NY: Doubleday, 1972.

Garrow, David. *Bearing the Cross: Martin Luther King, Jr., and the Southern Christian Leadership Conference*. New York: William Morrow, 1986.

———. "The FBI and Martin Luther King." *Atlantic Monthly*, July–August 2002, pp. 80–88.

———. *The FBI and Martin Luther King, Jr.: From "Solo" to Memphis*. New York: Norton, 1981.

Gentry, Curt. *J. Edgar Hoover: The Man and the Secrets*. New York: Norton, 1991.

Halberstam, David. *The Children*: New York: Fawcett Books, 1999.

Harvey, Robert. *A Short History of Communism.* New York: Thomas Dunne Books, 2004.

Haskins, Jim. *The Day Martin Luther King, Jr. Was Shot: A Photo History of the Civil Rights Movement.* New York: Scholastic, 1992.

Jackson, Thomas F. *From Civil Rights to Human Rights: Martin Luther King, Jr. and the Struggle for Economic Justice.* Philadelphia: University of Pennsylvania Press, 2007.

Johnson, Charles, and Bob Adelman. *King: The Photobiography of Martin Luther King, Jr.* New York: Penguin Putnam, 2000.

Jones, Clarence B., and Stuart Connelly. *Behind the Dream: The Making of the Speech That Transformed a Nation.* New York: Palgrave Macmillan, 2011.

Jones, Clarence B., and Joel Engel. *What Would Martin Say?* New York: HarperCollins, 2008.

Kamin, Ben. *Thinking Passover: A Rabbi's Book of Holiday Values.* New York: Dutton, 1997.

———. *Room 306: The National Story of the Lorraine Motel.* East Lansing: Michigan State University Press, 2012.

Karier, Clarence J. *The Individual, Society, and Education: A History of American Educational Ideas.* Champaign: University of Illinois Press, 1986.

———. "The Reassassination of Martin Luther King Jr." *Educational Theory* 38, no. 4 (1987): 463–75.

Kennedy, Caroline, ed. *A Patriot's Handbook: Songs, Poems, Stories, and Speeches Celebrating the Land We Love.* New York: Hyperion, 2003.

King, Coretta Scott, ed. *The Words of Martin Luther King, Jr.* New York: Newmarket Press, 1987.

King, Martin Luther, Jr. *Where Do We Go from Here: Chaos or Community?* Boston: Beacon Press, 1967.

Kotz, Nick. *Judgment Days: Lyndon Johnson, Martin Luther King, Jr., and the Laws That Changed America.* Boston: Houghton Mifflin, 2005.

Kurlansky, Mark. *1968: The Year That Rocked the World.* New York: Ballantine Books, 2004.

Lee, Wendy Lynne. *On Marx*. Belmont, CA: Wadsworth, 2002.

Lewis, John. *Walking with the Wind: A Memoir of the Movement*. New York: Simon and Schuster, 1998.

O'Neill, William L. *Coming Apart: An Informal History of America in the 1960's*. Chicago: Quadrangle Books, 1971.

Posner, Gerald. *Killing the Dream: James Earl Ray and the Assassination of Martin Luther King, Jr.* New York: Random House, 1998.

Powers, Georgia Davis. *I Shared the Dream: The Pride, Passion, and Politics of the First Black Woman Senator from Kentucky*. Far Hills, NJ: New Horizon Press, 2010.

Roberts, Gene, and Hank Klibanoff. *The Race Beat: The Press, the Civil Rights Struggle, and the Awakening of a Nation*. New York: Alfred A. Knopf, 2006.

Ro'i, Yaacov. *Jews and Jewish Life in Russia and the Soviet Union*. Abingdon, UK: Routledge, 1995.

Rowan, Cart T. *Dream Makers, Dream Breakers: The World of Justice Thurgood Marshall*. Boston: Little, Brown, 1993.

Salzman, Jack, ed. *Bridges and Boundaries: African Americans and American Jews*. New York: George Braziller and The Jewish Museum, 1992.

Schlesinger, Arthur M., Jr. *Robert Kennedy and His Times*. Boston: Houghton Mifflin Harcourt, 1978.

Schwartz, Leon. *A Scion of the Times: Personal Memoirs and Family Annals*. New York: Consortium House, 2010.

Service, Robert. *Comrades! A History of World Communism.* Cambridge: Harvard University Press, 2007.

Shatzkin, Mike, and Jim Charlton, eds. *The Ballplayers*. New York: Arbor House, 1990.

Sides, Hampton: *Hellhound on His Trail: The Stalking of Martin Luther King, Jr. and the International Hunt for His Assassin.* New York: Doubleday, 2010.

Talbot, David. *Brothers: The Hidden History of the Kennedy Years.* New York: Free Press, 2007.

Taylor, Clarence. *Reds at the Blackboard: Communism, Civil Rights, and the New York City Teachers Union*. New York: Columbia University Press, 2011.

Thomas, Gary. *Sacred Influence: How God Uses Wives to Shape the Souls of Their Husbands.* Grand Rapids: Zondervan, 2007.

Uchitelle, Louis. "For Blacks, a Dream in Decline." *New York Times*, October 23, 2005.

Woodward, C. Vann. *The Burden of Southern History*. Baton Rouge: Louisiana State University Press, 1960.

WSB-TV Newsfilm Collection, The Walter J. Brown Media Archives & Peabody Awards Collection, University of Georgia Special Collections Libraries, Atlanta.

Young, Andrew. *An Easy Burden: The Civil Rights Movement and the Transformation of America.* Waco, TX: Baylor University Press, 2008.

Federal Bureau of Investigation. *Stanley Levision—the FBI Files*. 5 vols. Lexington, KY: Filiquarian Publishing/Qontro, 2009.

Acknowledgments

This book could not have been written without the encouragement, help, and wisdom of Professor Clayborne Carson, the director of the Martin Luther King Jr. Institute for Research and Education, based at Stanford University. Clay, who was personally asked by Coretta Scott King to gather, save, and organize the papers of Martin Luther King Jr., is the singular living resource of the words and ideas of Dr. King. From the start of our working relationship and the warm friendship that has ensued, Clay has given me rare and privileged access to transcripts, files, letters, and statements associated with Dr. King—as well as his friends and enemies. I am so grateful.

The voice and heart of this work belong to Clarence B. Jones, one of King's "winter soldiers," the living link to that time and to the person of Stanley Levison. Clarence is my mentor, friend, and inspiration.

I am also appreciative for the input provided to me by Andrew Levison,

son of Beatrice and Stanley, a passionate voice for social justice in the best tradition of his parents.

Martha Bates, my longtime editor at Michigan State University Press, architect of my previous King-related books and the pioneer light for this one, is simply indispensable for me. When she happened to retire during the development of this project, I was further blessed to have the Press's director, Gabriel Dotto, step in as editor. And so, I went from strength to strength.

I could not have written anything without the unwavering encouragement and probing editorial assistance of my wife Audrey—who has made my hopes come true.

I am also deeply thankful for my daughters, Sari and Debra, who grew up hearing the stories. Now, my stepchildren, Samantha and Austin, are living The Dream.

Index